# New Media and the New Middle East

## Palgrave Macmillan Series in International Political Communication

**Series editor**: Philip Seib, University of Southern California (USA)

From democratization to terrorism, economic development to conflict resolution, global political dynamics are affected by the increasing pervasiveness and influence of communication media. This series examines the participants and their tools, their strategies and their impact. It offers a mix of comparative and tightly focused analyses that bridge the various elements of communication and political science included in the field of international studies. Particular emphasis is placed on topics related to the rapidly changing communication environment that is being shaped by new technologies and new political realities. This is the evolving world of international political communication.

**Editorial Board Members**:

Hussein Amin, American University in Cairo (Egypt)
Robin Brown, University of Leeds (UK)
Eytan Gilboa, Bar-Ilan University (Israel)
Steven Livingston, George Washington University (USA)
Robin Mansell, London School of Economics and Political Science (UK)
Holli Semetko, Emory University (USA)
Ingrid Volkmer, University of Melbourne (Australia)

**Books Appearing in this Series**

*Media and the Politics of Failure: Great Powers, Communication Strategies, and Military Defeats*
By Laura Roselle

*The CNN Effect in Action: How the News Media Pushed the West toward War in Kosovo*
By Babak Bahador

*Media Pressure on Foreign Policy: The Evolving Theoretical Framework*
By Derek B. Miller

*New Media and the New Middle East*
Edited by Philip Seib

# New Media and the New Middle East

*Edited by*

*Philip Seib*

NEW MEDIA AND THE NEW MIDDLE EAST
Copyright © Philip Seib, 2007.

First published in 2007 by
PALGRAVE MACMILLAN™
175 Fifth Avenue, New York, N.Y. 10010 and
Houndmills, Basingstoke, Hampshire, England RG21 6XS
Companies and representatives throughout the world.

PALGRAVE MACMILLAN is the global academic imprint of the Palgrave Macmillan division of St. Martin's Press, LLC and of Palgrave Macmillan Ltd. Macmillan® is a registered trademark in the United States, United Kingdom and other countries. Palgrave is a registered trademark in the European Union and other countries. `

ISBN-13: 978–1–4039–7973–5
ISBN-10: 1–4039–7973–1

Library of Congress Cataloging-in-Publication Data is available from the Library of Congress.

A catalogue record for this book is available from the British Library.

Design by Newgen Imaging Systems (P) Ltd., Chennai, India.

First edition: August 2007

10 9 8 7 6 5 4 3 2 1

Printed in the United States of America.

# CONTENTS

# LIST OF GRAPHS

# LIST OF TABLES

# PREFACE

This book was born at the 2005 annual conference of the Arab-U.S. Association of Communication Educators in Kuwait City. The vitality of the discourse at that meeting so impressed me that I asked a number of the young Arab scholars presenting papers to contribute chapters to the book. In addition, I recruited several Israelis and Westerners to bring their perspectives to the issues addressed in this volume.

The theme of the book is the role of new media—principally satellite television and the Internet—in stimulating change in the Middle East. The "new Middle East" referred to in the book's title differs from the political incarnation that Condoleezza Rice saw emerging from its "birth pangs" during the 2006 war between Israel and Hezbollah. Rather than being wholly a creature of conflict, this is a Middle East being shaped in part by the steadily growing and ever more accessible flow of information delivered by new communication technologies to people in the region.

As several contributors point out, these changes are affecting how those in the Middle East view the rest of the world and how they see themselves. Pan-Arab talk shows that challenge the region's governments as well as blogs and cell phone text messaging used to enhance women's political clout are just two of the ways that change is occurring. Despite such encouraging developments, progress does not proceed unimpeded. Governments have become more innovative in censoring information, and terrorist organizations have appropriated new media for their own evil purposes.

New media cannot in themselves bring about a new Middle East, but they can be valuable tools in the hands of people committed to democratization and other kinds of reform. That is why the topics examined in this book are so important. The authors are witnesses to change, and their tone is generally hopeful.

Throughout the world, the traditional structures of information cultures are changing. In the past, relatively few sources of news and other information were available to consumers. A small number of news organizations, which in some countries were merely mouthpieces for the government, delivered what they wanted when they wanted. News consumers in many countries had few options. Governments could exercise direct or more nuanced control over dissemination of information or at least had to deal with only a small number of providers.

That is no longer the case. During recent years, the flow of information has grown exponentially primarily because of the development of new media.

In terms of brand recognition, the best known international satellite TV channel is Al Jazeera, the Qatar-based station that began operations in 1996. After several years of dominating its region, Al Jazeera now has plenty of competition—more than 200 Arab satellite channels are on the air—but it remains an intriguing paradigm. Within a few years of its startup, Al Jazeera had established itself as the dominant television channel featuring the Arab viewpoint of major events, particularly those related to conflict. In 1998, when the United States and Britain bombed Iraq because Saddam Hussein was blocking the work of weapons inspectors, Al Jazeera was there. In 2000, during the Palestinian *Intifada*, Al Jazeera's graphic coverage attracted a large audience throughout the Arab world. And in 2001, when the United States attacked Afghanistan, the Taliban ordered all Western journalists to leave but allowed Al Jazeera to remain. By 2003 and the beginning of the Iraq war, Al Jazeera's success had encouraged rivals, such as Al Arabiya and Abu Dhabi TV, to emphasize live, comprehensive coverage. For the first time, many Arabs did not have to rely on the BBC, CNN, or other outside news sources when a big story broke. They could instead find news presented from an Arab perspective.

One of Al Jazeera's strengths has been its introduction of energetic and sometimes contentious debate into an Arab news business that was previously known for its drab docility. The high production values of the channel's newscasts and the lively exchanges in its talk shows have expanded the news audience and changed the nature of political discourse within the Arab public sphere. Getting more people to pay attention to and talk about news is an important facet of larger issues related to democratization.

The style and substance of Al Jazeera's programming has led its audience to become more engaged with the issues addressed in news coverage. This is largely due to the channel's being trusted more than many of its competitors. Critics of Al Jazeera, particularly in the West, often challenge the channel's objectivity, but such criticism misses the point in terms of understanding the channel's baseline strength. Rather than judging the news product they receive according to standards prescribed by outsiders, most of Al Jazeera's viewers consider *credibility* to be a news provider's most important attribute, and these viewers want news that is gathered independently for Arabs by Arabs and that sees events through *their* eyes. In the new era of proliferating satellite television channels, state-controlled and Western broadcasters have found that they are at a significant competitive disadvantage in the Arab world because they are not seen as being as credible as Al Jazeera and some of its Arab competitors. Furthermore, the presentation of news on Al Jazeera reflects a passion that is well suited for an audience that feels passionately about many of the issues and events that the channel covers.

During the 2006 war between Israel and Hezbollah, the Arabic channels—particularly Al Jazeera and Al Arabiya—provided more extensive coverage than was offered by other international channels. Their reports, which often featured graphic images of dead and wounded Lebanese civilians, affected the region's politics by stoking Arab anger toward Israel and the United States, and toward Arab governments that were slow to support Hezbollah. Al Jazeera's talk shows provided forums for public criticism of Arab leaders, and the overall coverage helped push countries such as Saudi Arabia and Jordan closer to Hezbollah's cause.[1]

Although Al Jazeera may be the best known player in the Middle East's media development, many others are in the game. Even more than satellite television, the Internet brings a whole new dimension to questions of media credibility. Plenty of online news providers offer detailed, sophisticated content, with greater depth than is found in print or broadcast sources. Beyond that, much of the news delivered on the Web—particularly the quasi-journalism of blogs—constitutes a populist approach to information dissemination that signals a significantly altered balance of media power.

The vast breadth of the blogosphere and its rate of growth make it difficult to evaluate. By mid-2007, Technorati—a Google-like search engine for blogs—was scanning more than 75 million blogs. By October 2006, the number had exceeded 54 million, and by early 2007 it had risen past 67 million. Some blogs are written by government officials, journalists, soldiers, and academics and convey valuable information. Some are musings of people with time on their hands and whose blogs range from personal confessionals to rumors, gossip, and conspiracy theories. Whatever they happen to be saying, bloggers are opening up discourse and creating new online communities linked by language, interests, and a growing commitment to free expression.

Many blogs provide an intriguing subtext to conventional news coverage. Just as reading a newspaper's "Letters to the Editor" section can provide insights into public attitudes, so too can an exploration of blogs. The results may not be as reliable as those from a properly constructed opinion poll, but they nevertheless are interesting as snapshots of what some people consider important. As the 2006 Israel-Hezbollah war was underway, bloggers in Israel and Lebanon kept talking. On the Face, a blog written by an Israeli, asked, "Will this turn out to be the first time that residents of 'enemy' countries engaged in an ongoing conversation while missiles were falling?"[2]

Blog-based conversation can become a significant undercurrent and may influence coverage by mainstream news media when the chorus of bloggers' voices becomes so loud that it attracts attention. If big news organizations are slow to pursue a story, bloggers may highlight bits and pieces of the story until conventional media take notice, investigate, and report it to a larger audience. Bloggers tend to have less tolerance for conventional wisdom and less trust of government and so are little affected by the relationships between governments and journalists that can influence the breadth and tone of coverage. But, by the same token, some bloggers are also less concerned than are professional journalists about commitments to accuracy and objectivity.

The various Internet-based modes of communication affect not only the Web-oriented public, but policymakers as well. Because anything on the Internet can have global reach, international news coverage and public attitudes can be affected by this vast new chorus of voices. During 2006, planners of Israel's public diplomacy efforts, for example, had to reckon with not just conventional international news coverage but also the international online audience's reaction to partisan Web sites and blogs from dissatisfied soldiers, civilians under fire in Gaza and Lebanon, and diverse commentators. Challenges to government pronouncements are more numerous and forceful, escalating the intensity of the competition for public opinion.

These are just some elements of the wildly dynamic world of new media. In the Middle East, media development must coexist with various tensions at many levels, but the growing pervasiveness and influence of new media are clearly among the most significant stimuli for change within the region.

Appraising different aspects of new media from different perspectives, the authors of this book provide much to think about as they offer a preview of tomorrow's Middle East.

Philip Seib

## Notes

1. Ali Khalil, "Major Arab News Channels Tested in Lebanon War," *Agence France Presse*, August 9, 2006.
2. Mike Spector, "Cry Bias and Let Slip the Blogs of War," *Wall Street Journal*, July 26, 2006; Sarah Ellison, "In the Midst of War, Bloggers Are Talking Across the Front Line," *Wall Street Journal*, July 28, 2006.

# Notes on the Contributors

**Samar al-Roomi** is a professor in the Department of Communications and Linguistics at Kuwait University's College for Women. She is a frequent contributor of opinion columns to Kuwait's *Arab Times*.

**Maura Conway** is a Lecturer in the School of Law & Government at Dublin City University, Dublin, Ireland. Her research addresses cyberterrorism and its portrayal in the media, and the functioning and effectiveness of terrorist Web sites.

**Ahmed El Gody** is senior lecturer and director of the New Media Lab at the Modern Sciences and Arts University in Cairo, Egypt.

**Mohammed el-Nawawy** is Knight-Crane endowed chair and assistant professor in the Department of Communication at Queens University of Charlotte and senior editor of the *Journal of Middle East Media*. He is coauthor of *Al-Jazeera: The Story of the Network that Is Rattling Governments and Redefining Modern Journalism* and author of *The Israeli-Egyptian Peace Process in the Reporting of Western Journalists*.

**Shahira Fahmy** is an assistant professor of electronic media publishing at Southern Illinois University. Her work has appeared in journals such as *Journalism and Mass Communication Quarterly, International Communication Gazette, Visual Communication Quarterly, Newspaper Research Journal* and the *Atlantic Journal of Communication*.

**Eytan Gilboa** is professor of international communication, director of the PhD program in communication, and senior research associate at the Begin-Sadat Center for Strategic Studies, all at Bar-Ilan University in Israel. Author and editor of numerous books and articles, he is on the editorial boards of *Journal of Communication* and *Communication Studies* and is the editor of the *USC Public Diplomacy Annual*.

**Thomas J. Johnson** is the Marshall and Sharleen Formby Regents Professor in the College of Mass Communications at Texas Tech University. He is the author of *The Rehabilitation of Richard Nixon: The Media's Effect on Collective Memory* and coauthor of *Engaging the Public: How Government and the Media Can Reinvigorate American Democracy*.

**Sahar Khamis** is the head of the Mass Communication and Information Science Department at Qatar University and has worked for international media organizations such as *The Wall Street Journal* and NHK-Japan Broadcasting Corporation.

**Yehiel (Hilik) Limor** is the chair of the School of Communication and Media Studies in the College of Judea and Samaria in Ariel, Israel. He is the author of several books including *The Mediators—The Media in Israel 1948–1990* (with D. Caspi), *Journalism* (with R. Mann), and *The In/Outsiders: Mass media in Israel* (with D. Caspi).

**Marc Lynch** is associate professor of political science at Williams College. He is the author of *State Interests and Public Spheres: The International Politics of Jordan's Identity* and *Voices of the New Arab Public: Iraq, Al-Jazeera, and Middle East Politics Today.*

**Orayb Aref Najjar** was born in West Jerusalem, Palestine in 1947 and is now an associate professor in the Department of Communication at Northern Illinois University, where she teaches international communication, digital photography, and graphics. She is the author of book chapters and journal articles on media in the Middle East and North Africa, censorship, and freedom of the press.

**Chanan Naveh** is senior lecturer and the academic counselor at the School of Communication, Sapir Academic College, and also teaches in the International Relations Department of the Hebrew University, Jerusalem. He has served as a senior managing editor of Israeli Radio's news department.

**Shawn Powers** is a PhD candidate at the Annenberg School for Communication at the University of Southern California, and is a research associate at USC's Center on Public Diplomacy.

**Ibrahim Saleh** is a member of the Journalism and Mass Communications faculty at the American University in Cairo. He is the author of several books and research papers about Middle East media.

**Philip Seib** is professor of journalism and professor of public diplomacy at the University of Southern California. His books include *The Global Journalist: News and Conscience in a World of Conflict, Beyond the Front Lines: How the News Media Cover a World Shaped by War*, and the edited volume *Media and Conflict in the 21st Century*. He is coeditor of the journal *Media, War and Conflict*.

CHAPTER 1

# New Media and Prospects for Democratization

*Philip Seib*

## INTRODUCTION[1]

New media are affecting democratization within the Middle East, particularly in terms of their transnational impact. This "Al Jazeera effect" is a relatively new phenomenon but may become more significant as the number of regional satellite television stations grows, along with the proliferation of other new communications technologies, such as the Internet and cell phones. Communications and information technologies can be potent tools in fostering political transformation, although they remain to varying degrees dependent on political institutions and other nonmedia factors.

Empowerment through information has been greater in recent years from the growing pervasiveness and influence of satellite television, the Internet, cell phones, and other such devices. The Internet, for instance, has been put to work by news organizations, governments, nongovernmental organizations (NGOs), terrorist groups, bloggers, and others and has had impact on political processes. Democratization does not, however, come easily, and it is important to resist the temptation to assume that technology can, in and of itself, transform political reality.

So, the effect of new media on democratization is very much a work in progress, as reflected in the Middle East by various elections during 2005, other political mobilization, and American public diplomacy efforts. Next steps in this process will include development of norms for media and other professionals who use these technologies.

## Media Effects and Transnational Presence

In the Middle East as elsewhere, politics sometimes receives an unexpected jolt that produces unanticipated consequences. This has happened during the past decade as information and communication technologies have become more pervasive and influential. This process is accelerating, pushed along in part by transforming events such as the American invasion of Iraq.

A key factor in this expansion of media reach and power is the growing irrelevance of borders. New media will facilitate transnational trends in politics and other facets of globalization because the media themselves are increasingly transnational. This will affect the dynamics of democratization by reducing the isolation of movements for political change and by facilitating detours around obstructions created by governments that have traditionally controlled the flow of information.

The complexity of democratization should be respected, however, and no single factor's impact should be overrated. Media effects, for instance, are just parts of a large political universe, the constituent elements of which must come into alignment if democratization is to develop. That said, the role of the media should also not be *under-*rated. Mohammed Jassim Al Ali, former managing director of Al Jazeera, has said: "Democracy is coming to the Middle East because of the communication revolution. You can no longer hide information and must now tell the people the truth. If you don't, the people won't follow you, they won't support you, they won't obey you."[2] That may overstate the situation, but the premise is sound in the sense that democratic reverberations are being felt in parts of the Middle East that have rarely been touched by such impulses in the past.

This is not merely a matter of theory. Media tools have been put to use in political protests in Lebanon, Egypt, Kuwait, and elsewhere. Transnational satellite television, for example, can—to a certain extent—evade controls imposed on news coverage within a country. The 2005 "Cedar Revolution" in Lebanon demonstrated how this can work on two levels. Regional/international coverage—such as is provided by Al Jazeera and Al Arabiya, among others—could provide information to Lebanese audiences with less concern about political repercussions that might deter some indigenous media organizations. By showing the size and energy of the protests, such coverage helped fuel the demonstrations and encouraged broader pressure for Syrian withdrawal. In addition, news organizations based outside the country may be trusted more than those that are presumed to be susceptible to localized political pressures.

The lines between national and transnational are not always sharply drawn; transnational media are not necessarily external media. In this case, Lebanese television channels, some of which are available on satellite, also intensively covered the post-assassination (of Rafik Hariri) story, as did radio stations and print media that reached regional and global audiences through the Internet. In Lebanon, as in any other country, indigenous news content is likely to be affected by the political, sectarian, and other interests of those who own and run media organizations. News consumers must take this into account when evaluating the information they receive.

The reports from Lebanon influenced longer-term political dynamics as the coverage reached viewers throughout the region, letting them see political activity that they might decide to emulate. During the following months, demonstrations elsewhere incorporated television-friendly tactics that were seen in the Beirut coverage. In Jordan, national flags were prominently displayed in front of the news media's cameras, which helped avoid having the protests dismissed as simply factional discord.[3] Overall, noted Bernard Lewis, television "brings to the peoples of the Middle East a previously unknown spectacle—that of lively and vigorous public disagreement and debate."[4]

Coverage of the Lebanon story is just one example that underscores the significance of the transnational nature of new media technologies. Some governments try to impose an intellectual sovereignty that ensures perpetuation of the status quo and prevents penetration by "discordant" ideas and actions. Freer movement of information, which is partly a function of globalization, works against repressive sovereignty of this kind and improves prospects for democratization. The increased flow of information does not, however, in itself guarantee a surge of democracy. Lebanon, for instance, continued to struggle in 2005 and then was wracked by war in 2006.

True democratization takes time to gain traction. Increased plurality of self-expression is useful, but sometimes it can be more a cacophony than a coherent, purpose-driven chorus. As with many of the elements of democratization, expanding public debate and participation is merely one of the numerous incremental steps needed in the process.

## GOVERNMENTS' REACTIONS

Communications pressures in the Middle East have been building for more than a decade, and governments have tried to control emerging technologies by licensing fax machines, blocking Web sites, finding friendly owners for satellite TV stations, and so on. But such measures can be circumvented as more satellite stations begin broadcasting, cell phone owners send text messages, and public ingenuity finds new ways to outdistance government controls.[5] For example, the London-based Saudi Human Rights Center has used satellite radio and television to encourage demonstrations in Riyadh. Islah Radio promoted Saudi reform in its broadcasts from shortwave transmitters at an unrevealed location (thought to be in Lithuania) and via the Hotbird satellite to take advantage of the substantial number of households with satellite reception in Saudi Arabia. Since most of the audience prefers even the most basic TV presence rather than merely words from a radio, Islah Television was born, initially presenting just its logo with text information scrolling on the screen and radio broadcasts as the audio. The station eventually provided programming with more audience appeal, including a call-in show featuring the station's driving force, Saad Al Faqih, who responded to viewers' emails, faxes, and phone calls placed through an Internet phone service (which allowed them to avoid government eavesdroppers). Al Faqih consistently criticized the Al Saud princes, at one point calling them "thieves who should be beheaded instead of petty criminals."

The Saudi government apparently fought back, as the shortwave and television signals were jammed and pressure was brought to bear on the European TV transmission providers to drop the station. In December 2004, the station was on the air with a new satellite home that let it be more insulated from economic pressure. As all this was going on, the station had achieved small but noteworthy results in its efforts to encourage demonstrations in support of human rights within Saudi Arabia.[6]

Without judging the merits of the station's content, its struggle for existence illustrates the kind of battle that can be expected as new media organizations jab at governments that are unaccustomed to being challenged. The on-and-off process will continue as each side finesses the other's latest technological gambit. Other Arab broadcasting and print news organizations that are based outside the region and compete against state monopolies are further expanding the amounts of information available to Middle East publics.[7] As journalist Youssef Ibrahim has observed, "The din of democracy talk has been amplified by satellite television, the Internet, and cell phones, and that is a new wrinkle for autocratic regimes experienced at quiet repression."[8]

## NEW MEDIA AS POLITICAL TOOL

Over the long term, the Internet may prove to be even more potent as a force for reform, although this will take time given the limited Internet access within most of the Middle East. As more widespread Internet access and use take hold in the region, the intrinsic political vitality of the World Wide Web is likely to change the way people view their own countries and the rest of the world. Information from news organizations and other sources that were previously out of reach will be tapped and the interactive nature of the Internet will foster the intellectual enfranchisement that opens the way to political change.

The Internet is an increasingly significant presence in international politics, but its lasting impact remains uncertain. Shanthi Kalathil and Taylor C. Boas noted that the Internet "is only a tool, and its specific uses by political, economic, and societal actors must be carefully weighed and considered,"[9] and Charles Kupchan observed that the "international effects of the information revolution, just like those of economic interdependence, depend upon the broader political context in which these technologies are deployed."[10] In other words, the Internet should not be viewed as a cure-all by advocates of democracy. As with any political enterprise, the abilities and character of participants, the resources available, other political occurrences near and far, and sometimes good or bad luck will affect any given democratization venture.

The Internet can generate political pressure because it is itself intrinsically democratic and can foster populist participation. That is not yet fully understood, but it can be seen in the fervor of political discussion that takes place on a scale and with an audacity new to politics in much of the world. People advocating change do not have to take the risks involved with public demonstrations in a police state, and they don't have to rely on slow and small-scale dissemination such as the *samizdat* endeavors in the Soviet Union. Instead there can be a political presence such as sprang up in late 2005 in Syria, where, according to *The Washington Post*'s David Ignatius, "Internet cafes are scattered through Damascus, allowing people to constantly share news and gossip. The security forces have been arresting dissidents, but that doesn't stop people from talking."[11]

Nevertheless, how much effect the Internet will have in the Arab political world remains speculative, particularly because Arab states lag far behind most of the rest of the world in taking advantage of this technology. As of 2003, there were only 18 computers per 1,000 people in Arab countries, compared to the global average of 78 per 1,000.[12]

Even when they have access, Internet users in some countries encounter government controls, with sites that are found officially bothersome blocked. The Saudi government's Internet Services Unit states that "all sites that contain content in violation of Islamic tradition or national regulations shall be blocked."[13] Among these blocked sites are Amnesty International's Web pages related to Saudi Arabia, the Encyclopedia Britannica's "Women in American History," *Rolling Stone* magazine, and Warner Brothers Records. In Egypt, some of the Muslim Brotherhood's Web sites, such as ikhwanonline, have occasionally been blocked, which is noteworthy given the putative efforts to make more open the Egyptian electoral process.

Besides blocking, some governments establish their own Web sites to present their version of issues and events that people may be learning about from other news media. How much credibility these quasi-news sites have with the public varies from country to country, but they provide a means for governments to compete with conventional news providers as sources of information.

Other entities such as NGOs effectively use the Internet to make their case to global audiences and for purposes ranging from stimulating news coverage to raising money. Terrorist organizations also use Web sites to recruit, raise funds, and proselytize. Despite government efforts to deny these groups access to the news media and the public, terrorist Web sites have proven successful in disseminating material such as pronouncements from Osama bin Laden, propaganda disguised as newscasts, online jihadist magazines, and video clips of executions of kidnap victims. Since the goal of these organizations is to instill terror in the public, the Web is a valuable device for delivering their message in sometimes horrific fashion.

The Internet is also important in recruiting, training, and communicating with terrorist groups' adherents, for example, the June 2005 online release of a forty-six-minute video, "All Religion Will Be for Allah," produced by Abu Musab Zarqawi's Iraqi branch of al Qaeda that featured a corps of suicide bombers-in-training. It was disseminated by a specially designed Web page with numerous links for downloading, including one for playing it on a cell phone.[14] Even cartoons depicting children as suicide bombers are easily accessible on the Web.[15]

## THE MECHANISMS OF INFORMATION DEMOCRACY

Open access to media venues and the easy dissemination of unmediated media may be viewed as information democracy, but because this freedom is available to all, regardless of their intentions, it may be abused, as can be seen in the terrorist examples. News organizations are sometimes inadvertently complicit in this as their coverage of terrorists' pronouncements reaches a much larger audience than could be achieved through the original webcast, videotape, or other message. This raises issues about mainstream media's gatekeeper role, and the European Union has urged media organizations to draw up a code of conduct to ensure that they do not become de facto propagandists for terrorists.[16]

Yet another use of the Internet with significant political potential is blogging. Blogs amplify voices that may have previously gone unheard. As such they foster a degree of democratic parity at least in terms of expanding audience access for those who feel they have something worthwhile to say. The blogging firmament is already crowded and becoming more so. As of October 2005, blog search engine Technorati covered roughly 19 million blogs; by January 2006 the figure was 25 million; in April 2007, it was 75 million.

Particularly in countries where governments have tried to suppress political organizing, blogging may prove to be valuable in orchestrating pressure for reform. In 2005, bloggers in Lebanon and elsewhere spurred debate about the perpetrators and aftershocks of the assassination of Rafik Hariri—debate that could be joined by anyone with Internet access, regardless of some governments' desire to stifle these discussions. Another example of political blogging could be seen in 2002 when Bahrainis dissatisfied with conventional media coverage of a scandal related to the national pension fund could read less constrained analysis on blogs such as "Bahraini blogsite" or "Mahmood's Den."[17] Many Bahraini villages have their own Web sites and chat rooms where discussions about the ruling Khalifa family are less restrained than they usually would be on street corners. By late 2005, BahrainOnline.org had become a go-to site for anyone interested in political news. Its iconoclastic success was evidenced when the irritated government jailed several of the site's Web masters for a few weeks.[18]

Talk about politics has expanded from the neighborhood coffee house to global proportions, enlisting participants and encouraging electronic speech and the thinking behind it. This is networking in the sense that likeminded activists can find each other and form partnerships of various kinds. Information—some of it solid, some of it wild—can be disseminated quickly and widely. Some time will have to pass before this phenomenon's long-term political impact can be determined, but if bloggers' talk leads to expanded bloggers' activism, this may be yet another way that mass media provide impetus for democratization.

While the Internet is put to increasing use, an even more common communications device is proving increasingly useful in mobilizing activists: text messaging on cell phones facilitates organization of demonstrations and circulation of political information. Particularly when political parties are restricted, text messages can be sent to unofficial membership lists. In Kuwait, women organizing protests about voting rights in 2005 found their effectiveness increased because they could summon young women from schools by sending text messages. (In May 2005, Kuwaiti women were granted the right to vote and to be candidates in parliamentary and local council elections). In Lebanon, text messages (and emails) were used as yet another means to mobilize anti-Syrian demonstrators in March 2005.[19] Fawzi Guleid of the National Democratic Institute in Bahrain observed that text messaging fosters expansion of speech because it "allows people to send messages that they would not say in public." It should also be noted, however, that text messaging lends itself to the spread of rumors and anonymous attacks. Rola Dashti, one of the organizers of the women's rights demonstrations in Kuwait, was the subject of widely circulated text messages that criticized her for her Lebanese and Iranian ancestry and alleged that she had received funds from the American embassy. Her response: "It means I'm making them nervous . . . and I'd better get used to it."[20]

## IS THE TIME RIGHT?

Advocates of democracy in the Middle East cannot ignore the reality of having many obstacles to overcome. In terms of Web access, there is a digital *wadi*, a deep and daunting canyon, between the region and much of the rest of the world.[21] Among the factors contributing to the level of technology use in the Middle East and some other parts of the world is the overall literacy rate and the usefulness of having a working knowledge of English.

Even a development as encouraging as the increased availability of satellite television is not a panacea for political problems. Hugh Miles has observed in his book about Al Jazeera that

> optimists theorize that satellite TV will sweep away traditional Arab obstacles to progress and dissolve seemingly intractable problems and that an 'Islamic Glasnost' will ensue . . . . But to believe that satellite television is automatically going to make Arab societies democratic is to presume that the current state of affairs in the Arab world results from an information deficiency, which is not true. Except in the most authoritarian Arab countries, the news has long been available to the

determined via the radio, and that has never brought about much democracy.

Miles added that even if Arab satellite television viewers see something on the air that leads them to change their minds about an issue, "there is still no political mechanism in place for them to do anything about it."[22] Miles makes a valid point, but it should be kept in mind that audience size is in itself important and the significance of sheer numbers with easy, frequent access to diverse sources of information should not be underestimated. When a critical mass has better access to information, political processes are more likely to change.

Nevertheless, optimism about prospects for media-inspired reform should be tempered with caution. As Jon Alterman pointed out, much of the debate that can be seen on Arab satellite television "is still largely about spectacle and not about participation." There are, as Alterman noted, some encouraging exceptions to this. He cited the example of Egyptian televangelist Amr Khalid who has cultivated a large following by eschewing the finger-pointing lectures favored by many Muslim clerics and instead quietly urging his audience to "sanctify the everyday." Alterman wrote,

> Through huge revival-style events in Egypt and increasingly via satellite television broadcasts beamed throughout the Middle East, Khalid has created not just a community of viewers, but also a community of participants. His followers do more than write and call in to his programs. His increasingly global audience participates in charity drives, organizes study groups, and seeks to apply his specific lessons to their daily lives.[23]

Khalid's success undermines the stereotype of the stern Islamic preacher with a forbidding television presence. Khalid's more modernist approach illustrates the multidimensional aspects of new media influence and the need to recognize that those who use these new media must be sensitive to the changing expectations of the mass audience.

No medium in itself can create change. It has to be used creatively and with an eye to its relationship with other social and political institutions. Along these lines Mohamed Zayani wrote,

> One should be skeptical about the often ambitious transformative claims for new media as well as the claims about its democratizing potential and its ability not just to increase and widen participation among the various social strata in the Arab world, but to transform social and political

organization. Real change cannot be expected solely or mainly from the media sector. Democracy cannot emanate just from the media; the political systems and institutions themselves have to change, evolve, and adapt . . . . We should not be under the illusion that satellite TV can dramatically change society or revolutionize its institutions.[24]

Similarly, Marc Lynch wrote: "What one enthusiast called 'the Democratic Republic of Al Jazeera' does not, in fact, exist. Al Jazeera cannot create democracy on its own, nor compel Arab leaders to change their ways. Television talk shows cannot substitute for the hard work of political organizing and institution building."[25] Looking at this from another angle, Mamoun Fandi noted that the proliferation of satellite television may create a virtual politics that citizens watch, like an event in an arena, rather than actually participate in. "Governments in the Arab world," wrote Fandi, "are encouraging the trend whereby the media become a substitute for real politics."[26]

All that may be true, but skepticism should not be allowed to slip into the cynical fatalism of the "Change will never happen" variety. Media might not make revolutions, but they certainly can contribute to them. In the end, the public's willingness to act is the most crucial factor in reform.

A more optimistic evaluation of media influence has been offered by Jon Alterman of the Center for Strategic and International Studies. He argued that "as literacy and bandwidth both expand dramatically, publics are exposed to a broad, often unregulated, spectrum of views that range from secular to religious, from nationalist to global, and from material to spiritual. Under the new paradigm, information is demand-driven rather than supply-driven, and the universe of available views is far broader than ever before." One consequence of more information being more widely communicated, wrote Alterman, is "greater political spontaneity. Whereas Arab politics have often been characterized by orchestrated demonstrations of solidarity, anger, sorrow, or joy, the regime's ability to organize such demonstrations in the future will be greatly diminished."[27]

Current and prospective effects of new media should be appraised in a politically holistic context. Writing about the liberalizing potential of the Internet, Shanthi Kalathil and Taylor Boas predicted that the Internet's influence "will complement many other, more long-standing potential forces for liberalization: greater contact with the outside world through tourism and travel, more integration with the global economy, and the increasingly modern outlook of a youthful population."[28]

## MEDIA AND DEMOCRATIZATION:
## A WORK IN PROGRESS

The 2004 Arab Human Development Report acknowledged that "formidable obstacles stand in the way of a society of freedom and good governance in Arab countries. And this is an undeniable truth. But at the end of this difficult journey, there lies a noble goal, worthy of the hardships endured by those who seek it."[29]

Despite the presence of those obstacles, the Middle East in 2005 provided fascinating illustrations of the ways that new media can surge and influence the political climate. The reverberations of the American invasion of Iraq continued and attracted much news coverage and angry attention. A parallel story could be found in the assertions of electoral freedom in Iraq and Palestine, and other democratic mani-festations (of varying degrees) in Lebanon, Egypt, Saudi Arabia, and elsewhere. Reform seemed to be developing momentum, sometimes on the level of headline-grabbing politics, as with the Iraq elections, and sometimes on a more incremental basis, as with the increasing assertiveness of some Arab women.

The new media played a critical role in all this; satellite television showed Egyptians, Syrians, and others that real elections were taking place in Palestine and Iraq, and showed Saudi women, among others, that Arab women in some countries might actually be allowed to hold positions in government (as in Bahrain) and even drive cars.[30]

Women's issues, long treated condescendingly, if at all, by many Arab media organizations, are gaining increased traction thanks partly to new media. A good example is the Lebanon-based Heya ("She") satellite television channel, which as of early 2005 was reaching a daily audience estimated at 15 million with a mixture of news, talk, and entertainment programming. About 70 percent of the station's staff members are women, with correspondents reporting from throughout the Arab world. Heya's founder, Nicolas Abu Samah, said the channel's goal "is to empower women. We want to question taboos and provoke controversy." Among the station's offerings is "Al-Makshouf" ("The Uncovered"), a talk show that addresses topics such as domestic vio-lence and workplace discrimination. A news program, "From Day to Day," examines news related to women from around the world. Abu Samah noted that the station proceeds carefully to avoid censorship; political leaders and religious authorities are not directly criticized on Heya programs.[31]

In addition to attention to women's issues, coverage of electoral politics is becoming more comprehensive and freewheeling. For the

2005 Iraq elections particularly, Middle Eastern television stations displayed their ambition and the strengths of their hardware. Al Arabiya broadcast from eight satellite trucks throughout Iraq, and used videophone links and live feeds from neighboring countries. Al Jazeera, despite being banned from broadcasting from within Iraq (an example of the political obstacles that continue to impede information flow), also offered heavy coverage.[32]

Supplementing television's influence, the Internet increasingly contributed to the new sense of intellectual community:

- From Lebanon, bloggingbeirut.com provided real-time Web video of the "Cedar Revolution" demonstrations against Syria's presence in the country. This case demonstrated again how the speed and pervasiveness of the Internet make it a valuable mobilization tool; along with cell phones it can keep people abreast of what is happening and bring them into the streets.
- Bitterlemons.org, founded in 2003, has provided an online venue for debate between Israelis and Palestinians, with the goal of contributing to "mutual understanding through the open exchange of ideas" and affecting "the way Palestinians, Israelis, and others worldwide think about the Palestinian-Israeli conflict." It emphasizes balance and draws financial support from the European Union and philanthropic sources outside the Middle East.[33]
- Kurds in Iraq, Turkey, and elsewhere used the Web to nurture a virtual state through online communication among members of the far-flung Kurdish population. Traditional borders lose relevance when they no longer impede the flow of ideas. Kurdistan may not appear on conventional maps, but communications technology helps make it real.
- On an even larger scale, extending far beyond the Middle East, satellite television and the Internet may be bringing a degree of virtual cohesion to the *ummah,* giving members of the worldwide Islamic population some easily accessible common ground despite the many differences within this global community. The conventional wisdom about such linkage has been that the Muslim in Cairo and the Muslim in Djakarta really don't have much to say to each other. Their languages, national cultures, and politics differ greatly. But they share Islam and the extent to which that may prove to be a transcending unifying factor is not known. If there might be an as yet unformed cohesion within the *ummah* that new media can galvanize, global geopolitical

balances could be altered significantly. Policymakers would be wise to ponder this, keeping in mind that the Internet as a unifying tool does not require uniformity. Members of dispersed groups can tie themselves tightly or loosely, as they choose, to a central cultural identity. The Internet connects on its users' terms.

It is significant that many examples of new media impact primarily involve indigenous media. Just a few years ago—as recently as the Gulf War of 1991—audiences in the Middle East remained largely dependent on Western news sources such as CNN and the BBC. By the time of the U.S.-led invasion of Iraq in 2003, Al Jazeera, Al Arabiya, and other Arab satellite stations had supplanted the Western television news providers as principal sources for war news within the Arab world. One of the keys to the increasing media influence within the Middle East is that new media organizations are providing information about Arabs that is produced and delivered by Arabs. Although there has been much harrumphing, especially from Western pundits, about the purported flaws in the objectivity of these news sources, the real issue is *credibility*. The audience is not caught up in considering the fine points of journalistic practice. They are prepared to trust news from people like them. On a larger scale, Western media hegemony is in decline and this aspect of globalization has significant ramifications in the Middle East and elsewhere.

These issues also are relevant to the public diplomacy efforts undertaken by the United States. American policy makers should recognize that public opinion in the Middle East is being galvanized not by the lavishly funded U.S.-based broadcasting projects—such as Al Hurra television and Radio Sawa—but rather by regional and local media sources that are taking advantage of new technologies. Audience preferences are clear. A survey conducted by the Arab Advisors Group, an Amman-based consulting firm, that found that among Cairo households with satellite television reception, 88 percent watch Al Jazeera while 5 percent watch Al Hurra. Similar figures appear in studies of other Arab audiences.[34]

Emerging from the rush of events and the shifting global and local political dynamics is a region that is clearly changing—often quietly and with small steps, but changing. If this is considered to be an area where, in Bernard Lewis's words, "things had indeed gone badly wrong,"[35] maybe these changes will be redemptive for those who live there. But if that is to happen, further steps must be taken.

## Moving Onward

The availability of communication and information systems is certain to keep expanding. That will affect how individuals live and how nations operate on intrastate, regional, and global levels. The Middle East will not be the only area where this transformation occurs, but the rate of acceleration and breadth of movement toward democracy will be particularly significant there. The information-influenced political climate is volatile as well as vibrant, making it hard to map the path toward constructive change. Clearly, conventional borders are of decreasing significance as the transnational communication flow increases and audiences can find information sources that match their cultural and political interests. In Bahrain, Shiites watch Al Manar, Hezbollah's Beirut-based channel, and increasingly tune in to Iraqi television that provides details about violence in that country. When Iraqi Shiites are killed in terrorist attacks, some Bahraini Shiites respond by wearing black.[36]

In 2006, as the situation in Iraq deteriorated and war broke out between Israel and Hezbollah, satellite television and online communication—particularly blogs—made their presence felt to an unprecedented degree. Their effects have yet to be measured: did they help to exacerbate tensions, or did their depictions of conflict encourage a desire for peace? As policy makers try to find an answer to this, they should keep in mind that the speed and pervasiveness of the new media may keep the public better informed, but these same media also may also increase the already high volatility in such situations.

The news media—with their audience expanding through new technologies—will be among the most important players in determining whether conflict or peace prevails, which will in turn affect the chances for expansion of democracy. Absent thoughtful standards that most journalists decide to observe, democratization could founder as tumult overwhelms progress. Gadi Wolfsfeld warned about this tendency toward spectacle: "The news media are a poor forum for public discourse over political issues. The rules of access and norms of debate are mostly designed to ensure a good show rather than an intelligent exchange of views." In a region of unresolved disputes, the tone and substance of journalism are important, wrote Wolfsfeld, because "journalists working in a more sensationalist media environment, for example, will construct very different stories about conflict and peace than those operating in a more reserved milieu." Wolfsfeld argued that "journalists have an ethical obligation to encourage reconciliation between hostile populations" by providing as much information as possible about roots of problems and encouraging rational public debate about options for solving those problems.[37] The obligation of journalists to recognize the effects of information must go hand in hand with the democratization process in the Middle East, or else progress will be hard to come by.

A related factor to be weighed when looking ahead is the question of who will best utilize and most benefit from new media. Jon Alterman wrote that "As control of public opinion increasingly slips away from governments' grasp, those who can organize and mobilize will find a far more receptive environment than any time in the recent past." It is important to note, he added, that this does not necessarily mean democratization, because "Islamist groups in the Middle East are among the most modern of political organizations, both in their techniques of organizing and in the sophistication of their communications strategies."[38]

This is an important point; democracy can be blocked or undermined by parties within and outside government. As the authors of the *Arab Human Development Report* 2004 noted,

> In Arab countries today, there seems to be a contradiction between freedom and democracy because many democratic institutions that exist have been stripped of their original purpose to uphold freedom in its comprehensive sense. . . . There are some media outlets that are little more than mouthpieces for government propaganda, promoting freedom of speech only if it does not turn into political activity. Such captive outlets fail to stimulate intelligent and objective debate, enhance knowledge acquisition, and advance human development among the public at large.[39]

Without the advancement of debate and enhancement of knowledge to which new media can make substantive contributions, prospects for democracy will weaken. For those contributions to be meaningful, all involved in the information process—from the individual blogger to the big media corporation—must retain independence. Government pressure is inevitable but it must be resisted if the democratic process is to gain a foothold.

These issues raise many complex questions that have few precise answers. New media's role in progressive political change is hard to define with certainty because the path toward democratization remains uncharted. Those who move in that general direction do so with more faith than certainty. They may yet get there, and their chances of doing so will certainly be affected by the ongoing evolution of new media in Middle Eastern societies.

## NOTES

1. An earlier version of this chapter appeared in *Transnational Broadcasting Studies (TBS) Journal*, no. 15 (January–June 2006).
2. Mohamed Zayani, "Introduction—Al Jazeera and the Vicissitudes of the New Arab Mediascape," in Mohamed Zayani (ed.), *The Al Jazeera Phenomenon: Critical Perspectives on New Arab Media* (Boulder, CO: Paradigm, 2005), p. 33.
3. Marc Lynch, "Assessing the Democratizing Power of Satellite TV," *Transnational Broadcasting Studies (TBS) Journal*, no. 14 (Spring 2005).
4. Bernard Lewis, "Freedom and Justice in the Modern Middle East," *Foreign Affairs*, vol. 84, no. 3 (May/June 2005): 46.
5. Steve Coll, "In the Gulf, Dissidence Goes Digital," *Washington Post*, March 29, 2005.
6. David Crawford, "Battle for Ears and Minds: As Technology Gives New Voice to Dissent, a Saudi Vies to Be Heard," *Wall Street Journal*, February 4, 2004, A 14; John Bradley, *Saudi Arabia Exposed* (New York: Palgrave Macmillan, 2005), pp. 193–195.
7. "Mass Media, Press Freedom and Publishing in the Arab World: Arab Intellectuals Speak Out," United Nations news release *Arab Human Development Report 2003*, October 20, 2003.
8. Youssef M. Ibrahim, "Will the Mideast Bloom?" *Washington Post*, March 13, 2005.
9. Shanthi Kalathil and Taylor C. Boas, *Open Networks, Closed Regimes* (Washington, DC: Carnegie Endowment for International Peace, 2003), p. 150.
10. Charles Kupchan, *The End of the American Era* (New York: Knopf, 2002), p. 106.
11. David Ignatius, "Careful with Syria," *Washington Post*, November 18, 2005, A 23.
12. United Nations Development Program, *Arab Human Development Report 2003: Building a Knowledge Society* (New York: United Nations Publications, 2003), p. 63.
13. Available online at: <www.isu.net.sa>
14. Susan B. Glasser and Steve Coll, "The Web as Weapon," *Washington Post*, August 9, 2005, A 1.
15. Various examples available online at: <www.memritv.org>
16. Nicholas Watt and Leo Cendrowicz, "Brussels Calls for Media Code to Avoid Aiding Terrorists," *Guardian*, September 21, 2005.
17. Madeleine K. Albright and Vin Weber, *In Support of Arab Democracy: Why and How* (New York: Council on Foreign Relations, 2005), p. 30.
18. Neil MacFarquhar, "In Tiny Arab State, Web Takes on Ruling Elite," *New York Times*, January 15, 2006, 1, 11.
19. Cathy Hong, "New Political Tool: Text Messaging," *USA Today*, June 30, 2005.

20. Coll, "In the Gulf, Dissidence Goes Digital."
21. *Arab Human Development Report 2003*, p. 64.
22. Hugh Miles, *Al-Jazeera* (New York: Grove, 2005), pp. 327, 328.
23. Jon Alterman, "The Key Is Moving Beyond Spectacle," *Daily Star*, December 27, 2004.
24. Zayani, "Introduction," p. 35.
25. Marc Lynch, "Watching Al Jazeera," *Wilson Quarterly* (Summer 2005): 44.
26. Miles, *Al-Jazeera*, p. 328.
27. Jon Alterman, "The Information Revolution and the Middle East," in Nora Bensahel and Daniel L. Byman (eds.), *The Future Security Environment in the Middle East* (Santa Monica, CA: RAND, 2004), p. 243.
28. Kalathil and Boas, *Open Networks, Closed Regimes*, p. 128.
29. United Nations Development Program, *Arab Human Development Report 2004: Towards Freedom in the Arab World* (New York: United Nations Publications, 2005), p. 22.
30. "A World through Their Eyes," *The Economist*, February 26, 2005, 24.
31. Will Rasmussen, "Heya Satellite Channel Tackles Women's Core and Controversial Issues in Middle East," *Daily Star*, February 25, 2005.
32. Hassan Fattah, "Voting, Not Violence, Is the Big Story on Arab TV," *New York Times*, January 30, 2005.
33. Available online at: <www.bitterlemons.org/about>
34. Arab Advisors Group, "48 Percent of Households in Cairo Use the Internet and 46 Percent Have Satellite TV," news release, January 26, 2005.
35. Bernard Lewis, *What Went Wrong?* (New York: Oxford University Press, 2002), p. 151.
36. MacFarquhar, "In Tiny Arab State, Web Takes on Ruling Elite," p. 11.
37. Gadi Wolfsfeld, *Media and the Path to Peace* (Cambridge: Cambridge University Press, 2004), pp. 102, 2, 5.
38. Alterman, "Information Revolution and the Middle East," p. 244.
39. *Arab Human Development Report 2004*, p. 65.

# CHAPTER 2

# The Arab Search for a Global Identity: Breaking out of the Mainstream Media Cocoon

*Ibrahim Saleh*

## INTRODUCTION

According to the *Wikipedia Encyclopedia*, "identity is an umbrella term used throughout the social sciences for an individual's comprehension of him or herself as a discrete, separate entity." In cognitive psychology, identity refers to the "capacity for self-reflection and the awareness of self." In sociology and political science, the notion of social identity refers to "individuals' *labeling* of themselves as members of particular *groups*—such as nationality, social class, subculture, ethnicity, gender, employment, and so forth. It is in this sense which sociologists and historians speak of a national identity of a particular country."

Arab identity has yet to come to grips with the concept of globalization. Arab identity and Islam are closely associated since most Arabs are Muslims. (However, not all Arabs are Muslims and most Muslims are not Arabs.) At the dawn of the twenty-first century, the Arab world faces many challenges, but none is more formidable than the issue of how to strike a balance between maintaining cultural integrity and religious identity, on the one hand, and absorbing the changes associated with the globalizing world on the other. Identity is a most valuable possession, but what could be more challenging than the issues related to the concept of identity: creating identities, managing them throughout their lifecycle, and keeping the whole process under control?

The Arab world is not, despite common perception, monolithic. Although the majority of Arabs share a common geography, religion, language, broad culture and history, the Arab world is made up of different states, governments and peoples, and ethnic groups. Truly, the Arab world has a dominant culture that distinguishes it from, say, the West; however, it also has its subcultures, characteristic of certain communities and radical groups. Although the majority of its inhabitants adhere to Islam, other religions exist within the Arab world, including Judaism, Christianity, and others. That is why it is difficult to deal with this heterogeneous region in one study, although it cannot be denied that the Arab cultures, on the whole, do share an underlying common fabric. In this respect, both commonalities and juxtapositions should be taken into consideration in realizing a global identity within this cocoon environment.

Halim Barakat supports this viewpoint:

["Identity"] refers to the sharing of essential elements that define the character and orientation of people and affirm their common needs, interests, and goals with reference to joint action. At the same time it recognizes the importance of differences. Simply put, a nuanced view of national identity does not exclude heterogeneity and plurality.

The search for identity is an empirical attempt to decipher the myths and symbols of any community. The controversy over the origin of characteristics of local identity and how far they have been affected by exogenous effects creates arguments about "original versus copy." These disputes may overshadow the fact that such analysis is based on the idea that identity and culture are static, while in truth they are dynamic and evolving and are affected by interaction with other countries and civilizations, particularly in this globalizing world. According to Sami Zubaida, since the Middle Ages history has marked a continuous journey by the Western powers to discover the *terra incognita* of other cultures. Hence, local cultures in the Arab world have been idealized, dominated, or destroyed by Western conquests. Accordingly, the quest for "social inclusiveness" is a crucial element in the search for a global identity that emphasizes balanced representation of all cultural groups and the interactions among them.

Literally, "cocoon" refers to "silky covering made by an insect larva to protect itself while it is a chrysalis" or "any soft protective coverage." Figuratively, media have become like a cocoon in the sense of isolating audiences from real experiences and immersing them in distorted realities. Arabs suffer from media cocooning on two different levels. On the national level, till recently, mainstream media in most of the Arab countries lacked transparency and plurality. The news was disseminated from the perspective that governments wanted their publics to see. A lot of issues were never unveiled until recently when the level of freedom significantly increased. Thus, national media cocooned the publics, keeping the complete picture related to national affairs away from them. In the international arena, the West has cocooned their publics by ingraining in their minds an unfair image of the Arabs by projecting the exceptional cases of extremism as the norm. On account of this, Arabs and Muslims have been facing a lot of attacks, discrimination, detention, and harassment. A prime example of the West's cocooning of the publics is cited by Godfrey Cheshire (2003) in his article entitled "Why Should We Care about Iranian Films." Cheshire states,

> The first response many Americans have on encountering Iranian films is, "I had no idea . . . ." That reaction often gives way to a realization that our electronic media cocoon us in images that reduce an intricate reality like contemporary Iran to a single, endlessly repeated visual cliché: bearded fanatics shaking their fists at the "Great Satan" in a staged street demonstration, say. Iranian movies thus confront us, sometimes uncomfortably, with how limited our views of other cultures are. No less strikingly, the films' profound humanism, gentleness and intelligence can't help but ask why such values in our cinema have largely been swept away by images of escapist fantasy, aggression and violence.

Unfortunately, virtual reality is manipulated by the hypocrisies of religious institutions, the injustice of political contenders, and the narrow outlook of the citizens who play the dual roles of victims and participants in the oppression generated by the institutions.

The dictatorial practices to which Arabs have been subjected internally and externally led to the fracturing of Arab culture into "beleaguered minorities." This term is used by S.J. Makielski, Jr. to describe those who feel themselves to be surrounded by a hostile environment and who have a very long history of being subjected to discrimination and deprivation, yet they have no power to change their condition. As a result, Arabs visualize their own identity as a menace, a terrorist, or a shadowy figure that operates outside the accepted value system and is accordingly feared and scrutinized.

## Theoretical Perspectives

Too little attention has been paid to the subject of cultural identity, and such attempts as those that exist are mostly confined to issues of national identity. Moreover, most of these works are often dominated by a dichotomy between commercialism and social commitment. Arab identity is perceived as an alienated concept that lacks authenticity even from the indigenous people's perspective.

There is little doubt that a nation's (or people's) image that is propagated in the international arena is related to the balance of power in the world. News media were invented in the West, and the West still plays the leading role in the technical and artistic development of media content. Through the media cocoon, Westerners have developed a distorted image of the Arabs. However, underlying the Arab identity are cherished cultural values that are challenged by the needs of the modern world. A continuous conflict emerges from the attempt to bridge the gap between traditional and modern values.

In addition, the self-image of Arabs is twofold: the romantic sentimental attachment to idealized beauties of Arab culture, on the one hand, and the growing rebellion against the rigidity of the classic aesthetic on the other. The new spirit of cultural revolt does not accept the former static framework of social norms. Conservatives and liberals seek to advance their own perspectives, and this entangles the news media in the struggle over the definition of social reality.

Taylor identified four major variables involved in such process. The first is one's opinion of an issue, the second is one's perception of the predominant public opinion, the third is one's assessment of the likely future course of public opinion, and the fourth is one's willingness to support with verbal statements and other signs of commitment. That is why it is vital to deal with this burning issue through independent, comprehensive, and well-informed coverage of the issues of governance, social trends, media frames and theories, as well as economic development. It is noteworthy that knowledge of the public world is mediated by broadcast news institutions that are in the business of making money and shaping political perception by routinizing the nonroutine into temporal/visual formats. News media accounts do not merely describe events or issues but are rather part of continuous processes of inscribing preferred meanings into the social reality.

The main conceptual framework relevant to this study is the Social Identity Theory developed by H. Tajfel and J.C. Turner in 1979. It was originally developed to understand the psychological basis of intergroup discrimination by identifying the *minimal* conditions that would lead members of one group to discriminate in favor of the in-group to which they belonged and against the out-group to which they did not. In this context, social identity is an individual-based perception of what defines the "us" associated with any *internalized group membership.* This can be distinguished from the notion of "personal identity" that refers to self-knowledge that derives from the individual's unique attributes. The quest for *positive distinctiveness* means that people's sense of who they are is defined in terms of "we" rather than "I." Individuals are likely to display favoritism when an in-group is central to their self-definition and a given comparison is meaningful or the outcome is contestable.

"Group think" is another pertinent issue here. This term was devised in the 1970s by the American psychologist Irving Janis who analyzed group decision making in the 1961 Bay of Pigs fiasco and used the term to describe a process by which a group can make bad or *irrational* decisions. He defined "group think" as a form of decision making characterized by uncritical acceptance of a prevailing point of view. In a group think situation, each member of the group attempts to conform one's individual opinion to what each believes to be the *consensus* of the group. This may result in the group ultimately agreeing upon an action that each member might individually consider unwise (the *risky shift*).

Group think is a severe problem in Arab society because it turns members of a group into believers and followers of rituals. They believe their group is right and others are wrong. It reduces the communication of the group with outsiders. In serious cases of group think, members may use force and violence to convince nonbelievers. Every day, governments and other institutions spend large amounts of resources to protect and promote their group think. To solve the problem of group think, we have to show people reality—the reality of how their group think relates to the prospects and demands of possible development.

## MILESTONES IN THE DEVELOPMENT OF ARAB IDENTITY

Over the centuries, the Arab world has confounded the dreams of conquerors and peacemakers alike. Its huge oil reserves have given it global economic importance and unique strategic value. Hence, historical and cultural discourses were formulated based on the constructions of "the other." Islam has always remained in the eyes of the West as a totally strange culture. Arabs themselves have perpetuated the idea of unilateral cultural import, that is, the belief that identity can be authentic only if its features spring from a particular environment and develop according to specific conditions. Such preserved original identity can exist only within an impermeable cultural environment that is cut off from foreign influences—an idea that exits among Arabs even today and can explain many of the phobias related to globalization.

In pre-Islamic Arabia, a person's social identity was derived solely from the membership in the tribe. That entailed taking part in all tribal activities, especially those involving the tribal cult. However, as Reza Aslan (2006) indicates, after the advent of Islam, the "Kharaijites," Shia't Ali, emerged as a small faction that represented the first self-conscious attempts at defining a distinctive Muslim identity. They based their leadership on the most pious person in their community irrespective of the tribe, lineage, and ancestry.

During the eighteenth and the nineteenth centuries, religion and the state were unified entities. At that time, religion was culture, ethnicity, and social identity; hence, it was citizenship. This was the case among Zoroastrians, the Jews, Christians, Muslims, and others, as each group tried to enforce a specific vision of its beliefs. In the Arab world, territorial expansion was always associated with religious proselytizing, and each religion was the "religion of the sword." In fact, "holy war" did not originate from Islam but through the Crusaders who gave a purported theological legitimacy to what was in reality a battle for land and trade routes.

Currently, Western media cluster Arabs and Muslims as proponents of terrorism and other violence for political gain, although Islam actually calls for universal brotherhood, equality, and social justice. As Azmi Bishara points out,

> One cannot help but notice in the course of the ongoing debate on democracy and reform in the Arab world that those who are most adamant in denying the existence of such a thing as Arab identity are the quickest to lump all these countries together when it comes to criticizing them. Arab, as a collective designation, is okay as long as it is used in a negative context.

The ignorance of journalists covering the region is one principal reason for misunderstanding the Arab identity and culture, thus developing media bias as well as promoting the notion of Islamophobia. Even when foreign news agencies attempt to place the events in a historical context, they often get facts wrong and create an inaccurate or misleading impression. In addition, photographers and television camera crews seek the most dramatic pictures they can find, and the context is often missing. The media routinely adopt the news frames that fit their agendas. Once an image or impression is ingrained in someone's mind, it is often difficult, if not impossible, to erase it.

George Stanth contends that the current Arab identity has evolved out of the relation between the synergetic popular culture and elite culture, in addition to relationships with indigenous catalysts and exogenous influences over the years. Within the framework of this newly appearing Arab identity, the former isolated one has become increasingly obsolete because Arab culture has increasingly converged with "consumer culture."

This conversion to consumer culture can be attributed to the growing use of the Internet and satellite technology in the Arab world. In a field study conducted for the British Council by A. C. Nielsen, as a vital part of the project titled "Social Issues in the Eyes of the Media," one question investigated media habits in the Middle East and North Africa.

As graph 2.1 illustrates, watching TV seems to be the most common activity (100 percent), followed by listening to the radio (73 percent), then surfing the Internet (62 percent), and finally reading (55 percent). Though surfing the net comes in the third position, its percentage is significant, and it reflects the growing audience consumption of Internet content among the people in the MENA (Middle East and North Africa) region.

Reviewing the top six reasons for using the Internet (graph 2.2), communication through email comes on top of the list (67 percent). However, following up the latest news and looking for information have considerable percentages—59 percent and 49 percent respectively.

It should be noted that, as Jon Alterman states, major Western networks such as MSNBC and NBC as well as important print and broadcast sources such as Al-Ahram and Al Jazeera have Arabic Web sites. This makes them easily accessible to a great number of Arabs.

In another question about the most-watched TV channels, the results (graph 2.3) indicated that there is not one truly dominant

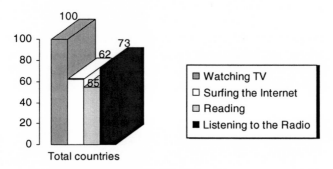

**Graph 2.1**  Media Habits in the Middle East

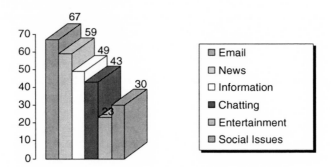

**Graph 2.2**   Top Reasons for Using the Internet

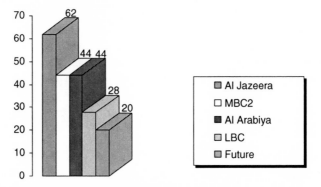

**Graph 2.3**   Most-Watched TV Channels

terrestrial or local channel among respondents' preferences. All the channels are transnational channels that range from those presenting just news to those presenting entertainment or a package of different programming. Al Jazeera dominates the Arab market (62 percent) followed by Al-Arabiya (44 percent).

With this boom in Arab satellite television channels and growing Internet usage, which enabled more Arabs to have access to real-time information, it is crucial to examine issues such as the type of audiences that the Arab media address, the advantages they brought about to the audiences, if any, and the role they play in breaking away from the cocoon environment nationally and internationally.

Concerning the audiences, satellite channels fiercely compete for market share and most of them target Arab audiences in general rather than a particular national category, and the viewers are of all ages. With respect to the Internet, the majority of users are youth and young adults. While the first category uses the Internet mostly for emailing, downloading entertainment material, chatting, and other such features, most of the young adults use it for following up the news or looking for information.

It cannot be denied that the role of satellite stations and access to the Internet in the Arab world is remarkable because they have opened the doors to the outside world and made available information to the Arab peoples. In the recent past, connecting to the rest of the world was a farfetched dream; however, one can now communicate with people from the other side of the world as if they were just next door. Besides, online stores have made buying anything from any place in the world more than easy. Through satellite channels, many people have come to know things about "the other" they could have never dreamt of before. In addition, in the past, the Arabs were exposed only to "official" news through media that were mouthpieces of their governments. Now, thanks to the Internet and international satellite channels, there is less constraint on news dissemination. Any person can gain access to the news from all possible perspectives.

Exposure to such media has, however, redefined the kind of identity the Arabs used to adhere to in traditional mainstream media. Despite offering a window on the world, the breakthrough into the international media universe has led to growing extremism in the region as people have become either neoliberals, seeking Westernization in the copycat manner, or conservatives, blocking change and sticking to the historical interpretation of identity. The first group perceives the West from a glittering generalized perspective, which leads them to attempt to imitate it. This has led to sociopolitical problems and disintegration of societal values. For example, the latest statistics indicate that more than 40 percent of the couples in Egypt divorce as a result of men being dissatisfied with their wives and seeking women that fit the *Bay Watch* and *The Bold and the Beautiful* image.

Unfortunately, in this copycat process only the negative side of Western values is assimilated while great values such as the appreciation of hard work, commitment, and punctuality are ignored. The other side of extremism is incarnated in those gripped by sectarian or extremist thought and a preference for certain ethnic groups or sects—a realization of what Samuel Huntington calls "fault lines." The coexistence of these two poles together is rather difficult, and it has produced social tension and political agitation.

Speaking of transnational channels' breaking out of the mainstream media cocoon, there is no doubt such channels have led to increased access to information and have loosened state monopoly over media content. Due to the lack of political responsiveness to citizens' true needs and problems, some talk shows in some satellite channels try to be the principal forum for genuine public debate. Thus, the motto of Al Jazeera, for example, is "opinion and counter-opinion."

The communications revolution, in some cases, has helped challenge the official record of history and has created a forum of expression beyond the reach of the state censor. Until the boom in electronic media, the news was transmitted through traditional means that could be easily distorted. Currently, the declining monopoly of information has encouraged daring journalists and other media persons to break the typical social and political taboos, exposing the most conservative households to debates ranging from women's rights to gay marriage.

In a way, it can be said that these channels respond to their audiences' demands; however, they still cannot fully serve as watchdog over the government, and the content in many of them is still restrained by political or business considerations. As stated in "Arab Media: Tools of the Governments; Tools for the People,"

> For journalists to raise objections to the picture of regime rectitude and regional solidarity is to risk censorship, jail, or worse. Strict self-censorship reigns as the modus operandi among media professionals; some might say that it takes the place of the journalistic ethics practiced where a free press exists.

With regard to the role of such new media in attempting to penetrate the international arena and expressing the Arab voice and identity, it is sad that Arab channels have given much space to Western affairs while they have neglected issues related to neighboring Arab countries. As a result, many Arabs now know more about Americans than they know about their fellow Arabs.

> The media do not delve into national or local issues because these are the issues that most threaten their governments' authority and legitimacy. Coverage of specific problems in individual Arab countries is absent. The justification offered is that people in one country—Oman, for example—would not be interested in Morocco's national issues. ("Arab Media: Tools of the Governments; Tools for the People")

Similarly, many Web sites rely on Western news wires such as Agence France-Presse, the Associated Press, and Reuters rather than present an Arab perspective. Further, Internet technology is used by young people mostly for chatting about meaningless matters rather than for trying to enlighten "the other" about the true Arab identity and the essence of Islam, even though making fruitful use of such technology can lead to wonderful results.

Dr. Martin Luther King said, "We fear each other because we have not communicated with each other! We do not communicate with each other because we fear each other!" The first part of the quotation expresses one main reason for the Western view of Arabs. In an attempt to make use of Internet technology to break out of the international media cocoon and help bridge the knowledge gap between the West and the Middle East, the American University in Cairo (AUC) and Soliya—a nongovernmental nonprofit organization based in the United States—arranged a Web conferencing program involving students from the United States and the Middle East. The program provided university students with an opportunity for cross-cultural dialogue. They collaboratively explored the relationship between their regions with a view to improving intercultural awareness and understanding. Prior to the program, 42 percent of the Arab students and 23 percent of the American students rated their knowledge of the issues affecting the U.S.-Arab/Muslim relations as high. After the program, the figures changed to 83 percent and 70 percent respectively (graph 2.4).

The program also had a positive impact on drawing respondents' attention to the fact that the media have had a significant role in misleading the public and swaying public opinion against "the other." A Qatari female student stated, "I learned that the American media is the main reason why there are many stereotypes and false ideas on Islam and the Arab world." Similarly, an American student admitted, "I learned that the media can greatly misinform both Americans and people in the Middle East." The program also offered students an opportunity to

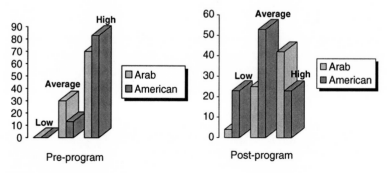

**Graph 2.4** Knowledge of Issues

examine their own prejudices by trying to discover "the other" through first-hand experience. Another female Qatari student expressed her opinion about the aspect she liked best about the program saying,

> Respecting each other's opinions is what attracted me most in this program. I'm glad it ended up without any misunderstanding or serious disagreement. I was happy to see how my American partners in this program could express themselves freely and were brave to tell us all about the stereotypes they had. I enjoyed answering all their questions about Islam and the Arab world and discussing our perspectives on the Arab-American relationship.

## INDIRECT INDICATORS OF ARAB IDENTITY THROUGH EMPIRICAL OBSERVATIONS

A survey conducted in 2005 at the American University in Cairo by Mirray Fahim and Karim Zein El-Abdien under the supervision of Ibrahim Saleh using a sample of 200 university students of different ages, religions, nationalities, and majors sought answers to five questions:

Q.1 Can we develop identity away from Religion?

| Yes | No | Don't Know | No Response |
| --- | --- | --- | --- |
| 40% | 38% | 18% | 4% |

Q.2 What is the importance of democracy for identity development?

| Important | Not Important | Don't Know | No Response |
| --- | --- | --- | --- |
| 54% | 28% | 6% | 12% |

Question 1 asked about the possibility of dissociating identity from religion. Although some scholars insist that Arab identity is not based on religion but on issues such as ethnicity, the responses highlight the dichotomy among the youth.

Question 2 asked about the link between democracy and identity, which is explained by Azmy Bishara who defines democracy as a group of values empowered by a number of principles and systems—the separation of powers, judiciary autonomy, civil rights, the peaceful rotation of authority though the elections, mechanisms for checking and punishing the abuse of power, and others. He argues, "In the context of democratic thought, there is scope for asserting national identity, so long as such confirmation promotes the processes of modernization and democratization and helps resistance against Western domination."

Q3. How can we empower identity development?

| Freedom | Diversity of Views | Standard of Living | Other |
|---------|--------------------|--------------------|-------|
| 24% | 31% | 27% | 18% |

Though the respondents rated "diversity of views" higher than the other elements, the percentages indicate that young people are collectively undecided about the foundation for identity development.

Q4. What are the elements of one's own identity?

| Religion | Race | Social Class | Sex | Other |
|----------|------|--------------|-----|-------|
| 24% | 22% | 16% | 20% | 18% |

Q5. How do you label one another?

| Religion | Race/Ethnicity | Social Class | Educational Level | Occupation |
|----------|----------------|--------------|-------------------|------------|
| 27% | 21% | 25% | 19% | 8% |

In the responses to questions 4 and 5, it can be inferred that "religion" plays a slightly higher role in "labeling one another" (27 percent) than in "identifying oneself" (24 percent). With regard to "race," the percentages are very close in both "labeling one another" (21 percent) and "identifying oneself" (22 percent). The surprising point is that the "social class" variable is rated much higher in "labeling one another" (25 percent) than in "identifying oneself" (16 percent). These three elements represent the double standards used in defining current Arab identity.

Another pan-Arab study of media professionals and media students was conducted as part of a project entitled "Social Issues in the Eyes of the Media" sponsored by the British Council. The sample was a purposive nonprobability one composed of 1210 persons fromsix countries (Egypt, Saudi Arabia, Palestine, Jordan, Syria, and Lebanon).

The first question asked about the major social issues that affect one's life and accordingly have an impact on one's identity. The respondents gave priority to unemployment (88 percent), while poverty (47 percent) came second, and marriage and divorce came third (46 percent). The list is long, but this triad indicates a causal relation between identity and development. This makes the economic factors followed by the social problems main obstacles in the way of any possible improvement.

The second question asked about the respondents' goals in life. The respondents cited getting a suitable job (36 percent), being successful in life (27 percent), raising a family (23 percent), and living a happy life (6 percent). This illustrates how economic issues affect the lives of Arabs and their perception of the future.

The third question asked about the kinds of activities that Arab citizens typically get involved in. Some of the answers were prestige answers such as "reading newspapers" or "reading magazines" because of the high rates of illiteracy and the poverty in the region. However, other responses such as "watching TV" or "listening to the radio" seem very true and several of them provide insight into the Arab identity. One has to do with the increasing rates of activities such as going to cafés (40 percent) or watching TV (100 percent) that are group oriented, while others such as playing sports (31 percent) or going to the parks (18 percent) emphasize the decreasing levels of personal interests. Limited economic resources presumably constrain the type of the activities that individuals engage in.

## Concluding Remarks

Globalization can be conceptualized on different levels of theory building, because it is shaped by the capitalist economy, the nation-state system, the military order, and the whole global information structure. Many hypotheses have focused on local, national, and regional institutions and markets, although they often emphasize expressions of resurgent nationalism and separate cultural identities. There are serious doubts about whether the internationalization of media technology and networks is contributing to creation of a new Arab identity.

Priority should be given to strengthening local community control over processes of ecological, cultural, and social change. Synergy between indigenous and global scientific knowledge could enhance biological and cultural diversity, reinforce equity in resource governance, and strengthen comprehensive cultural, social, and environmental impact assessments. The search for Arab identity involves identifying the customary rules and processes that govern knowledge access and control in order to develop appropriate normative instruments for protecting traditional knowledge.

Although it is school that we associate most often with learning and education, communities themselves provide open learning environments. Learning as a basic human activity is no longer associated only with formal and structured schooling: enclosed spaces, individual assessment, rigid timetables, and the like. The notion of the open learning community sees learning as a group or social activity rather than a strictly individual one. Every culture teaches its young how to behave; every family shares its knowledge of the world with its younger members; every society has specialized moments of learning at different stages of life. All of us are lifelong learners. Communities of learning can build upon cultural institutions as diverse as the societies to which they belong or can create new forms of cultural expression, thanks mainly to the new technologies. The challenge is for education systems to adapt to the complex realities and provide a quality education that takes into consideration learners' needs and political demands. While uniform solutions for plural societies may be both administratively and managerially simpler, they disregard the risks involved both in terms of learning achievement and loss of linguistic and cultural diversity.

Arabs perceive globalization as a power game from which great powers draw immense gains and to which the rest of the world is subjugated. In this regard, the traditional Arab identity represents a collective form of resistance to globalization. This is invariably intertwined with the rise of counterhegemonic consciousness. Nevertheless, the mainstream media, even in the Arab world, stipulate that this region has no choice but to adjust to the modern times and their accompanying changes. Another school of thought presumes that globalization is a paradigm shift from which there is no escape. This shift requires changes in the lifestyle, value systems, as well as the cultural and mental attitudes toward the local, the national, and the universal. None can deny the fact that globalization has caused serious deterioration in the Arab culture, yet it has intensified the local cultural politics.

For Arabs, the issue of identity must be more a matter of recognition rather than self-assertion. It is important to bear in mind that the dialectic of local and global experiences is bound to produce divergent yet understandably paradoxical effects. However, the Arab identity is constructed in a dynamic process, and it assumes multiple forms that permit individuals and societies to uphold both cultural diversity and global norms such as protection of human rights and democratization.

It should be noted that a reassertion of the Arab identity in this global age may simply be a reaction to the extant social discrimination, racism, and high unemployment rates. It is equally important to remember that some Western countries have straddled multiculturalism and assimilation policies, but they have failed to effectively pursue either.

Since the 9/11 terrorist attacks in the United States, Arabs too, and not just Muslim immigrants living in the United States, have become the targets of indiscriminate media attacks. Ironically, however, such media bias has strengthened Muslims' religious identity. Consequently, many Muslims have turned to their own local networks and local identity as an effective way to safeguard themselves against social stigmatization and discrimination. The upshot has been huddling through one's enclave— ethnic, religious, or otherwise—to feel secure and safe.

The Arab culture, and accordingly Arab identity, has strong links with its many subcultures and identities. The struggle is to redefine or discover such identities in this dynamic changing world of globalization in which the rules of the media game are in the hands of non-Arabs. A common syndrome among Arabs is their continuous disagreements about everything except identity: the quest for and the assertion and affirmation of identity, regardless of variant ethnic, religious, or political ideologies.

The acquisition of electronic media was a sign of progress in Arab identity, though its negative impact cannot be overlooked. No doubt, Arab identity is going through a dynamic evolution, moving away from the previous rigid identity that has become incompatible with the changes in an increasingly globalized society. However, this identity should not develop in isolation from Arabs' own identity as a distinct group. It should be one that pertains to Arab history and culture but with a capacity for change and growth. The dynamic evolution of Arab identity means that society is moving ahead and undermines the claims that the West and the Arabs cannot find common ground.

Breaking out of the current media cocoon requires a broader critique of the Arab society. There is a necessity for developing a causal relation between the dynamic evolution of Arab identity and the creation of a critical domestic media environment. This is a long process because it first appeals to the elite public and gradually penetrates to the other strata. This potential reform has to stem from a constitutional structure that recognizes an international ethical journalism standard that endorses respect for cultures and religions and promotes tolerance.

The Arabs have failed so far, with the exception of a few successful attempts, to project an image that is not idealistic but successful in changing the stereotypes of Arabs as terrorists, old-fashioned, rigid, and anti-Western. The reasons for this failure are the lack of the know-how about structuring sound discourse, the failure in achieving full participation in the arena of international satellite communication, the lack of professional skills that can pursue this kind of communication, weak media financing, and the underestimation of the potential effects of dialogue across cultures, in addition to the overwhelming romantic fallacy that Arabs have culture, history, and identity that need not be modified as part of strategic planning or marketing. The real challenge facing the recognition of the true Arab identity is establishing a crisis management policy that considers the strategic public diplomacy and military censorship employed by most players in the region, providing access to alternative sources of information as well as boosting multinational professional dialogue.

## BIBLIOGRAPHY

Alterman, J. *New Media, New Politics: From Satellite Television to the Internet in the Arab World* (Washington, DC: Washington Institute for Near East Policy, 1998).

Aslan, Reza. *No God But God: The Origins, Evolution and Future of Islam* (New York: Random House, 2006).

Atwater, N., and Green, N.F. "News Source in Network Coverage of the International Terrorism." *Journalism Quarterly*, vol. 65, no. 3 (Autumn 1998): 967–971.

Bishara, A. (July 28–August 3, 2005). "Opinion, Identity and Democracy." *Al-Ahram Weekly Online*, 753, available online at: <http://www.ahram. org./2005/753/op31.htm> (Accessed: June 2, 2006).

Cohen, S., and Young, J. (eds.) *The Manufacture of News: Deviance, Social Problems and Mass Media* (London: Sage, 1981), pp. 118–137.

Dennis, D. (2001). "The War on Perceptions: Exploiting U.S. Media and Governance Practices," available online at: <www.ctheory.net/articles. aspx?id=319> (Accessed: November 27, 2001).

Edelman, M. "Contestable Categories and Public Opinion." *Political Communication*, vol. 10 (1993): 231–242.

Entman, R. "Framing: Towards Clarification of a Fractured Paradigm." *Journal of Communication*, vol. 43, no. 4 (1993): 51–58.

Feldman, S., and Zaller, J. "Political Culture of Ambivalence: Ideological Responses to the Welfare State." *American Journal of Political Science*, vol. 36 (1992): 268–307.

Gibran, G.K. *The Vision: Reflections on the Way of the Soul* (New York: Penguin Books, 2004).

Graber, D. "Content and Meaning." *American Behavioral Scientist*, vol. 33, no. 2 (1989): 144–152.

Haleem, B. "Arab Identity: E. Pluribus Unum." *The Arab World: Society, Culture and State* (Berkeley: University of California Press, 1993).

Herman, E., and Chomsky, N. *Manufacturing Consent: The Political Economy of the Mass Media* (New York: Pantheon Books, 1988).

Janis, I. *Victims of Groupthink: A Psychological Study of Foreign-Policy Decisions and Fiascoes* (Boston: Houghton Mifflin, 1972).

Kennamer, D.J. "Self Serving Biases in Perception of the Opinions of Others." *Communication Research*, vol. 17(1990): 393–404.

Krippendorf, K. *Content Analysis an Introduction to its Methodology* (Beverly Hills, CA: Sage, 1980).

Lodge, M., and Hamil, R. "A Partisan Schema for Political Information Processing." *American Political Science Review*, vol. 80 (1986): 505–519.

Makielski, S.J., *Beleagured Minorities: Cultural Politics in America*. San Francisco: W. H. Freeman, 1973.

Mansfield, P. *A History of the Middle East*, 2nd edition (New York: Penguin, 2003).

Moscovici, S. "Silent Majorities and Loud Minorities," in J.A. Anderson (ed.), *Communication Yearbook*, vol. 14 (Newbury Park, CA: Sage, 1991), pp. 298–308.

Pipes, D. *The Long Shadow: Culture and Politics in the Middle East.* (Piscataway, NJ: Transaction Publishers, 1988).

Said, E. *Covering Islam: How the Media and Experts Determine how We See the Rest of the World* (New York: Pantheon Books, 1981).

———. *The End of the Peace Process: Oslo and After* (New York: Pantheon Books, 2000).

Saleh, I. *Unveiling the Truth of Middle Eastern Media. Privatization in Egypt: Hope or Dope?* (Cairo: Cairo Media Center, Modern Sciences and Arts, 2003).

———. *The Geo-political Self-image of Israel* (Cairo: Cairo University Press, 2004).

———. *Prior to the Eruption of the Grapes of Wrath in the Middle East: The Necessity of Communicating Instead of Clashing* (Cairo: Teeba Corporation, 2006).

Scheufele, D. "Framing as a Theory of Media Effects." *Journal of Communication*, vol. 49, no. 1 (1999): 103–122.

Shafiq, V. Arab *Cinema: History and Cultural Identity* (Cairo: AUC Press, 1988).

Shamir, J. "Information Cues and Indicators of the Climate of Opinion: The Spiral of Silence Theory in the *Intifada*." *Communication Research*, vol. 22, no. 1 (February 1995): 24–30.

Shoemaker, P., and Reese, S. *Mediating the Message: Theories of Influences on Mass Media Content* (White Plains, NY: Longman Publishers, 1996).

Solomon, J. *Signs of Our Time* (Los Angeles: Jeremy P. Tarcher, 1988).

Stanth, G. "Local Communities and Mass Culture," in George Stanth and Sami Zubaida (eds.), *Mass Culture, Popular Culture and Social Life in the Middle East* (Boulder, CO: Westview Press, 1987).

Stempel, G.H. "Content Analysis," in G.H. Stempel and B.H. Westley (eds.) *Research Methods in Mass Communication* (Englewood Cliffs, NJ: Prentice-Hall, 1989).

Tajfel, H., and Turner, J.C. "The Social Identity Theory of Inter-Group Behavior," in S. Worchel, and L.W. Austin (eds.), *Psychology of Intergroup Relations* (Chicago: Nelson-Hall, 1986).

Thayer, G. *The War Business: The International Trade in Armaments* (New York: Avon, 1969).

Tiffen, R. *News and Power* (Sydney: Allen & Unwin, 1989).

The United States Institute of Peace (September 2005) "Arab Media: Tools of the Governments, Tools for the People?" *The International Journal of Not-for-Profit Law*, vol. 7, no. 4, available online at: <http://www.icnl. org/ijnl/vol7iss4/special_3.htm> (Accessed: May 15, 2006).

Valkenburg, P., Semetko, H., and De Vreese, C. "The Effects of News Frames on Readers' Thoughts and Recall." *Communication Research*, vol. 26, no. 5 (1999): 550–569.

Werner J., S., and Tankard, J.W., Jr. *Communication Theories: Origins, Methods and Uses in the Mass Media* (New York: Longman, 2001).

*Wikipedia: The Free Encyclopedia*, available online at: <http://enwikipedia. org/wiki/Identity_(social_science)> (Accessed: June 1, 2006).

Wimmer, R.D., and Dominick, J.R. (1997). *Mass Media Research: An Introduction*. Belmont, CA: Wadsworth, 1997.

Wodak, R. (ed.) *Language, Power and Ideology: Studies in Political Discourse* (Amsterdam: Benjamins Publishing, 1989).

Zhu, J. "Issue Competition and Attention Distraction: A Zero-Sum Theory of Agenda Setting." *Journalism Quarterly*, vol. 68 (1998): 825–836.

Zubaida, S. "Comparisons of Popular Culture in the Middle East," in George Stanth and Sami Zubaida (eds.), *Mass Culture, Popular Culture and Social Life in the Middle East* (Boulder, CO: Westview Press, 1987).

Zuckerman, M. "Looking with Both Eyes." *U.S. News & World Report*, April 21, 1997.

# CHAPTER 3

# The Role of New Arab Satellite Channels in Fostering Intercultural Dialogue: Can Al Jazeera English Bridge the Gap?

*Sahar Khamis*

Previous research dealing with the images and "stereotypes" of Arabs and Muslims in Western media has largely verified "that lurid and insidious depictions of Arabs as alien, violent strangers, intent upon battling nonbelievers throughout the world, are staple fare. Such erroneous characterizations more accurately reflect the bias of Western reporters and image-makers than they do the realities of Muslim people in the modern world."[1]

Studying the distorted media images of Arabs and Muslims in the Western media is not a new topic. In fact, it is a topic that has been tackled extensively in media research. However, the new international events and developments that took place in recent years, starting with the September 11 attack and ending with the current troubled conditions in postwar Iraq, the violence in the occupied Palestinian territories, and the war on Lebanon, necessitate (re)addressing and (re)visiting this issue. This is especially important in light of how new "realities" could lead to either creating new distorted "images," or reinforcing old ones.

It is particularly important to acknowledge the power of the international news coverage presented by major American television networks, such as CNN, ABC, NBC, and CBS, in shaping American public opinion toward political issues and developments, in general, and toward Arab and Muslim nations and people, in particular. This post-9/11 coverage by global American TV networks, which also coincided with America's declared "war against terrorism," has to a large degree reinforced some of the negative images of Arabs and Muslims, especially images of "violence" and "terrorism." This means that many Americans when they think of Islam, especially these days, they "tend to visualize media-driven images of violence."[2]

The importance of media coverage and media images also extends beyond the domain of shaping public opinion to the domain of shaping public policy and diplomacy. That is mainly because U.S. media elite tend to follow U.S. policy, while, at the same time, those responsible for shaping policies are influenced in part by the stereotypical media images and pictures in their heads.[3]

On the other hand, it is equally important to examine the other side of the coin, which comprises the images and stereotypes formed in the minds of Arab and Muslim people about America as a nation and the Americans as a people, and about the role Arab satellite channels play in shaping these images. This is a particularly important aspect to address taking into account the growing tide of "anti-Americanism," which is currently prevailing through many parts of the world, in general, and through the Arab and Islamic world, in particular.[4]

Complex political, economic, and cultural factors contribute to this negativism toward the United States, which has even made some of the traditionally pro-American groups in the Middle East, such as Western-educated elites, severely critical of current U.S. policies in the region. However, out of these many factors, one is of particular importance and significance, which is the fact that the United States is not just the "lone hyperpower" in today's modern world; rather, it has also become the only "defining" power of the world.[5]

This was confirmed in a public opinion survey conducted in Egypt after 9/11 and after President Bush's declaration of the "war on terrorism." It showed that 96.3 percent of the total sample of 1083 Egyptians covered in the survey disagreed with the American definition of terrorism, since they felt that the most serious form of terrorism is the kind of state terrorism that is exercised by Israel against the Palestinian people.[6] Moreover,

> The power to define also extends to representation: America defines the way in which other people should be seen and characterized. The US is the storyteller to the world . . . This power to define others in terms of American perceptions and interests often leads to the dehumanization of entire groups of people. Consider the way in which all Arabs are seen as "fundamentalists."[7]

Therefore, the birth of Arab satellite channels signified the start of a new era of self-definition and self-representation for Arabs and Muslims. Studies dealing with Arab audiences' motivations for watching these satellite channels indicated that the most important source of credibility and attractiveness in these channels is the fact that they present news from an Arab perspective and defend Arab interests.[8]

In fact, a survey covering audiences in a number of Arab countries revealed that 90 percent of the respondents' main reason for preferring Arab satellite channels over all other channels is the "authenticity" of these channels in terms of reflecting the "cultural fabric and traditions" of the Arab nation.[9]

Additionally, the significant changes in the media environment in the Arab world since the early 1990s, especially the legalization of private sector ownership of satellite channels, brought about a new era of diversity and relative freedom, away from direct state ownership and control.[10] This is another important factor to be considered in analyzing the depiction of the "Other" through these channels, and in exploring the complexity of intervening factors that could potentially influence media images and representations.

It clearly emerges from the previous discussion that there is an introduction of both new political realities as well as new types of media that are likely to contribute to the formation of new media images, and the reinforcement or challenging of already existing ones. It is, therefore, important to assess the interplay of these complex and dynamic factors, and their potential impact on the process of cross-cultural communication and understanding between the West and the East, in general, and between the Arab world and the United States, in particular.

## THE CHALLENGES CONFRONTING ARAB SATELLITE CHANNELS

So far, these "Pan-Arab" satellite channels, which broadcast mainly in Arabic and address a predominantly Arab audience, have not successfully challenged the negative images and false stereotypes on both sides. On one hand, some studies, drawing upon the theoretical background of "cultural cultivation" research, have verified the strong impact of TV images of Arabs and Muslims, as presented through major American TV networks, on shaping American public opinion about the Arab and Islamic nations and their people.[11] It is a fact that the largely "pan-Arab" satellite channels have not been successful in changing, or even challenging, the negative stereotypes of Arabs and Muslims that are cultivated by different segments of American society through television in light of various international political developments since September 11, 2001.

It can be argued that the Arab satellite channels have not managed, so far, to deploy effective "media diplomacy," which is as much needed as effective "public diplomacy," to arrive at better cross-cultural communication and understanding.[12] On the other hand, it is equally true that various segments of the Arab public cultivated false media images and negative stereotypes about America and Americans through Arab satellite channels' coverage of international political events since 9/11. Therefore, it is vital to assess the role played by these primarily pan-Arab media outlets in shaping Arab public opinion trends and attitudes toward the West in general and the United States in particular.

Taking into account the fact that no single factor leads to the creation of false images and negative stereotypes on both sides, we should consider the complexity of factors that could contribute to false stereotyping and (mis)perceptions of the "other" in the first place. Within this context, we can argue that it is essential to analyze the multiple challenges that are confronting these "new media," namely Arab satellite channels, in building better bridges of cross-cultural understanding.

These challenges are multidimensional and they could be divided into three main categories: political challenges, cultural and educational challenges, and professional challenges.

Regarding the political challenges, it could be argued that despite the relative atmosphere of freedom that has permitted private ownership of satellite TV channels in many Arab countries, there are still many political limitations and restrictions on freedom of the press in many Arab countries. This is clearly demonstrated by the fact that many Arab governments retain direct and indirect control over the media, and that the general pattern of media ownership in a good number of Arab countries is still predominantly characterized by public, governmental ownership.[13] Therefore, the Arab world's attempts to communicate with the outside world have been largely inadequate and unsuccessful because government officials in most cases tell the media what they should do and say, which makes the media unable to make the required "cultural jump" and negatively affects the credibility of Arab media.

This explains why the most successful and most popular media in the Arab world today are the semi-independent media, such as Al Jazeera and Al Arabiya, which were able to get around direct governmental control for the first time and to present an alternative, free voice, thus presenting news from a "pan-Arab" perspective that is different from the official, governmental perspective.[14]

One major criticism that can be voiced against these Arab satellite channels, however, is that they are still largely restricted to a regional audience, due to their inability to address a wide, international audience. This reinforces the image of Arabs who are "talking to themselves," rather than to the rest of the world.

One of the counterarguments is that "these channels were not created for the purpose of communicating with the outside world; rather, they were created in order to present a new model of media freedom within the Arab world, which is different from the classic model of having a government official telling the story."[15] In other words, the main argument here is that despite the fact that these channels did not fill the gap in terms of creating a successful international dialogue, they were to a large degree successful in terms of breaking away from the traditional model of direct governmental censorship and hegemony. This, in turn, helped to boost Arab media's credibility to a large degree, not just within the Arab world, but also abroad—a factor that could have positive implications on the Arab media's international image and their ability to effectively communicate with the outside world.

The second major challenge confronting many of the Arab media is cultural and educational, which could be crystallized in what is called the "knowledge crisis" in the Arab world. This term refers to the fact that there are still many obstacles to gaining knowledge and spreading it in most Arab communities.

> There is still a shortage in the various areas of gathering and spreading information in the Arab world, whether in the fields of education, translation, or media. This is due to a number of factors including the limited resources which are available to individuals and institutions in terms of gaining the required knowledge, in addition to many governmental and bureaucratic restrictions and limitations. All of these factors lead, in turn, to an inability to provide the right atmosphere for knowledge production in the Arab world.[16]

This "knowledge crisis" is exacerbated by another equally important obstacle that is the "educational crisis." This refers to the very high illiteracy rates in many Arab countries, especially among population segments such as women and children in rural areas and Bedouin communities. These rates are very high, even compared to other developing nations in other parts of the world. Additionally, the report mentions that this educational crisis is not just quantitative, in terms of the high illiteracy figures, but it is also qualitative, due to the poor quality of education that is offered in many Arab countries and the fact that it still needs reform in terms of encouraging creativity, independent thinking, and the use of modern skills.[17]

The third type of challenge is the professional challenge, which involves the absence of good "strategic planning" in most Arab media. This refers to a lack of sufficient clarity in setting general goals, targets, and objectives. Here, it could be added that there is a significant lack of coordination between the various Arab media in terms of coming up with one unified general media policy that represents the "Arab point of view" regarding the ongoing issues and the political challenges on the regional and the international fronts.[18]

Additionally, there is still a need for better recruitment and selection criteria for those who work in the Arab media, particularly the Arab satellite channels, since they do not always meet educational and professional standards for such key positions. This problem is exacerbated by the fact that there is a shortage of the required training and preparation for these media professionals, and many of them report that they do not always receive the necessary on-job training in key areas, such as mastering foreign languages and acquiring the computer skills.[19]

Arab media still need more qualified and highly trained professional communicators who can address the Western world with its own languages and with the necessary understanding and awareness of Western culture, mentality, and lifestyle.

All the previously mentioned factors—coupled with a number of financial, administrative, and organizational obstacles and handicaps that still plague some of the Arab media—lead to a general condition of "job dissatisfaction" among many communicators in key media positions, which negatively affects their ability to carry on an enlightening and constructive dialogue with the outside world. Therefore, professional challenges including issues such as ignorance of the other side's culture, civilization, and background, especially among image-makers and communicators, as well as the inability of the Arab side to successfully address international and American public opinion, so far, due to linguistic and cultural barriers, have made the new Arab satellite channels primarily pan-Arab, rather than global, in their reach.

After exploring some of the most important obstacles and challenges that confront Arab satellite channels in terms of constructing effective intercultural dialogue, it is equally useful to turn our attention to some of the attempts that are currently being made to build better bridges of cross-cultural understanding.

## AL JAZEERA ENGLISH: A POSSIBLE CROSS-CULTURAL BRIDGE

One of the possible bridges that could enhance cross-cultural understanding on the Arab side is the birth of Al Jazeera English, a new Arab satellite channel broadcasting in English.

Al Jazeera has been the most successful Arab satellite news network,[20] and wishes to enter the English-language news market. The Qatar-based Arab satellite channel is taking the big step from being a regional Arab news network to becoming a global English news channel, competing with existing media giants such as BBC World and CNN International. Al Jazeera English aims on giving a "Third world-perspective," as well as offering a "Fresh perspective on world news."[21]

Most importantly, it also aims to challenge the existing Anglo-American dominance in the global public sphere. Today, the majority of news flows from the developed to the developing world, that is, from the West to the East. If Al Jazeera English succeeds, the new channel will represent a counterflow of information from the Arab world to the rest of the world, especially to developed Western countries. In other words, it will represent in this case the first viable and competitive attempt to challenge the existing Anglo-American news hegemony and to offer a credible alternative to global Anglo-American news channels.[22]

Al Jazeera English defines itself as follows:

A 24-hour English-language news and current affairs channel, headquartered in Doha. It will start broadcasting throughout the world in 2006. Presenting a fresh perspective on world news, Al Jazeera English is an objective and independent news channel, covering all sides of the story from all parts of the world and revolutionizing viewer choice.

Al Jazeera English is also the world's first English-language news channel to be headquartered in the Middle East. From its unique position within the Arab and Muslim world, looking outward, Al Jazeera English reports inclusively, examining all perspectives of a story and providing a fresh 360 degree approach to news coverage. With broadcasting centers in Doha, Kuala Lumpur, London and Washington D.C., and supporting bureaus worldwide, the channel provides both a regional voice and an international perspective to a potential global audience of over one billion English speakers. The station broadcasts news, current affairs, features, analysis, documentaries, live debates, entertainment, business and sport. Building on the Al Jazeera Network's ground breaking developments in the Arab and Muslim world that have changed the face of news within the Middle East, Al Jazeera English is now extending this fresh perspective from regional to global through accurate, impartial and objective reporting.[23]

The philosophy behind launching this new channel is not just another ambitious broadcaster starting a new service. According to Nigel Parsons, managing director of Al Jazeera English, this new channel is created "to fill a unique role as a builder of bridges."[24] Similarly, a spokesperson for the new channel, Charlotte Dent, emphasized that Al Jazeera English "will be catering to a global audience and will be committed to presenting all sides of an issue."[25]

The same point was emphasized by Ahmed Al-Sheikh, editor-in-chief of Al Jazeera channel. When asked in an interview whether he thinks Al Jazeera could have any impact outside ethnic Arab communities, he answered "I think yes; I met so many people who watch Al Jazeera . . . . People used to tell us, 'If only we could understand Arabic. We watch you for the pictures.' . . . I think people sometimes just see the pictures and they are waiting for Al Jazeera English to be launched."[26]

Al Jazeera English has said it would be editorially independent of its Arabic sister organization but would draw on its resources "where appropriate." The channel's managing director Nigel Parsons said that while more than half of the network's funding comes from the emir of Qatar, the government has never tried to interfere with programming.[27]

Al Jazeera, which styles itself as an independent voice in a turbulent region that is short on press freedom, is shaping Al Jazeera English in the same spirit: outspoken and unwilling, in its own words, "to sanitize war." Al Jazeera's aggressive journalistic style has led to its reporters being banned from Iraq, Iran, and Saudi Arabia. It has also inspired new competition from the likes of the BBC, which announced plans to start a news channel in Arabic.[28] In a surge of hiring intended to make Al Jazeera English palatable to Western viewers and advertisers, the channel secured the services of high-profile television personalities such as David Frost, the veteran BBC interviewer, and Josh Rushing, who was a United States military spokesman in the war on Iraq. From CNN, it added the prominent anchor Riz Khan, and from Sky News of Britain, the reporter David Foster.[29]

Therefore, it could be said that through broadcasting in English and addressing a global audience, as well as by hiring prominent international media figures, Al Jazeera English is attempting to overcome some of the previously discussed professional and cultural obstacles and challenges that are confronting Arab satellite channels. However, this possible new bridge also faces a number of major challenges.

## CHALLENGES FACING AL JAZEERA ENGLISH

The most important challenge facing Al Jazeera English is the "image problem," due to the fact that the Arabic Al Jazeera channel's approach complicates the job of selling the English-language service to broadcast outlets and potential advertisers, especially in the United States. Al Jazeera has made headlines throughout the world with its raw and often controversial coverage of international conflicts. Despite its sweeping popularity in the Arab world, there have been many controversies about its content and style, as well as criticisms of its editorial policy. Given Al Jazeera's notoriety, will the English-language service be able to persuade enough satellite and cable services to carry it, particularly in the United States market? Will advertisers sign up, or will they prefer to steer clear of associations with Al Jazeera?[30]

"Al Jazeera is a controversial channel, and I don't think the positions of the new version will be all that different," said Oussama Jamal, managing director of Starcom Egypt, a company that buys TV time on behalf of advertisers. "Some clients don't want to associate themselves with news and politics in this way," he added.[31] Veteran BBC interviewer David Frost said that before taking a job with Al Jazeera English he had checked out the company with U.S. and British government officials, "all of which gave Al Jazeera a clean bill of health in terms of its lack of links with terrorism."[32] Frost added, "For all the people who think it's anti-American, there are various countries in the Middle East who think it's too pro-Western. I would say the jury's out on Al Jazeera. Obviously, we all suffer from the handicap of not being able to sit there and watch in Arabic."[33]

It is for this reason that Frost senses that the importance of the new Al Jazeera English channel is its ability to address an international audience in English, as well as to bring a totally different perspective to coverage of world events. "I think it's good to have another 24-hour news network in the world bringing a different point of view, a 360-degree point of view," Frost said.[34]

The channel's managing director Nigel Parsons admits that "there is an image problem to be overcome. We hope we would be judged on our merits, but recognize that we may be seen as a 'sister channel' of the original, controversial Arabic-language channel." However, he also agrees with Frost's opinion by saying, "We're certainly not anti-West or anti-America." As for Middle East coverage, he asserts "People forget most Arabs had never seen an Israeli before Al Jazeera, and we allow Israelis to give their side of the story."[35] The prominent TV anchorman Riz Khan also voiced a similar opinion by saying that he is aware of Al Jazeera's reputation in the United States but views this as a "new channel" staffed by credible and extremely professional journalists. "Any concern people have that it's going to be slanted one way or anti-American, they'll be appeased once they realize it's a proper international channel," he said.[36]

However, the "image problem" is not the only challenge facing Al Jazeera English. Even without Al Jazeera's controversial reputation, it will be difficult for the new network—which has deals to be carried in Europe, Asia, and Africa—to get widespread access to U.S. cable and satellite outlets.[37] That is mainly because of the dominance of a few American cable companies, which limits who can get through to the American viewers. "We don't expect to be on in 25 or 30 million homes on Day One," Nigel Parsons, the channel's managing director, said. "I'll be delighted if we've got 5 million homes and can build on that," he added.[38]

Also complicating Al Jazeera English's status is the communication stalemate between the Arab world and the United States, which comes from the fact that "the inability to effectively communicate from the Arab side is coupled with an unwillingness to listen on the American side. This is mainly due to the fact that many Americans do not want to hear that there are negative feelings and hatred toward America abroad, and if they hear it, they don't want to believe it."[39] This situation is made worse by the minimal interest in foreign news among Americans. In fact, "many studies show that at least 60 percent of Americans do not read foreign news because they don't understand it, so they simply tune out."[40]

Confirming the same point, Nigel Parsons said that patching together a global distribution platform through cable and satellite operators remained "a work in progress and a significant challenge." He noted that "cable operators, rather sadly, say Americans are not interested in international news, which is a shame, because we want to be a conduit for understanding between different cultures."[41]

How far can Al Jazeera English succeed in achieving its declared goals of reaching out to a diverse, global audience and bridging the communication gap between the Arab world and the rest of the world? Answers to this and similarly crucial questions will emerge over time.

## CONCLUSION

In investigating the cultural role and influence of relatively "new media" (i.e., Arab satellite channels) and their strengths and weaknesses, especially in terms of affecting international public opinion, it is clear that the channels face numerous challenges. First, political challenges, since despite the significant changes in the media environment in the Arab world recently, in many Arab countries media state ownership is the pattern and the governments in most Arab countries exercise direct or indirect forms of control over the media. Second, cultural and educational challenges, due to the barriers facing the Arab public in accessing suitable education and acquiring basic and background knowledge. Third, image-makers and communicators face professional challenges related to their ignorance of the other side's culture, civilization, and background. This problem is exacerbated by lack of sufficient training, as well as administrative, technical, and financial problems.

It should be recognized, however, that Arab media professionals sincerely desire to reconsider their role and to improve their performance in reaching out to the other side. Case in point is the potential role that the emerging Al Jazeera English channel could play in fostering intercultural dialogue and bridging the existing communication gap. This provides hope that effective cross-cultural dialogue between the Arab world and the rest of the world might slowly start to get off the ground.

If there is any hope of replacing the ongoing discourse of "clash of civilizations" in favor of a new discourse of "dialogue between civilizations," it could only be achieved through arriving at a better and deeper understanding of the "other," which facilitates fruitful and constructive interaction, cooperation, and exchange of ideas. This, in turn, requires exerting a huge effort, on both sides, to overcome all of the previously discussed barriers.

The role that transnational television channels could play in this regard is, indeed, vital and influential. The managers of Al Jazeera English seem to appreciate this. As Nigel Parsons notes, "While America is often bad at understanding the rest of the world, the rest of the world is often bad at understanding America."[42]

Therefore, it is vital to contribute to the process of changing and challenging negative stereotypes and distorted images among both Arabs and Americans at a sensitive time when negative feelings and sentiments are escalating on both sides. This is a goal that is, of course, of utmost importance to Arabs and Americans equally.

## NOTES

1. Jack Shaheen, "Hollywood's Muslim Arabs," *Muslim World*, vol. 90, no. 1, 2 (Spring 2000): 22–43.
2. Paul Findley, *Silent No More: Confronting America's False Images of Islam* (Amana Publications/International Graphics: Maryland, 2001), p. 88.
3. Shaheen, "Hollywood's Muslim Arabs," p. 40.
4. Noam Chomsky, *9/11: An Open Media Book* (New York: Seven Stories Press, 2001), pp. 10–20.
5. Ziauddin Sardar and Merryl Wyn Davies, *Why Do People Hate America?* (Cambridge: Icon Books Ltd., 2002), pp. 25–30.
6. Middle East Research Center, Ain Shams University, Cairo, "A Public Opinion Survey on the Reactions of Egyptian People to the 9–11 Attack," *Journal of Middle Eastern Affairs*, vol. 1 (January 2002): 2–12 (Arabic).
7. Sardar and Davies, *Why Do People Hate America?* p. 203.
8. Douglas Boyd, *Broadcasting in the Arab World: A Survey of the Electronic Media in the Middle East*, 3rd edition (Iowa University Press, 1999).
9. Suzan El-Kalliny, "Arab Audiences Usage of Satellite Channels in the Era of Globalization," *Journal of Middle Eastern Affairs*, vol. 4 (April 2002): 2–20 (Arabic).
10. James Napoli, Hussein Amin, and Luanne Napoli, "Privatization of the Egyptian Media," *Journal of South Asian and Middle Eastern Studies*, vol. 18, no. 4 (1995): 30–57.
11. George Gerbner, "Political Correlates of Television Viewing," *Public Opinion Quarterly*, vol. 48, no. 2 (1984).
12. Mohamed El-Nawawy and Leo A. Gher, "Al-Jazeera: Bridging the East-West Gap through Public Discourse and Media Diplomacy," *Transnational Broadcasting Studies (TBS) Journal*, no.10 (Spring 2003), available online at: <http://www.tbsjournal.com>
13. Salih Al-Kallab, "The Arab Satellites—The Pros and Cons," *Transnational Broadcasting Studies (TBS) Journal*, no. 10 (Spring 2003), available online at: <http://www.tbsjournal.com>
14. Lawrence Pintak, Director of the Adahm Center for Television Journalism, The American University in Cairo, personal interview with the author, November 2005, Doha, Qatar.
15. Ibid.
16. Arab Human Development Report (UNDP: United Nations Development Program, 2003), pp. 9–10.
17. Ibid., pp. 10–12.
18. Mohamed Nabil Teleb, "The Communicators in Specialized Satellite Channels in Egypt," *Journal of the Faculty of Arts*, vol. 25 (1999): 81–132 (Arabic).

19. Suzan El-Kalliny, "The Staff of Arab Satellite Channels: Training Methods and Selection Criteria," *Journal of Arts and Humanities*, El-Menya University, Egypt, vol. 15 (1998): 30–50 (Arabic).
20. Naomi Sakr, "Contested Blueprints for Egypt's Satellite Channels," *Gazette*, vol. 63, no. 2/3 (May 2001): 149–167.
21. Ahmed El-Sheikh, editor-in-chief of Al Jazeera Satellite Channel, personal interview with the author, November 2005, Doha, Qatar.
22. David Hoffman, "Beyond Public Diplomacy," *Foreign Affairs*, vol. 81, no. 2 (2002): 83–95.
23. Al Jazeera International, Media Pack, 2006, p. 3.
24. Eric Pfanner and Doreen Carvajal, "The Selling of Al Jazeera TV to an International Market," *International Herald Tribune*, October 31, 2005.
25. Ibid.
26. Ahmed El-Sheikh, personal interview with the author.
27. Pfanner and Carvajal, "Selling of Al Jazeera TV."
28. Ibid.
29. Ibid.
30. Ibid.
31. Ibid.
32. Howard Kurtz, "Al Jazeera Finds Its English Voice: David Frost Joins New International Television Network," *Washington Post*, October 8, 2005.
33. Ibid.
34. Ibid.
35. Ibid.
36. Ibid.
37. Ibid.
38. Ibid.
39. Lawrence Pintak, personal interview with the author.
40. Ibid.
41. Pfanner and Carvajal, "The Selling of Al Jazeera TV."
42. Ibid.

# CHAPTER 4

# The Public Diplomacy of Al Jazeera

*Shawn Powers and Eytan Gilboa*

## INTRODUCTION

Al Jazeera is one of the most important news organizations in the world today. This chapter suggests that the Arab network also functions as a significant political actor in the international sphere with a clear agenda and means to accomplish it. Moreover, the study further argues that Al Jazeera has adopted two discreet roles: internal and external. The internal is exemplified by the network's initiation of discussion on controversial and taboo topics in the Arab and Muslim public sphere, as well as by its continued scrutiny of Arab regimes. The external role is exemplified by Al Jazeera's claims to represent to the world Arab and Muslim perspectives on regional and international events. It manages the images and representations that much of the West draws on when thinking of the Muslim world, as well as its coverage of political events of geopolitical importance to Western nations, such as the war in Iraq and the Palestinian-Israeli violent confrontation (Second *Intifada*). Al Jazeera's self-adopted dual roles have won considerable support for the network in the Arab street, but also severe criticism from many circles. Arab governments have ignored Al Jazeera's external role and have severely criticized the internal role of liberating political debates; while Western governments have largely ignored Al Jazeera's internal democratizing role and have severely criticized the external representation including the network's depictions of the American-led war efforts in Iraq and its alleged connections and/or support for fundamentalist Islamic terrorist organizations. In light of these criticisms, Al Jazeera has utilized public diplomacy techniques in order to maintain the credibility necessary for its regional and increasingly global roles and to promote its image in the international arena.

Drawing from several bodies of literature, this study is an effort to join international relations and communications scholarship that have largely failed to cross paths. Through an examination of Al Jazeera's public statements, interviews, online discourse, actions and responses to public controversies, Al Jazeera's rise as an international actor is mapped and examined in the context of the changing nature of the global political environment. Similarly, the network's public discourse is examined in light of theories of new public diplomacy, with a particular focus on strategies for branding state and nonstate political actors, as well as on the process and possibilities of two-way communications strategies. Accordingly, this multilevel analysis offers new insight into the strategies and sources of Al Jazeera's power and reputation, an investigation that provides an important contribution to a growing body of literature documenting Al Jazeera's popularity and influence. By examining the methods by which the network grew, and contextualizing it in both international relations and communications literature, this study provides a model for analyzing news organizations as an international nonstate actor.

First, the study begins with an overview of the rise of Al Jazeera as a transnational news organization, looking both at the significant events that contributed to its rise in importance, as well as at the numerous indicators of the network's political and social influence throughout the Arab world. Second, the study outlines the controversies in which Al Jazeera has been embroiled, separated by criticism stemming from actors both inside and outside the Middle East. This examination of the controversies demonstrates that other international actors often treat the network as a transnational political actor, a fact that details the necessity for Al Jazeera to combat criticism using advanced and untraditional communications techniques. Third, this study connects international relations scholarship calling for further exploration of the role of transnational actors in international politics to communications research on the growth in importance of transnational media organizations. Accordingly, drawing from Al Jazeera's public discourse, several clear political objectives are identified, differentiating the network from the traditional conception of the media as the fourth estate, while also providing significant evidence for our argument that Al Jazeera is a transnational political actor. Finally, Al Jazeera's public discourse will be examined and contextualized in terms of new public diplomacy.

Drawing from the concepts of branding and two-way communications, it is revealed that Al Jazeera's communications largely represent an expressive and effective model of new public diplomacy, a rarity in today's highly contested geopolitical environment.

## THE RISE OF AL JAZEERA

Established in 1996 with an initial contribution of $147 million from the Qatari emir Sheikh Hamad bin Khalifa Al Thani, Al Jazeera started out as a small competitor on the Arab transnational satellite television scene. Emir Al Thani's hope was to establish a news organization similar to CNN, but one that was focused on issues directly related to the Arab world, offering an independent Arab perspective. Having one of the most liberalized media environments in the region, Qatar was the perfect launching point for such an endeavor. Benefiting from the collapse of the BBC's Arab World Service news channel broadcast from London, Al Jazeera was able to lure many of the newly unoccupied journalists and newsmakers into the network, as well as from the shrinking Voice of America and BBC Arabic Radio services.[1] Yet, it was not until December 1998, with the American-led Operation Desert Fox, that this Arab broadcaster started challenging the Western international agenda. As American and British airplanes began pounding Saddam Hussein's purported facilities for making and hiding Iraq's weapons of mass destruction (WMD) inventory, Al Jazeera was the only news organization with camera crews on the ground in Iraq, ready and able to capture rather graphic images of the consequences that the campaign had on the Iraqi infrastructure. Desert Fox was to Al Jazeera what the first Gulf War was to CNN; it put it on the regional and global communications map. Another wave of violence in September 2000, the Palestinian Second *Intifada*, offered Al Jazeera its second major opportunity to show firsthand images of the consequences of war, images that were relayed with lightening-fast transmission to an eager Arab citizenry.[2] Yet, it was not until the terror attacks of 9/11 that the news organization truly started to become a significant player in international politics, at least in the eyes of the Arab and the Western worlds.

At the onset of the American-led invasion of Afghanistan, Al Jazeera was the sole international news organization with an operating bureau in Kabul, providing it with firsthand access to images of the events taking place as the Taliban was being overrun by Western military forces. As the violence escalated, major transnational news organizations were forced to partner with Al Jazeera in order to have

access to footage of the conflict in Afghanistan, ensuring that the organization's portrayal of the conflict would not only be seen throughout
the region, but also throughout the Western world. Similar to its
approach in covering Operation Desert Fox in Iraq and the Second
*Intifada*, Al Jazeera's cameras focused on the civilian and the infrastructural damage caused by the American-led invasion, producing
images that were seen quite unfavorably by an American government
struggling to build international support for their newfound military
endeavor.[3]

Al Jazeera has been widely popular among citizens of Arab states. A
widely cited survey conducted by Gallup in 2002 found that viewers
in Kuwait, Saudi Arabia, Jordan, and Lebanon are most likely to turn
to Al Jazeera first for information on regional and world events,[4] and
more broadly, that "Al Jazeera is regarded positively in the Arab
world."[5] A more recent survey measuring the comparative importance
of Al Jazeera, determined by whether it is considered as one of the
three most important sources for news, demonstrates the widespread
popularity of Al Jazeera across the region: 42.7 percent of Egyptians,
67.3 percent of Jordanians, 58.6 percent of Kuwaitis, 45.8 percent of
Moroccans, 64.1 percent of Saudi Arabians, 46 percent of Syrians,
and 78.8 percent of citizens in the United Arab Emirates ranked Al
Jazeera as one of their three most important sources for news.[6] Even
among Israeli Arabs, Al Jazeera is the most popular channel. When
asked to rank the three news channels they watch most, 57 percent
of Israeli Arabs put Al Jazeera in the first place and 21 percent
placed it in the second place, far ahead of any other local or foreign
channel.[7]

Perhaps more interesting is the number of Arabs who consider the
information from Al Jazeera trustworthy: 89 percent of Bahrainis,
93 percent of Egyptians, 96 percent of Jordanians, 95 percent of
Kuwaitis, 90 percent of Moroccans, 94 percent of Saudi Arabians,
93 percent of Tunisians, and 96 percent of citizens of the United Arab
Emirates.[8] Or, as a young man from Cairo recently described it: "With
Al Jazeera, I do not need to look for anything else because it simply
answers all the questions I have. When we think of the word news, we
automatically think of Al Jazeera because . . . it reflects the true and
exact news . . . I would describe it as a mirror reflecting exactly what
happens."[9] Another recent poll conducted in Jordan, Lebanon,
Morocco, Saudi Arabia, Egypt, and the United Arab Emirates by
Zogby International and Shibley Telhami found that Al Jazeera was
the first choice for international news for 45 percent of those polled,
far and away more popular than its competitors.[10]

Lynch helps put the survey's findings in perspective, pointing out that the Zogby/Telhami poll's significance is not that it found Al Jazeera to be the most popular broadcaster, but rather that a mere 10 percent of those surveyed said that they never watch it: "if you asked how many people actually like Al-Jazeera the most, that number would be a lot lower. But the fact is that everybody has to watch Al-Jazeera to know what's going on, and that's not true of any other station."[11] Telhami summarizes the survey's results by saying "Al Jazeera is by far the number one most-watched station in every category that we tested on. Al-Arabiya is a very distant second right now . . . . There is no question that Al Jazeera has more impact than any other channel."[12] The Gallup poll also suggests that Al Jazeera's popularity stems mostly from the perception that it is honest and fair in its approach toward reporting the news. The main reason for Al Jazeera's reputation, however, is the poor standing of most Arab national media systems. Most of the Arab media are controlled by corrupt and ineffective regimes and systematically distort the news, particularly with regard to domestic and regional events. In comparison to the failed Arab media, Al Jazeera is a bastion of free and independent press. In addition, ordinary Arabs are pleased with Al Jazeera's external role, and they admire the challenge the network mounts against the Western media coverage of international and Middle Eastern events.[13]

This perception of credibility and the overwhelming popularity of the Arab satellite broadcaster bring with it a tremendous bit of influence and power. This survey of the network's recent controversies highlights the fact that "Al-Jazeera is more important as a regional power than the State of Qatar.[14] Miles describes the organization as "the most powerful, non-state actor in the Arab world today," arguing that if Al Jazeera was a political party, it would give Hamas or Muslim Brotherhood a run for their money.[15] Similarly, Zayani suggests that by "tapping into the Arab identity during times marked by Arab disunity, Al Jazeera has emerged as a key opinion maker."[16] Poniwozik agrees, arguing, "Among all the major influences on Arab public opinion—the mosque, the press, the schools—the newest and perhaps most revolutionary is Al Jazeera."[17] Moreover, in 2005, the world's leading brand-monitoring survey organization found that Al Jazeera was voted the world's fifth most influential "brand," beating out prestigious companies such as Finland's Nokia, United Kingdom's Virgin, and the American-based Coca-Cola. Adding to its fame, "the most identifiable Arabic brand in the world" was also the world's most searched-for Web site in the last week of March 2003, soon after the American-led campaign in Iraq began.[18]

There is a clear sense among scholars and policymakers that Al Jazeera has become a critical opinion leader in the region, offering up programming, images, commentary, and discussions that determine both what is on the public's political and social agendas, as well as the ways in which actors receive praise and blame in the eyes of millions of Arabs. In some cases, this influence manifests itself in subtle ways, and in others, it may be more direct. For instance, news broadcasts by Al Jazeera have translated "into popular pressure on Arab governments to step up their efforts to act on certain issues and to alter their tame policy."[19] In 2000, Al Jazeera's coverage of the second Palestinian *Intifada* sparked public protest across and "united Arabs behind a single issue for the first time since the early 1970s," a fact that was recognized by both scholars and governments in the region.[20] Regardless of the exact mechanisms guiding its leverage, Al Jazeera's ability to influence the Arab and international political agenda has become clear.

## AL JAZEERA: CONTROVERSIES AND CRITICISMS

Despite its widespread popularity, and because of its influence in and beyond the Middle East, Al Jazeera's coverage of events and journalistic flair has triggered repeated criticisms both within and outside the region. Prior to 9/11, Al Jazeera's critical and, comparatively speaking, independent approach to covering the Arab world caused diplomatic havoc throughout the region. Soon after its inception the network was recognized as a thorn in the side of regimes that had grown accustomed to controlling the news flow. Al Jazeera quickly established a reputation for challenging governments and taboos in the region, with a particular emphasis on programs featuring debate segments where opposing guests are encouraged to argue. By holding to its motto of "the opinion and the other opinion," guests were often ideologically opposed and encouraged to argue about such controversial and taboo topics as corruption, sex, religion, and politics.[21]

One of the network's first significant public controversies took place in November 1998. Al Jazeera's most popular show *The Opposite Direction* featured a debate, between a former Jordanian foreign minister and a Syrian critic, that resulted in a series of accusations tying Jordan to an Israeli plot to eradicate the Palestinian territories. The day after the show, the Jordanian minister of information declared that until the Qatari government took steps to prevent the show's moderator, Dr. Faisal al-Qasim, from his "intentional and repeated campaign against Jordan," that he would shut down Al Jazeera's bureau in Amman. Similarly, criticisms and condemnations of Al Jazeera's news were featured prominently early on in the Saudi press, which were widely considered to be an extension of the government's opinion. In an article titled "Arabsat and Another Kind of Pornography," the Saudi Press analogized Al Jazeera to a form of entertainment pornography, arguing that it should be regulated and banned in a fashion similar to that of traditional pornography.[22] The severity of Arab criticism of the organization increased considerably after its coverage of the American-led Operation Desert Fox, where Al Jazeera not only transmitted exclusive coverage of the seventy-hour bombing campaign throughout the region but also gave high-level Iraqi officials access to their airwaves in an unprecedented fashion. Saudi Arabia, the free Kurdish community, and Kuwait all opposed the coverage, seeing it as "unacceptable propaganda" that could be used to "rehabilitate the Iraqi regime."[23] Interestingly, American officials leveled no such criticism against the network.

Saudi Arabia was perhaps one of the most pronounced critics of the network. Saudi Crown Prince Abdullah once accused Al Jazeera of being a "disgrace to the [Gulf Cooperation Council] countries, of defaming the members of the Saudi Royal family, of threatening the stability of the Arab world and of encouraging terrorism."[24] Other members of the Saudi government have similarly criticized Al Jazeera for its coverage of deaths relating to Arab pilgrimages in Saudi Arabia, calling it "a dagger in the flank of the Arab nation."[25] Saudi Arabia also took some of the most dramatic measures in its efforts to limit Al Jazeera's success. While Al Jazeera's journalists were prohibited from reporting from within the kingdom almost since its inception, Saudi officials started speaking out publicly against the network and its alleged propaganda. Interior Minister Prince Nayif declared that Al Jazeera "is a distinguished high-quality product but it serves up poison on a silver platter." Saudi mosques supposedly followed up, criticizing the organization and issuing a "political fatwa forbidding Saudis from appearing on the Station's shows."[26] The kingdom went as far as to prohibit watching satellite television in coffee shops in an effort to restrict the network's reach. Perhaps most importantly, the Saudi regime, along with Kuwait, is largely considered responsible for organizing a widespread boycott on businesses that advertise on Al Jazeera, a measure that has dramatically curtailed the network's ability to gain the necessary revenue required for more formal independence.[27]

Kuwait's criticisms of Al Jazeera similarly escalated in response to a talk show that featured a discussion of women's rights that was exceptionally critical of the Kuwaiti emir Sheikh Jaber al-Ahmad Al Sabah. The emir was so outraged with Al Jazeera's handling of the show that he promptly went to Qatar to argue that Al Jazeera had "violated the ethics of the profession and harmed the State of Kuwait," a disregard of Kuwaiti law that resulted in the banning of the network's operations within Kuwaiti jurisdiction. Yet, while Kuwait and Saudi Arabia were the two most pronounced critics of Al Jazeera in the Arab world, every government in the region—save Saddam Hussein's Iraq—had at one time or another lodged formal criticisms against the network or taken action to restrict Al Jazeera's ability to gather or distribute the news. Libya "permanently withdrew" its ambassador from Qatar in response to Al Jazeera's airing of a discussion that included one guest who called Colonel Qadhafi a "dictator." Morocco also withdrew its ambassador, accusing the network of leading "a campaign against . . . its democratic revolution," and Tunisia went as far as to sever diplomatic ties with Qatar after a show that aired views of members of the Islamic opposition that were critical of human rights conditions in Tunisia.

The Egyptian and Algerian governments accused the network of supporting the cause of Islamic extremists by offering ideological and extremist group leaders access to the mass media airwaves. Algeria was so afraid of the influence that Al Jazeera wielded that it once was forced to cut the power to several major cities in the middle of an episode of *The Opposite Direction* that featured criticisms of the government's human rights abuses during the country's civil war.[28] Bahrain banned Al Jazeera from covering its 2002 elections, arguing that the network had been "penetrated by Zionists."[29] Iraq shut down Al Jazeera's bureau in Baghdad because, according to interim prime minister Ayad Allawi, the network is an advocate of violence, "hatred and problems and racial tension."[30] All in all, Al-Qasim observes, "six countries [Jordan, Saudi Arabia, Kuwait, Tunisia, Libya, and Morocco] withdrew their ambassadors from Doha because of [*The Opposite Direction*]. They were protesting against what was said [on] the program."[31] Having failed to curtail the network's critical journalism through public criticisms and pressure on the Qatari government, an unnamed Gulf state went as far as to offer Qatari foreign minister Sheikh Hamad bin Jassem bin Jabr Al-Thani US$5 billion to shut down the station.[32]

However, after 9/11, criticism of the network's journalism started coming in heavy doses from governments and critics outside the Middle East, primarily the Bush administration. Days after the attacks on the Pentagon and World Trade Center, Al Jazeera aired an interview with Osama bin Laden that had been recorded in December 1998. Four days later, editors aired a letter, written by bin Laden, calling for "Muslims all over the world to defend Afghanistan" against Western imperialism.[33] Concerned that the messages contained hidden codes for al Qaeda operatives around the world, not to mention that they could shore up support for bin Laden's cause, the Bush administration was quick to criticize Al Jazeera's editorial decisions. After broadcasting the first bin Laden tape, the Arab satellite broadcaster felt the wrath of the American diplomatic entourage, with American policymakers and scholars labeling it as "Osama's mouthpiece," "Hate America Television," or simply "Jihad TV."[34]

These criticisms were just the beginning. As Al Jazeera's popularity and influence grew throughout the region, and as the Bush administration began to realize the importance of winning the support of the Arab world for its foreign policy goals in the region, controversies surrounding Al Jazeera's newsmaking erupted throughout the public discourse. Criticism from high-ranking U.S. officials became especially commonplace during the most recent war in Iraq. Deputy Defense Secretary Paul Wolfowitz suggested that al Jazeera's coverage was "inciting violence" and "endangering the lives of American troops" in Iraq.[35] Secretary of Defense Rumsfeld followed up by accusing the organization's coverage of the War on Terror as being "vicious, inaccurate, and inexcusable," arguing that Al Jazeera has repeatedly cooperated with the insurgents in Iraq to portray U.S. soldiers as occupiers "randomly killing innocent civilians."[36] Moreover, Secretary of State Colin Powell contended that the network showed videotapes from terrorists "for the purpose of inflaming the world and appealing to the basest instincts in the region,"[37] concluding a meeting with visiting Qatari foreign minister by saying that Al Jazeera had "intruded on relations" between the United States and Qatar.[38] Hostility toward the network finally reached a pinnacle in 2004, when President Bush himself took time out of his much-prized State of the Union address to comment that Al Jazeera's coverage of the war in Iraq was "hateful propaganda," a comment that fueled rumors that he had at one point suggested to Prime Minister Blair that the Western coalition add Al Jazeera's headquarters in Doha to a list of the coalition's military targets in the war on terror.[39]

Al-Jazeera's controversial performance also surfaced on the Internet. Friends of Al Jazeera, a grassroots, nonaffiliated organization, was formed in 2005 (www.friendsofaljazeera.org). The Web site's contents feature mostly articles about the barriers that Western and Arab governments are imposing on the network; it is also an open forum where anyone can discuss Al Jazeera–related issues and ask questions about the network. At the other end, Accuracy in Media established a Web site critical of the network, calling it "Terror Television: The Rise of Al-Jazeera and the Hate America Media" (www.stopaljazeera.org). The site offers videos, documents, and blogs and asks Americans to support legislation banning Al Jazeera English from broadcasting in the United States.

The sheer volume and tone of the criticism leveled at Al Jazeera, especially from external sources, has only strengthened the popularity of the network among Arabs and Muslims. It also clearly demonstrated that the network was not functioning only as a news organization but has been recognized as a significant transnational political actor in the world. Contemporary scholarship on international relations has devoted considerable attention to nonstate actors and produced definitions, methods, and theories to analyze their position, behavior, and influence. Hence, international relations literature may be helpful to understand the performance of Al Jazeera in world affairs.

## AL JAZEERA AS A POLITICAL ACTOR

International relations scholars have come to recognize the growing number and importance of nonstate actors on the conduct and flow of international politics. Very few, however, have viewed transnational media organizations as international actors. In his survey of the last thirty years of scholarship, Risse found that "the significance of cross-border interactions involving nonstate actors—multinational corporations, [international nongovernment organizations], epistemic communities and advocacy networks—is not longer seriously contested in an age of globalization."[40] However, the emerging relationships between traditional and nontraditional international actors are challenging the methods of analysis deployed by international relations theorists. Rather than relying on a two-tiered system of state and nonstate actors, where state actors are considered the primary players, globalization and its associated political and social transformations demand a rethinking of the ways relationships and power are negotiated in the international sphere.[41] Willetts argues that the emergence of powerful nongovernment international actors, ranging from transnational corporations to terrorist groups, demands a systems-based method of analyzing international affairs. Rather than privilege the nation-state as the primary actor in international affairs, a pluralistic approach acknowledges "all organized groups as being potential political actors," while calling for scholars to analyze the "processes by which actors mobilize support to achieve policy goals."[42] Unfortunately, "most of the literature is still prominently concerned with proving against a state-centric picture of world politics that [transnational actors] matter. As a result, more interesting questions—when and under what conditions do they matter?—are rarely asked."[43]

Transnational and global media organizations, however, do not fit neatly into any of the categories of nontraditional actors identified by international relations scholars, nor have they been identified as important and autonomous political actors in the international sphere. In contrast with other nonstate actors, the goals of media organizations are more difficult to define. For instance, according to Nicholson, a transnational company's primary goal is to "satisfy shareholder and the managers themselves whose incomes are oftentimes tied to the earnings of shares and thus the profits of the firm."[44] Transnational media organizations, however, often have goals that may at times surpass their desire for profits and/or popularity among other international actors. The case of Al Jazeera is an exemplar in that it continues to rely on state aid from Qatar in order to continue to broadcast and report news throughout the Arab world and has oftentimes aired content knowing that it would result in less advertising revenue.[45] At the same time, international advocacy networks, nongovernmental organizations (NGOs), and epistemic communities, which use "constructions such as the reframing of issues or shaming in order to mobilize people around new principled ideas and norms," better describe the role that some transnational media organizations play in the international arena. Yet, despite the similarities, most international relations scholars continue to view media organizations as tools of other international actors, rather than as autonomous political actors in the international system.[46]

Risse concludes his survey of recent developments in international relations theory by prescribing that "future research on TNAs needs to take into account that these actors—whether MNCs or principled INGOs—have lost their innocence and have become part and parcel of international governance structures."[47] Communications scholars, however, have inadvertently responded to this call, most often through discussions and debates surrounding the "CNN effect." Emerging out of the growth of twenty-four-hour cable news networks, CNN in particular, several prominent scholars have proposed the existence of a "CNN effect" in international politics, referring to the dominant role that news coverage of international events can play in forcing policymakers to adopt particular policies.[48] The examples most often cited are the several humanitarian crises of the 1990s, most notably the massacre at Tiananmen square and the ethnic violence in Bosnia and Somalia, to argue that images made available through transnational media dramatically influence the ways in which many nation-states and international organizations respond to these international events. While several important flags have been raised with regards to the verifiability of any such influence, it is hard to dispute that transnational media networks were playing a role in international politics, at least in the eyes of many policymakers.[49] United Nations secretary general Boutros Boutros-Ghali once commented, "CNN is the sixteenth member of the Security Council." Former secretary of state Madeleine Albright similarly acknowledged the growing importance of media coverage in relation to American policy in Somalia, commenting "Television's ability to bring graphic images of pain and outrage into our living rooms has heightened the pressure both for immediate engagement in areas of international crisis and immediate disengagement when events do not go according to plan. Because we live in a democratic society, none of us can be oblivious to those pressures." Another former secretary of state James Baker III noted in his memoirs that "in Iraq, Bosnia, Somalia, Rwanda, and Chechnya, among others, the real-time coverage of conflict by the electronic media has served to create a powerful new imperative for prompt action that was not present in less frenetic time."[50] While it may be difficult to detail the empirical nature of the relationship between media coverage of events, communication scholarship has in many ways begun to answer Risse's call for "future research" to "evaluate competing explanations and specify the conditions of TNA impact on the various levels of governance."[51]

Al Jazeera's controversial newsmaking and widespread popularity and credibility have led some to begin thinking of the network along similar lines, a fact exemplified by calls of the possible existence of an "Al Jazeera effect."[52] Evidence of the political role of and politics surrounding Al Jazeera's coverage is abundant in its brief ten-year tenure. Not only has its coverage sparked geopolitical tensions between other nation-states and its hosting country, Qatar, but it has also endured military actions against its reporters and bureaus, and is increasingly talked about and treated as a powerful political actor in the region. According to Miles, "Arab ambassadors in Doha . . . spent so much time complaining about Al Jazeera that they felt more like ambassadors to a TV channel than ambassadors to a country."[53] Moreover, during the second *Intifada*, Egyptian president Mubarak accused Al Jazeera of trying to trap Egypt into joining the conflict through its framing of events, commenting, "Let Al-Jazeera go to war. We are not going to war."[54] From the perspective of the Bush administration, Al Jazeera is one of the critical political players in the region, so much so that the State Department and Department of Defense have separate dedicated working groups for monitoring the network's programming twenty-four hours a day, seven days a week.[55]

Along these lines, Kai Hafez contends that Arab satellite broadcasters operate in a different environment from Western media organizations and, as such, require new types of normative tools for measuring their political and social functions. As opposed to news organizations such as CNN and the BBC, the role of Arab satellite broadcasters "is not just objective and balanced reporting but also . . . to take over the tasks that are usually fulfilled by political parties." Broadcasters such as Al Jazeera envision their role beyond functioning merely as a mass medium; rather, Arab satellite broadcasters are increasingly considered "agent[s] of change and its role is in many ways not comparable to Western media."[56] This argument is better understood in the context of the discourse on Western journalistic norms. As BBC's Hosam El-Sokkari has argued, "In the BBC we don't see ourselves as a medium with a political message. We are a platform for debate . . . We don't see that our job is to mobilize forces or mobilize the streets against governments."[57] Contrastingly, Al Jazeera has a self-stated explicit democratic political purpose. For instance, the "About Al Jazeera" page of their English Web site reads:

> In the rest of the world, often dominated by the stereotypical thinking of news 'heavyweights', Al-Jazeera offers a different and a new perspective. Al-Jazeera's correspondents opened a window for the world on the millennium's first two wars in Afghanistan and Iraq. Our expanded coverage competed with and sometimes outperformed our competitors bringing into the spotlight the war's devastating impact on the lives of ordinary people.[58]

This mantra of Al Jazeera as an agent for democratic governance is found throughout the network's public discourse. Wadah Khanfar, managing director of Al Jazeera, is clear about the democratic motivations guiding editorial decisions: "Al-Jazeera has changed the political landscape in the Middle East. People now receive the opposition's discourse directly. Al-Jazeera opened it up for intellectuals, thinkers, critics to speak their mind. It was the first democratic exercise in the region."[59] Ahmed Al-Sheikh, editor-in-chief, differentiates Al Jazeera's work from that of other news organizations by saying that "our talk show programmes . . . are always focused on democracy and freedom of speech and the necessity for a greater degree of transparency in the Arab world."[60] While there is a raging debate among scholars and policymakers as to whether or not Al Jazeera serves a democratic or anti-American agenda, among a range of other potential agendas, there does seem to be consensus that the news organization is most certainly a powerful advocate with particular (albeit varied) political ambitions.

The case of the war in Iraq offers a more specific example of Al Jazeera's political leanings. This Arab satellite broadcaster has distanced itself from other transnational media organizations by occasionally acknowledging that its coverage and framing of the war's events are guided by a particular worldview that resonates with its target audience. Faisal Bodi, editor of Al Jazeera's online content, described the organization's approach: "Of all the major global networks, Al Jazeera has been alone in proceeding from the premise that this war should be viewed as an illegal enterprise. It has broadcast the horror of the bombing campaign, the blown-out brains, the blood-spattered pavements, the screaming infants and the corpses."[61] Similarly, Asaad Taha, an investigative reporter for Al Jazeera, has defended the inflammatory and oftentimes partial nature of his journalism by arguing that he "is adamantly against the notion of neutrality. There is no such thing as a neutral journalist or a neutral media for that matter."[62] Jihad Bailout, former Al Jazeera spokesperson, defended the organization's portrayal of the war in Iraq by arguing, "Our audience actually expects us to show them blood, because they realize that war kills . . . If we were not to show it, we would be accused by our viewers . . . of perhaps hiding the truth or trying to sanitize the war."[63]

Inadvertently, these statements prove that Al Jazeera has a political agenda and is a political actor. If horrors of violence and warfare are the main driving criterion, then Al Jazeera discriminates among different types of blood. The network has constantly failed to document the horrors, torture, and mass killings of innocent citizens by the regimes of the Taliban in Afghanistan and Saddam Hussein in Iraq. It has also failed to cover the terrible genocide in Sudan, perhaps because Muslims are carrying it out, and it offered only very limited and partial coverage of the death and destruction caused by Palestinian suicide bombing in Israel during the second *Intifada*, and the bloody consequences of the Hezbollah missile attacks on Israeli cities and towns in the 2006 Hezbollah war.[64]

While often claiming to offer an objective view of current events, Al Jazeera is also quick to argue that its agenda represents that of a

Pan-Arab citizenry, and that its perspective, while offering "the opinion and the counter-opinion," serves as a counterweight to the predominance of Western media organizations the decade prior. El-Nawawy and Iskandar describe this perspective as "contextual objectivity," defined as "the necessity of television and media to present stories in a fashion that is both somewhat impartial yet sensitive to local sensibilities." Thus, according to the idea of contextual objectivity, although Al Jazeera's coverage may condone several clear political biases, such biases occur in every media organization, and Al Jazeera's particular biases are justified in that they compensate for the partisan worldviews presented in powerful Western media outlets such as CNN and Fox News.[65] Al Jazeera's managing editor Mohammed Jasim Al-Ali described the process as one where journalists "take their experience from the BBC, but their background as Arabs means we can adapt this experience and apply it to the Arab world. We know the mentality of the Arab world—but we also want the expatriate Arab audience who are used to the Western media."[66] Faisal Bodi explains Al Jazeera's approach to news in similar terms, arguing that it as "a corrective" to the official line that the Western media embraces.[67] Al-Ali contends that the difference between CNN and Al Jazeera "is that they look first to international news, then maybe to Asian, Middle Eastern specific issues. We look first to Arab and Islamic issues in detail, and after that to international questions."[68]

Yet, despite what seem to be several conspicuous political leanings, Khanfar argues that his news organization carries no political agenda. When asked about Iraq, Khanfar contends that, despite being legally blocked from operating from within the country, "our coverage has never changed—never pro or against."[69] Although there seems to be a lack of consistency on the specific journalistic goals among Al Jazeera's reporting core, what is clear is an over-the-top effort to portray their coverage as objective and nonbiased while at the same time playing to the desires and demands of its target audience. The tension between these two goals explains the diverging descriptions of Al Jazeera's political and social roles in the region and also illuminates underlying factors for several of the major controversies that the organization has been embroiled in during its young yet distinguished incumbency. In order to maintain its popularity with its main audience in the Arab world, Al Jazeera has needed to portray itself as representing a pan-Arab worldview with independently tailored and democratically oriented intentions. The network's self-presentation as the sole news organization in the region that operates independent of the control of both Western and Arab governments, a medium for and of the people, comes through time and again in its public discourse and branding efforts. At the same time, however, in order to maintain functioning relations with at least some Arab and Western governments, the organization has to play down its political messages and portray itself as being an objective and responsible international player. These two competing dynamics define both the types of controversies that Al Jazeera has been involved in, as well as the constraints that govern their public responses to such controversies.

## AL JAZEERA RESPONDS TO CRITICS: A NEW PUBLIC DIPLOMACY

Today, despite such widespread criticisms from governments around the world, or perhaps because of it, Al Jazeera stands as the world's fifth most popular brand. With an audience hovering around 40 to 50 million prior to the launching of its international, English-language services, Al Jazeera has won over the hearts and minds of an Arab citizenry like no other actor in today's geopolitical environment. In order to counter a plethora of criticisms over the last ten years, the network has made many changes to improve its journalistic practices, as well as its image. While in traditional terms Al Jazeera's communicative strategies may be considered public relations exercises, the network's unique political role in the international community combined with its particular methods of image building and promotion requires a new lens for observation and evaluation. Al Jazeera's communications strategies may be best identified with the emergence of a new public diplomacy—that which can be "characterized as a blurring of traditional distinctions between . . . public and traditional diplomacy, and between cultural diplomacy, marketing and news management."[70]

While traditional public diplomacy refers to the efforts by nation-states to communicate with and persuade foreign publics, most often associated with the international broadcasting and propaganda efforts of the cold war era, new public diplomacy describes a set of communicative activities that are utilized by states and nonstate actors in the international sphere in order to effectively communicate with and persuade any number of foreign audiences.[71] No longer confined to the domain of nation-states, NGOs, international organizations, and even transnational corporations are capable of conducting new public diplomacy, oftentimes with more success than the traditional leaders of the international community. Grounded in Joseph Nye's concept of "soft power," new public diplomacy refers to the tactics employed by states and nonstate actors to "influence the attitudes and behaviors of others," using "attraction, seduction and persuasion." In the case of a transnational media organization, new public diplomacy is best understood drawing from two elements of effective international communication: two-way communications and actor-branding. Whereas traditional public diplomacy was unidirectional, relying on one actor to deliver a message to the masses, the new public diplomacy is grounded in a concept of reciprocal and respectful two-way communication as well as in "strategic communications, including the scientific measurement of public opinion and persuasion techniques."[72] Branding is also becoming an increasingly utilized and essential element of new public diplomacy, where actors are "giving products and services an emotional dimension with which people can identify."[73] Importantly, while two-way communications refers to the method by which direct communications take place, the concept of branding refers more broadly to the substance of what is being communicated. By drawing on these two complimentary levels of analysis, this study provides a holistic and dynamic understanding of Al Jazeera's new public diplomacy. What is revealed is a synergistic relationship between the two methods of new public diplomacy, where the method of communications strengthens the credibility of the messages being communicated, while the messages being emphasized simultaneously emphasize the bi-directional nature of the communications.

Branding is nothing new for transnational media networks, as CNN, Fox News, and the BBC have all developed advanced marketing techniques for promoting their networks abroad. The case of Al Jazeera, however, is distinct in that Al Jazeera's network represents a far more politically motivated and targeted actor in the international arena, and because its transnational success suggests a change in strategies from the more traditional networks. According to Melissen, "the art of branding is . . . about reshaping a country's self-image and molding its identity in a way that makes the re-branded [actor] stand out from the pack. Crucially, it is about the articulation and projection of identity."[74] Accordingly, understanding Al Jazeera's brand requires an analysis of the networks self-described aspirations and identities, qualities elucidated throughout its public discourse.

One important element of Al Jazeera's identity revealed in its public discourse is that it is grounded and constructed around the idea that the network engages in specific public diplomacy practices. For instance, Joanne Tucker, managing director of the network's English Web site, suggests that "There was a need to reach the West . . . A huge slice of life gets overlooked . . . We are trying to provide a bridge to the Arab world"[75] Along similar lines, Nigel Parsons, the managing director of Al Jazeera English, says that one of the primary purposes behind the launching of the English newscast is to "be a conduit to greater understanding between different peoples and different cultures."[76] These statements make clear that Al Jazeera places its role as a public diplomat in the international sphere at the center of its self-presentation and organizational identity, a quality that emphasizes the need to analyze the network using tools typically reserved for nation-states and other political actors in international politics. The motto behind the network's new advertising campaign, "Al Jazeera: setting the news agenda," reinforces this identity while engendering a strong sense of responsibility and distinction associated with its brand.

Essential to all the network's branding efforts is its message of independence, a rhetorical trope of importance for news organizations in general, but one that takes on particular significance in the context of the Arab world. Always keen to emphasize the network's democratic and autonomous identity, Khanfar agues, "We have been punished by governments. Our bureaus were closed. Our journalists were detained, but we have never compromised on the editorial integrity or balanced reporting when it came to the Arab governments, and we are not going to do it for any other government in the world."[77] Drawing on Western journalistic norms, suggesting that Al Jazeera has been "entrusted in relating the truth" to the world, Khanfar defuses critics by speaking directly to his audience and showing no hesitation in expressing his opinion about the governments in the region. Indeed, Al Jazeera rarely hides from public criticisms of its journalistic practices. Offering spokesman an opportunity to further publicize Al Jazeera's independence from unpopular governments; "every criticism or restriction lumped upon it by a U.S.-government organization, news service or ally is the equivalent of free advertising for the brand. And while few Arabs are tuning out, Western viewers disenfranchised with their own nations' coverage are beginning to tune in."[78]

Coinciding with its independence-identity is Al Jazeera's image as a news network whose primary concern is that of the public writ large. It is not merely that Al Jazeera is independent from existing nodes of power in the international community. The brand's popularity is due not only to Al Jazeera's independence from existing nodes of power, but also to the network's identity being tied to serving an imagined pan-Arab community. Endorsing the popularity of the channel, two middle-aged women living in the east of Cairo say, "we watch Al Jazeera because they are working for us."[79] Jihad Bailout, Al Jazeera's former head of media relations and principle spokesman, spent most of his time with the network defending it from accusations of bias and collusion. In response to criticisms that Al Jazeera's coverage of the war in Iraq was sensationalized, Bailout counters, "What we are trying to do is provide a comprehensive picture of what's happening in as much of a balanced way as possible."[80] Similarly, responding to criticisms of the network's coverage of the conflict in Fallujah, Khanfar argues, "the fact that [the Americans] don't like to see [civilian casualties] on the screen, doesn't mean that me as a journalist should take these sensitivities and political considerations into account, because I have a duty towards the people."[81] The network's public discourse reveals a consistent theme emphasizing Al Jazeera's obligation to its transnational Arab and Muslim audience, part of a rhetorical trope that taps into one of the defining characteristics of today's new public diplomacy: understanding communication as dialogue.

Grounded in the Habermasian concept of communicative action, and often called two-way communication, this manner of constructing messages that are part of a larger dialogue contribute to a discussion or integrate the many points of view of the receiver is an essential characteristic of successful public diplomacy in the twenty-first century. By firmly and consistently articulating Al Jazeera's purpose as one that is part of a process of two-way communication, the network actively constructs an image of not only being independent from the corrupt politics of the Arab world, but also running an organization that is for and of the people. Part of what makes Al Jazeera's particular efforts at two-way communication credible is that they not only emphasize their obligation to the Arab citizenry, but they also demand that "the audience must be engaged in the issues."[82] Indeed, the network's official motto, "the opinion and the other opinion," a reference to the fundamentals of any dialogue, represents Al Jazeera's grounding in and dedication to a strategy of two-way communication. Al Jazeera's two-way communication is further elaborated through its selective use of interactive features on its shows and Web site, both of which feature sections that encourage input from the Arab citizenry. Some of the network's most popular programs include call-in segments, and its Web site includes interactive features that allow for feedback with regard to any particular article or image as well as a provision to get in touch with a range of Al Jazeera's editors. This communicative strategy is further reinforced through its online discourse, which states that the network's "ultimate goal is to set up a more proactive relationship with our audience, where the audience is not simply a visitor at the other end of the line. They are and they will always be an integral part of the news reporting and news making process."

The interactive nature of Al Jazeera's news, while in and of itself an essential element of its new public diplomacy, is also part of a larger rhetorical strategy of branding the network as representative of the diverse and authentic voices of the Arab people. Al Jazeera's ability to represent an imagined, pan-Arab identity has been demonstrated by its popularity, and in research that indicates a strong parasocial relationship between the network's audience and journalists, as well as by the perception among a large majority of viewers that Al Jazeera represents a "local" source of news.[83] According to Zayani, "this . . . notion of Arabism manifests itself to a certain degree in the very image the network projects of itself—its staff, its language, its name, and its location. Al Jazeera employs people from various Arab nations . . . from every corner of the Arab world, with no apparent domination of any single group . . . naturally, the lack of a dominant group gives the network a Pan-Arab ring."[84] Moreover, "the channel promotes an Arab nationalist discourse wrapped in a democratic style which makes it easy for viewers to palate . . . it projects an inclusive identity which crosses national borders."[85] Al Jazeera's ability to effectively represent its pan-Arab public is best explained by Iskandar's analysis of the network's mainstreaming of the "discourse of dissent," an operating strategy that allows Al Jazeera to incorporate the various sects of dissent in the Arab world in ways that boost its image as an independent and trustworthy news organization. Yet, unlike other so-called alternative media in the region, through incorporating a multiplicity of views and its treatment of communication as a dialogue, Al Jazeera is able to transcend accusations of bias and boost its image as an independent political force in regional and, increasingly, international politics.[86]

Finally, critical to Al Jazeera's self-presentation and branding efforts is its ability to adopt advanced Western communications technologies and formats while simultaneously utilizing them to express the news "from the Arab point of view." At the outset, Al Jazeera drew from CNN and the BBC and modeled itself after the Western format of round-the-clock news service. It has since adapted and has consistently been at the cutting edge of technological advances in communication, exemplified by their use of satellites and mobile technologies to facilitate real-time broadcasts from wherever they have journalists on the ground. Moreover, the network also has a robust online presence, or e-image, both in English and in Arabic. Drawing controversies similar to their on-air content, focused around the images and language surrounding the wars in Iraq and Afghanistan, the network's online operations exemplify much of the network's brand as far as it offers an advanced communications platform, alongside messages targeted at a pan-Arab audience, and interactive online mechanisms that allow for viewers to respond and react to what they see. Ibrahim Helal, Al Jazeera's chief editor, is quick to point out: "Technically speaking our direct link from DC to Doha is two seconds faster than anybody else's, so we have the sharpest edge in time."[87] Oftentimes described under the banner of "glocalization" or "cultural hybridity," the negotiation of Western influence into local and regional institutions is of critical importance to the identity of any organization, especially in the Arab world. Al Jazeera's success at branding itself as Arab in outlook and Western in method and platform functions as a "sign of symbolic equilibrium between the Occident and the Other."[88] In this particular context, Al Jazeera's brand not only represents an example of successful hybridization but also serves as a symbolic champion of globalization, providing the only major Arab brand known to the outside world as an example of the possibility of utilizing parts of globalization's offerings in ways that enhance local or Arab culture.[89]

## CONCLUSION

For such a widely successful and popular transnational news network, the amount of scrutiny Al Jazeera has endured is truly unprecedented. The network has dealt with political, diplomatic, economic, and military pressures to change the nature of its operations, and even its organizational identity. Yet, despite the efforts of Arab and Western governments, Al Jazeera has not only survived but has also capitalized on its controversial status by reaching out directly to citizens of the Arab and Western worlds, showing little respect for the opinions of foreign leaders. Today, Al Jazeera channels, both in Arabic and English, stand poised to become the world's most watched news network, a feat of tremendous consequence. For citizens of the Arab world, the network represents a champion of global reach, the sole globally recognized Arab brand, and a trusted and powerful institution in international politics. They feel that the network well represent them, perhaps, better and more effectively than their own governments, in challenging Western politics and foreign policy, particularly toward the Middle East. For governments, both in and outside the Arab world, Al Jazeera represents challenge and competition, a network whose status has resulted in it being treated as an established international political actor. Finally, for scholars, Al Jazeera's rise and success represent both the changing nature of international politics as well as the changed demands of international communications, a new type of organization and communicator that challenges the existing categories and methods of analysis.

Although much has been written about the rise and successes of Al Jazeera as well as about the many obstacles it has overcome, what has been lacking is a thorough contextualization of the network's political role and self-presentation strategies. This study utilizes concepts from international relations theory, the new public diplomacy and communications, to offer an analysis and explanation of Al Jazeera's perfor-mance and a criticism of its journalistic practices and politics, as well as of its continuing dramatic successes. Through a systematic examination of Al Jazeera's public statements, interviews, online discourse, actions and responses to public controversies, and a corresponding contextualization of Al Jazeera's public discourse in international relations and communications literature, this study makes three primary arguments:

First, Al Jazeera is not merely a transnational media organization, but also a network that acts and is treated as a powerful actor in international politics, a fact that demands a new set of methods for examination and interrogation of its operations, goals, and role in social and political change.

Second, the network has adopted a political agenda relating both to the internal matters of the Arab world and to the external affairs of the rest of the world, primarily the West. The internal agenda promotes debates on values, customs, and norms in Arab society and politics. The external agenda offers critical coverage and opinion on international events such as military interventions and wars in Afghanistan and Iraq. The network also challenges Western values and behavior. Al Jazeera's internal and external political agenda has drawn criticism and sanctions from inside and outside the Middle East. Yet, although the Arab governments may have favored the external representation of Arab interests, they have been much more concerned with the internal agenda, which directly questioned their autocratic governance and leadership. Thus, they focused their criticism on the internal role of the network. The United States on the other hand may have favored the internal agenda, which is compatible with the idea of democratizing the Middle East, but has been much more concerned with the external agenda, which in American eyes has undermined public support in the Arab world for the wars in Afghanistan and Iraq. Thus, American and other Western leaders focused their criticism on Al Jazeera's external political agenda.

Third, related to its status as an international political actor facing severe criticism from both inside and outside the Middle East, Al Jazeera has engaged in a widespread and thorough communications campaign to overcome the many controversies that it has been involved in. This campaign is best understood as a successful example of new public diplomacy. Relying on a coordinated effort, both in form and content of its communications, at branding the network's identity to become synonymous with independence and a diverse yet united pan-Arab citizenry, Al Jazeera represents perhaps an effective example of the design and importance of new public diplomacy in contemporary international politics.

This study suggests a new methodology for analyzing global news organizations. It argues that some of them, such as Al Jazeera, should be viewed as nonstate actors pursuing self-adopted political agendas. Like any other international actor, they develop goals and interests and use public diplomacy to achieve them. Close collaboration between international relations and communication scholars is required to explain these functions of global news organizations in world affairs. This collaboration means adding global news organizations to lists of nonstate actors, and using both international relations and communication theories to effectively study them.

## NOTES

1. Norbert Wildermuth, "Defining the 'Al Jazeera Effect': American Public Diplomacy at a Crossroad," *In Media Res*, vol. 1, no. 2 (February 2005).
2. Marc Lynch, "Watching al-Jazeera," *The Wilson Quarterly*, vol. 29, no. 3 (Summer 2005): 36–46.
3. Ibid.
4. Richard Burkholder, "Arabs Favor Al-Jazeera Over State-Run Channels for World News," *Gallop Poll*, November 12, 2002, available online at: <http://www.galluppoll.com/content/?ci=7210&pg=1>
5. Mohamed Zayani, *The Al Jazeera Phenomenon: Critical Perspectives on Arab Media* (Boulder, CO: Paradigm Press, 2005), p. 3.
6. Mark Rhodes and Rola Abdul-Latif, "Al Jazeera and Al Arabiya: A Comparative Study," *Intermedia Research* (2005).
7. Amal Jamal, *The Culture of Media Consumption Among National Minorities: The Arabs in Israel* (Nazareth: Ilam, 2006), p. 177.
8. Rhodes and Abdul-Latif, "Al Jazeera and Al Arabiya," pp. 1–37.
9. Interview, cited in Rhodes and Abdul-Latif, "Al Jazeera and Al Arabiya," p. 36.
10. Shibley Telhami. "The Cambridge Arab Media Project: The Media and Political Change in the Arab World," *Transnational Broadcasting*

Studies (TBS) Journal, no. 13 (Fall 2004), available online at: <http://www.tbsjournal.com/Archives/Fall04/camptelhami.html>

11. Brooke Gladstone, "Al-Nielsens," On the Media, National Public Radio, December 16, 2005, available online at: <http://www.onthemedia.org/transcripts/transcripts_121605_neilson.html>

12. Telhami, "The Cambridge Arab Media Project."

13. Mohammmed el-Nawawy and Leo A. Gher, "Al Jazeera: Bridging the East-West Gap through Public Discourse and Media Diplomacy," Transnational Broadcasting Studies (TBS) Journal, no. 10 (Spring 2003), available online at: <http://www.tbsjournal.com/Archives/Spring03/nawawy.html>

14. S. Abdallah Schleifer, "Al Jazeera Update: More Datelines from Doha and a Code of Ethics," Transnational Broadcasting Studies (TBS) Journal, no. 13 (Fall 2004), available online at: <http://www.tbsjournal.com/Archives/Fall04/aljazeera_schleifer.html>

15. Hugh Miles, "Arab Television News and Al Jazeera," Roundtable discussion at The Frontline Club, Transnational Broadcasting Studies (TBS) Journal, no. 14 (March 2, 2005), available online at: <http://www.tbsjournal.com/Archives/Spring05/frontlinetranscript.html>

16. Zayani, Al Jazeera Phenomena, p. 8.

17. James Poniwozik, "The Battle for the Hearts and Minds: Even before bin Laden's Tape, the US Was Losing the Propaganda War in the Arab World," Time Magazine, October 22, 2001, p. 65.

18. Abram Sauer, "Al Jazeera: Tough Enough?" Interbrand (2005), available online at: <http://www.brandchannel.com/features_profile.asp?pr_id=122>

19. Zayani, Al Jazeera Phenomena, p. 9.

20. Mohammmed El-Nawawy and Adel Iskandar, Al-Jazeera: The Story of the Network That Is Rattling Governments and Redefining Modern Journalism (Boulder, CO: Westview Press, 2003), p. 56.

21. Marc Lynch, Voices of the New Arab Public (New York: Columbia University Press, 2006).

22. Hugh Miles, Al-Jazeera: The Inside Story of the Arab News Channel That Is Challenging the West (New York: Grove Press, 2005), pp. 45–47.

23. Ibid., p. 54.

24. "Crise larvée entre Ryad et Doha," Translated by BBC, AFP Dispatch, January 17, 2002.

25. Naomi Sakr, quoted by Ethan Zuckerman in "Al Jazeera in the Mirror," February 2, 2006, available online at: <http://www.ethanzuckerman.com/blog/?p=358>

26. Miles, Al-Jazeera, p. 53.

27. Olivier Da Lage, "The Politics of Al Jazeera or the Diplomacy of Doha," in Mohammed Zayani (ed.), The Al Jazeera Phenomenon (Boulder, CO: Paradigm Publishers, 2005), p. 54; Philip Seib, "Hegemonic No More: Western Media, the Rise of Al-Jazeera, and

the Influence of Diverse Voices," *International Studies Review*, vol. 7 (2005).

28. Davan Maharaj, "How Tiny Qatar Jars Arab Media," *Los Angeles Times*, May 7, 2001.
29. British Broadcasting Corporation, "Bahrain bans Al Jazeera TV," May 10, 2002.
30. Associated Press, "Iraq shuts al-Jazeera's Baghdad office," August 7, 2004.
31. Faisal Al-Qasim, interviewed by Amy Goodman, "The Opposite Direction: Why This Al Jazeera Talk Show Draws Fire from Arab and Western Governments," *Democracy Now*, February 2, 2006, available online at: <http://www.democracynow.org/article.pl?sid=06/02/02/147208>
32. Ian Urbina, "Al Jazeera: Hits, misses and ricochets," *Asia Times*, December 25, 2002, available online at: <http://www.atimes.com/atimes/Middle_East/DL25Ak01.html>
33. Wildermuth, "Defining the Al Jazeera Effect."
34. Catherine Cassara and Laura Lengel, "Move over CNN: Al Jazeera's View of the World Takes On the West," *Transnational Broadcasting Studies (TBS) Journal*, no. 12 (Spring 2004): 3.
35. Robert Fisk, "The US Moves to Close Down Al Jazeera TV: Wolfowitz the Censor," *The Independent*, August 1, 2003.
36. Donald Rumsfeld, Remarks at the Chicago Council on Foreign Relations, U.S. Department of State, August 8, 2004, available online at: <http://www.uspolicy.be/Article.asp?ID=44FBBCF6-C1B6-4B60-93C0-F67E2B988EB6>
37. E.A. Torriero, "US, Media at Odds over Iraq Coverage," *Chicago Tribune*, August 1, 2003.
38. Reuters, "Colin Powell Registers US Complaints about Al Jazeera," *Los Angeles Times*, April 28, 2004.
39. Neil Mackay, "Wartime Secrets: Did President Bush Want to Bomb Television Station," *The Sunday Herald*, November 27, 2005.
40. Thomas Risse, "Transnational Actors in World Politics," in W. Carlsnaes, T. Risse, and B.A. Simmons (eds.), *Handbook of International Relations* (London: Sage, 2005), p. 268.
41. Ibid., p. 259.
42. Peter Willetts, "Transnational Actors and International Organizations in Global Politics," in J. Baylis and S. Smith (eds.), *The Globalization of World Politics* (Oxford: Oxford University Press), p. 358.
43. Risse, *Handbook of International Relations*, p. 268.
44. Michael Nicholson, *International Relations: A Concise Introduction* (New York: New York University Press, 1998), p. 40.
45. Lynch, *Voices of the New Arab Public*; Da Lage, "The Politics of Al Jazeera."
46. Risse, *Handbook of International Relations*; Willetts, "Transnational Actors."

47. Risse, *Handbook of International Relations*, p. 269.
48. Eytan Gilboa, "Global Communication and Foreign Policy," *Journal of Communication*, vol. 52, no. 4 (December 2002): 731–748; Eytan Gilboa, "The CNN Effect: The Search for a Communication Theory of International Relations," *Political Communication*, vol. 22, no. 1 (2005): 27–44; Samuel Feist, "Facing Down the Global Village: The Media Impact," in Richard L. Kugler and Ellen L. Frost (eds.), *The Global Century: Globalization and National Security* (Washington, DC: National Defense University Press, 2001).
49. Eytan Gilboa, "Television News and US Foreign Policy: Constraints of Real-Time Coverage," *Harvard International Journal of Press/Politics*, vol. 8 (Fall 2003): 97–113; Eytan Gilboa, "Effects of Global Television News on U.S. Policy in International Conflict," in P. Seib (ed.), *Media and Conflict in the 21st Century* (New York: Palgrave Macmillan, 2005), pp. 1–31.
50. Eytan Gilboa, "Global Communication and Foreign Policy: Debating the CNN Effect," *International Studies Perspectives*, vol. 6, no. 3 (2005): 325–341.
51. Risse, *Handbook of International Relations*.
52. El-Nawawy and Gher, "Al Jazeera: Bridging the East-West Gap"; Robert D. Alt, "The Al Jazeera Effect: How the Arab TV network's coverage of the Coalition is influencing opinion in Iraq," *The Weekly Standard*, April 21, 2004, available online at: <http://www.weeklystandard.com/Content/Public/Articles/000/000/003/992hodmd.asp>; E.C. Nisbet, M.C. Nisbet, D.A. Scheufele, and J.E. Shanahan, "Public Diplomacy, Television News and Muslim Opinion." *Press/Politics*, vol. 9, no. 2 (2004): 11–37; Wildermuth, "Defining the Al Jazeera Effect."
53. Miles, *Al-Jazeera*, p. 57.
54. Ibid., p. 81.
55. Interview with senior level State Department media analyst Joe Norris, May 27, 2006.
56. Kai Hafez, "Arab Satellite Broadcasting: Democracy without Political Parties?" *Transnational Broadcasting Studies (TBS) Journal*, no. 13 (Fall 2004), available online at: <http://www.tbsjournal.com/Archives/Fall05/Hafez.html>
57. Quoted in Morand Fachot, "Conference Report: News Xchange 2004, Arab Media Take Centre Stage," *Transnational Broadcasting Studies (TBS) Journal*, no. 13 (Fall 2004), available online at: <http://www.tbsjournal.com/Archives/Fall04/newsxchange_fachot.htm>
58. Al-Jazeera.net, "About al-Jazeera," available online at: <http://english.aljazeera.net/NR/exeres/5D7F956E-6B52-46D9-8D17-448856D01CDB.htm>
59. Wadah Khanfar, interviewed by Vibhuti Patel, "The Last Word: Al-Jazeera, all the time," *Newsweek International*, April 10–17, 2006.

60. Ahmed Al-Sheikh, "The Diversity of Arabic Media," *Transnational Broadcasting Studies (TBS) Journal*, no. 13 (Fall 2004), available online at: <http://www.tbsjournal.com/Archives/Fall04/mediaxchange.html>

61. Faisal Bodi, "Al-Jazeera Tells the Truth about War," *The Guardian*, March 28, 2003.

62. Zayani, *Al Jazeera Phenomena*, p. 18.

63. Jacqueline E. Sharkey, "Al-Jazeera under the Gun," *American Journalism Review*, vol. 26, no. 5 (October/November 2004): 19.

64. Ike Seamans, "'Fair and balanced' Muslim-style," *Jewish World Review*, September 3, 2004. For more on Al Jazeera's biases, see: Miles, *Al-Jazeera*; Lynch, *Voices of the New Arab Public*; Muhammad Ayish, "Political Communication on Arab World Television: Evolving Patterns," *Political Communication*, vol. 19 (2002): 137–154; Rasha El-Ibiary, "Television Coverage of the 2003 US-Led Invasion of Iraq: Content Analysis of Al-Jazeera and CNN," 55 Annual PSA Conference, Leeds (2005).

65. El-Nawawy and Iskandar, *Al-Jazeera: The Story of the Network*, p. 54, 202.

66. Ibid.

67. Bodi, "Al-Jazeera Tells the Truth about War."

68. Mohammed Jasim Al-Ali, interviewed be S.A. Schleifer, "A Dialogue with Mohammed Jasim Al-Ali," *Transnational Broadcasting Studies (TBS) Journal*, no. 7 (Fall 2001/Winter 2001–2002), available online at: <http://www.tbsjournal.com/Archives/Fall00/al-Ali.htm>

69. Wadah Khanfar, "Al Jazeera's Brand Name News," *Foreign Policy* (April 2005), available online at: <http://www.foreignpolicy.com/story/cms.php?story_id=2822>

70. Rhiannon Vickers, "The New Public Diplomacy: Britain and Canada Compared," *British Journal of Politics and International Relations* vol. 6 (2004): 151–168.

71. Eytan Gilboa, "Public Diplomacy: The Missing Component in Israel's Foreign Policy," *Israel Affairs*, vol. 12 (Winter 2006–2007): 718.

72. Ibid., p. 719.

73. Peter Van Ham, "The Rise of the Brand State: The Post Modern Politics of Image and Reputation," *Foreign Affairs*, vol. 80 (2001); Jack Yan, "Branding and the International Community," *Journal of Brand Management*, vol. 10 (2003): 447–456.

74. Jan Melissen, "Wielding Soft Power: The New Public diplomacy," Netherlands Institute of International Relations, Clingendael Diplomacy Papers, no. 2 (May 2005), p. 24.

75. Josef Federman, "Al Jazeera's Web Site Looks West with Launch in English," *Wall Street Journal*, February 4, 2003.

76. Lawrence Pintak, "Interview with Nigel Parsons, Managing Director of Al Jazeera International," *Transnational Broadcasting Studies*

*(TBS) Journal*, no. 15 (October 2005), available online at: <http://www.tbsjournal.com/Parsons.html>

77. Amy Goodman, "Why Did You Want to Bomb Me Mr. Bush and Mr. Blair? Al Jazeera Director Demands More Information on Secret Memo," *Democracy Now* (February 3, 2006), available online at: <http://www.democracynow.org/article.pl?sid=06/02/03/154219>

78. Sauer, "Al Jazeera: Tough Enough?"

79. Interview, Cairo, July 8, 2006.

80. Quoted in Jacqueline E. Sharkey, "Al-Jazeera Under the Gun."

81. Kanfar, "Why Did You Want to Bomb Me?"

82. Hafez Al-Mirazi, Al Jazeera's Washington bureau chief, quoted in E. Kelley, "Al Jazeera: Mouthpiece for Terrorists, Lackey for Israel, or Voice for Democracy?" *Washington Report on Middle East Affairs*, vol. 21 (2002).

83. Philip J. Auter, Mohamed Arafa, and Khalib Al-Jaber, "Identifying with Arabic Journalists: How Al-Jazeera Tapped Parasocial Interaction Gratifications in the Arab World," *Gazette*, vol. 67, no. 2 (2005): 189–204; Ralph D. Berenger, "Book Essayy: Al Jazeera: In Pursuit of 'Contextual Objectivity,'" *Transnational Broadcasting Studies (TBS) Journal*, no. 14 (2005), available online at: <http://www.tbsjournal.com/ReviewsBerenger.html>

84. Zayani, *Al Jazeera Phenomena*, p. 7; Philip Seib, "The News Media and the 'Clash of Civilizations,'" *Parameters*, vol. 34, no. 4 (Winter 2004–2005): 80.

85. Zayani, *Al Jazeera Phenomena*, p. 7.

86. Adel Iskandar, "Is Al Jazeera Alternative? Mainstreaming Alterity and Assimilating Discourses of Dissent," *Transnational Broadcasting Journal (TBS) Journal*, no. 15 (2005), available online at: <http://www.tbsjournal.com/Iskandar.html>

87. S. Abdallah Schleifer, "Interview with Ibrahim Helal, Chief Editor, Al Jazeera," *Transnational Broadcasting Studies (TBS) Journal*, no. 10 (Spring/Summer 2003), available online at: <http://www.tbsjournal.com/Archives/Spring03/helal.html>

88. Ali Bayramoglu, "Al Jazira: Vecteur d'une globalization islamique," *Sabah*, October 9, 2001, translated in Zayani, *Al Jazeera Phenomena*, p. 31.

89. Zayani, *Al Jazeera Phenomena*, p. 30.

# CHAPTER 5

# The Caged Bird Sings:
# How Reliance on Al Jazeera
# Affects Views Regarding
# Press Freedom in the
# Arab World

*Shahira Fahmy and Thomas J. Johnson*

With millions of viewers from Arab and Muslim states, Al Jazeera Arabic-language news channel has been very critical of countries in the Arab world, loosening the controls on freedom of speech in many Arab countries. Since the 9/11 attack, the U.S. invasion of Afghanistan, and the Iraq War, many officials and policymakers around the world have identified the Al Jazeera as a possible contributor to democracy in the Middle East.

In this study, the researchers examine the perceptions of the audience of Al Jazeera, with a special focus on how viewers assess press freedom in the Arab world and how they compare it to freedom of the press in the United States. This study also examines the degree to which viewers believe Al Jazeera has contributed to press freedom in the Arab world. Using the data of an Arab-language survey gathered from 53 different countries in Fall 2004, the authors examine the relative contribution of reliance on Al Jazeera to attitudes toward press freedom in the Arab world after controlling for political ideology and individual-level demographic factors.

## SUPPORT FOR PRESS FREEDOM
## IN THE ARAB WORLD

Before the 1991 Gulf War, Arab countries enjoyed few press free-doms. Arab governments held a monopoly over television, guided by the belief that television should serve as a government operation designed to promote national development goals. Television stations operated within ministries of information and were funded by the government. Employees were viewed as part of the government bureaucracy and therefore enjoyed few press rights.[1]

Scholars suggest that the 1991 Gulf War served as a catalyst for the rise of satellite news stations that have eliminated the governments' monopoly over the news.[2] Although scholars agree that the rise of satellite networks, most notably Al Jazeera, and the emergence of the Internet have caused the government to encourage more Western-style news gathering and presentation, there are debates about whether Arab governments have significantly lifted controls on the press.

For instance, Ayish[3] argues that the rise of satellite news stations such as CNN and the BBC, as well as independent Arab stations such as Al Jazeera, has spurred Arab governments to encourage news operations to adopt a more professional style mirroring Western news networks within a continued government monopoly. Until recently, most television stations presented protocol news, that is, shots of heads of state delivering long, dry speeches toeing the government line on policy. Government-sponsored stations such as Saudi Arabia's Abu Dhabi satellite channel have adopted a more Western-style broadcasting with state-of-the art technology, advertising revenue, a wide range of news and public affairs programming shows, as well as entertainment and family-oriented offerings. Also, several Arab coun-tries have opened media "free zones" where Arab governments boast that media are able to operate without legal restrictions.

But although new Arab satellite news stations such as Abu Dhabi TV may look like Western news outlets with bureaus in major Arab and international cities, field reports, and live studio or satellite-relayed interviews, the governments still greatly influence content. Indeed, Miles indicates,

> . . . some assert that the information revolution might actually be bolstering oppressive Arab regimes' control over their people: the public vents its anger on *Al-Jazeera*'s talk shows, while real power remains entrenched in the hands of the regime.[4]

Governments may have modified censorship laws, but government actions and certain religious and sexual topics as well as discussions of political corruption remain out of bounds.[5] Sakr argues that broadcast stations operating in the media free zones may be free from financial restrictions such as taxes, custom duties and building restrictions, but they are still subject to censorship.[6] Indeed, in Freedom's House rankings of press freedoms throughout the world, all Middle Eastern countries except Turkey (52) and Kuwait (57) were judged as "not free," with Saudi Arabia (80) and Libya (94) topping the list.[7] The score for Saudi Arabia matched China (80) and Libya was just below Cuba (96).

Perhaps because press freedoms have been severely restricted in Arab nations, press freedom may be valued more in the Arab world than in the United States. A Pew Global Projects attitude survey[8] found that those in predominately Muslim countries place a high priority on having the right to criticize the government and that the press should operate without the specter of government censorship. However support for press freedoms differs greatly by country. For instance, in Turkey 83 percent of those surveyed supported the people's right to openly criticize the government and 68 percent believed the media should be able to report without government censorship. However, figures for Jordan, a monarchy with a limited parliament, were much lower (32 percent and 35 percent).

## AL JAZEERA AND PRESS FREEDOM

On its Web site, Al Jazeera boasts,

> Free from the shackles of censorship and government control *Al Jazeera* has offered its audiences in the Arab World much needed freedom of thought, independence and room for debate. In the rest of the world, often dominated by the stereotypical thinking of news "heavyweights," *Al Jazeera* offers a different and a new perspective.[9]

Al Jazeera's supporters have credited the station with creating a revolution in the political life of Arab countries by being the first network to provide Arab viewers an uncensored round-the-clock news service that has offered them a chance to express their opinions through live phone-in shows as well as to hear the perspectives of opposition leaders, dissidents, and intellectuals.[10]

Indeed, Middle East scholar Marc Lynch characterizes 1998 to 2002 as the Al Jazeera era, crediting the station with helping to create a new Arab public that

> has already conclusively shattered the state's monopoly over the flow of
> information, rendering obsolete the ministries of information and the
> oppressive state censorship that was smothering public discourse well
> into the 1990s . . . . The new public has forced Arab leaders to justify
> their positions far more than ever before, introducing a genuinely new
> level of accountability to Arab publics.[11]

Ironically, Al Jazeera has achieved credibility and a reputation for helping open Arab societies by adopting Western style journalistic techniques and values. Al Jazeera has employed BBC and CNN as models
in developing news-gathering techniques such as seeking out multiple
perspectives on the news, relying heavily on video and slick graphics to
tell the story as well in creating news shows such as *The Opposite
Direction* (based on CNN's *Crossfire*). Indeed, most of Al Jazeera's
reporters were initially recruited from the BBC Arabic TV service and
they brought with them the BBC's editorial spirit and style.[12]

While Al Jazeera admits that it presents the news from an Arabic
perspective to counter the Western slant presented by networks such as
CNN and Fox,[13] Al Jazeera officials argue they try to cover all view-
points of an issue with objectivity, integrity, and balance and to allow
audience members to make up their own minds on issues. It presents
the views of Western leaders, and it was the first Arab network to interview top Israeli officials. Furthermore, while some have criticized political talk shows such as *The Opposite Direction* for providing a forum for
extremists who invite conflict rather than compromise, others have
praised the network for their willingness to criticize Arab governments
and their officials and for covering taboo topics such as sex, polygamy,
and government corruption.[14] Furthermore, Al Jazeera has opened up
its phone lines to allow Arab citizens to express their views without fear
of censorship or filters. For instance, after the fall of Baghdad, *Minbar
Al-Jazeera* opened up its lines to its viewers to get their views on the
future of Iraq, spurring impassioned, heated discussions among people
ranging from those who celebrated the fall of Saddam Hussein and
hoped the former Iraqi leader would be slaughtered in the streets of
Baghdad, to those who claimed the coalition came to Iraq to protect
its oil and would abandon Iraq to civil war.[15]

Al Jazeera scholar Marc Lynch argued, "The anguished, excited,
angry, delirious discussions, in which Arabs struggled to make sense of
events, constitutes perhaps the most open and accessible debate in
Arab history."[16] The network credited with ushering in a period of

freedom of discussion in the Arab world has itself been the victim of attempts to censor its message by both Arab governments and the United States. Arab governments, which in the past depended on government-controlled media to serve as their mouthpieces, have criticized Al Jazeera for negative coverage of Arab governments. Consequently, several Arab governments have closed their embassies in Qatar, where Al Jazeera is based, and have at least temporarily shut down Al Jazeera bureaus in their country.[17] For instance, interim Iraqi prime minister Ayad Allawi closed the Baghdad bureau offices of Al Jazeera for a month.[18]

The United States government, which before 9/11 hailed Al Jazeera as a beacon of freedom for adopting Western reporting techniques,[19] has castigated the network for what it perceives as an anti-American bias. Al Jazeera has been accused of aiding terrorists by airing tapes of Osama bin Laden and other anti-American figures. England's *Daily Mirror* reported that during the siege of Fallujah, George W. Bush approached Prime Minister Tony Blair about a plan to bomb Al Jazeera's headquarters, a report Bush denied and the British government would not comment on, citing its Official Secrets Act. But Al Jazeera has been the victim of earlier bombings. In Fallujah and Basra, the U.S. military had bombed hotels where Al Jazeera reporters had stayed; it also bombed the network's studios in Kabul and Baghdad in an attack that killed reporter Tareq Ayoub. Further, the U.S. forces have seized several Al Jazeera reporters, imprisoning them in Abu Ghraib and Guantanamo, where the reporters claim they were tortured.[20]

## PRESS FREEDOM AND MEDIA RELIANCE

Those who rely heavily on the media, particularly newspapers, are more likely to support journalistic rights and oppose media censorship.[21] Numerous studies have linked newspaper use to increases in political knowledge[22] and the ability to process information more deeply.[23] Those who are more knowledgeable may have a greater understanding of the media's role in promoting the democratic process and see it as a watchdog to protect individuals from government abuses.

Media use also predicts levels of media credibility, with individuals judging their most used medium as the most credible.[24] Scholars within the United States have debated whether credibility is directly linked to press freedom. Gaziano and McGrath[25] discovered that those who rated the media low in credibility were more likely to agree that the media abuse their First Amendment rights and that the media enjoy too much press freedom. However, studies by Blake, Wyatt and associates[26] failed to find a direct connection between support for journalists' rights, newspaper and TV news, and general media credibility. One possible explanation why support for freedom of the press has not predicted perceived credibility in the United States is that press freedoms are enshrined in the First Amendment and therefore may be taken for granted. However in countries such as those in the Middle East where the press had enjoyed few freedoms, researchers have found stronger links between credibility and press freedom. For example, Arab audiences put little trust in government-controlled media, and give high marks to outside Internet sources and pan-Arabic satellite news.[27]

Reliance on Al Jazeera emerged as the strongest predictor of credibility of both the Arab- and English-language Al Jazeera Web sites.[28] Viewers watch Al Jazeera faithfully because, unlike Western sources, it provides an Arab perspective on the news. Similarly, unlike most Arab sources, it provides round-the-clock uncensored news and has been willing to take controversial issues and allow viewers to call in to freely express their views.

Johnson and Fahmy argue that reliability may be more important for Al Jazeera than Western news sources because Al Jazeera does not follow Western standards of taste.[29] For instance, the network has tried to present a human perspective on the Iraqi War by showing scenes of bloody, wounded civilians, including children. Infrequent viewers may be jarred by such graphic content, judging it sensationalistic. Indeed, when Fahmy and Johnson[30] examined public support for graphic coverage, heavy viewers of Al Jazeera were more likely to support such content, as they contended that it provided truer pictures of wars and military conflicts in the Middle East than the Western media who sanitize coverage.

## POLITICAL VARIABLES AND ATTITUDES TOWARD PRESS FREEDOM

Other than political ideology, scholars have not extensively examined the influence of political variables on censorship views. Liberals have consistently supported press rights more than conservatives, as liberals have been found to be more tolerant of views and behaviors they do not necessarily agree with.[31] However, studies of Al Jazeera viewers have found that while liberals outnumber conservatives, most viewers consider themselves independents, which may limit the impact of ideology on views toward censorship.[32]

Little attention has been paid to the influence of other political measures such as political interest and activity. However, those who are more politically interested and active are more likely to rely on the media, which in turn, may be linked to higher support for media rights. Indeed, Johnson and Fahmy[33] found that those who were politically interested were more likely to rely on Al Jazeera than those politically disinterested. On the other hand, research has not indicated political interest and activity to be strong predictors of media credibility, which has also been linked to support for press freedom. Therefore political attitudes may serve, at best, as weak predictors of attitudes toward press freedom in the Arab world.

## DEMOGRAPHICS AND ATTITUDES TOWARD PRESS FREEDOM

Studies have consistently shown that men with high education and income support media rights on issues of censorship. While younger individuals may show more support for individual rights in general, studies suggest that those near retirement age voice the strongest support for media rights.[34] The portrait of media supporters coincides with the characteristics of heavy news users.

Studies suggest that Al Jazeera users tend to be young men with high education, but low incomes.[35] However, Auter and Associates[36] found that heavy viewers of Al Jazeera tend to be middle-aged (35–44) with lower education and income. They argued that while those with low education and incomes would turn to Al Jazeera as a convenient, inexpensive method of keeping up with world news, wealthier individuals with higher income might rely on a multitude of sources for news and information.

Because audience characteristics of heavy viewers of Al Jazeera do not match the portrait of those who traditionally support media rights, demographics may have less of an impact in the Arab world than it does in Western studies. Indeed, Fahmy and Johnson[37] reported that demographic variables such as age, gender, and education did not serve as mediating factors in determining whether those who supported press freedom and who relied heavily on Al Jazeera would support the network's use of graphic images in its broadcasts.

## RESEARCH QUESTIONS (RQ)

RQ1. How do viewers of Al Jazeera TV judge the level of press freedom in the Arab world?

RQ2. How do viewers of Al Jazeera TV compare the level of press freedom in the Arab world to the level of press freedom in the United States?

RQ3. Do heavier viewers of Al Jazeera TV perceive more press freedom in the Arab world than lighter viewers do?

RQ4. To what degree does reliance on Al Jazeera TV correlate with attitudes toward press freedom in the Arab world after controlling for political ideology (political activity and political interest) and demographic variables (age, education, gender, English-language proficiency, and income)?

## METHOD

In summer 2004, the researchers contacted senior executives of Al Jazeera network in the Middle East, requesting their assistance in putting a hyperlink on the Arabic Web site of the news organization. An Arabic-language survey examining the perspectives of viewers toward press freedom was posted on the Web site (http://www.aljazeera.net), free of charge. The survey hyperlink was posted for three weeks—from September 21, 2004 to October 12, 2004. With the exception of a relatively few violent incidents in the Palestinian territories, the Gaza Strip and Iraq, a search on the Lexis-Nexis database reveals no major events occurring during that time period in the Arab world that would have influenced the results of this survey.

The questionnaire was first written in English and then translated into Arabic and then translated back into English. Back-translation was done to ensure accurate translation and cultural compatibility. The questionnaire was then pre-tested. To ensure that valid and reliable data was collected, the survey hyperlink was first sent to 10 viewers of Al Jazeera TV residing in the Arab world. Overall, 731 respondents completed the final online questionnaire. Ninety-three survey samples were eliminated because they were duplicates or were incomplete, leaving 638. The survey's respondents were Al Jazeera television viewers who seek more information from the Al Jazeera Arabic Web site. Using an online questionnaire proved to have been the preferred method for this study as it allowed the researchers to directly survey Al Jazeera viewers who spoke Arabic. Attempting to select a group of Al Jazeera viewers through traditional means would be extremely difficult because most of the Arab governments restrict who can conduct surveys and because of the limited degree of freedom enjoyed in the Arab world overall.[38] Furthermore, because data collection via the

Internet allows more anonymity than other means of gathering responses, respondents might be more likely to offer honest answers.[39] Finally, electronic surveys offer potential efficiencies over mail and telephone surveys, including reduced costs, timeliness, as well as unhindered access across international boundaries.[40]

This study's respondents, therefore, can be classified as a purposive sample of Al Jazeera viewers who have access to the Internet. Results, therefore, might not be representative of the larger Arab culture or even of all Al Jazeera viewers, so care must be taken not to generalize the results to the population at large.

To answer the research question examining press freedom, respondents were asked to rate the freedom of the press in the Arab world and the United States on a scale from 0 to 10. Respondents were also asked to state their level of agreement with statements dealing with the following: whether the channel has led to an increase in press freedom in the Arab world, whether the Arab media should be allowed to publish free from government control, and whether the Arab media should be allowed to freely criticize their governments. The five-point scale ranged from "strongly agree" to "strongly disagree."

To test the relationship between media reliance and press freedom, a press freedom index was computed. The index was composed of two measures: Arab media should be allowed to publish free from government control and Arab media should be allowed to freely criticize their governments.

- *Al Jazeera Reliance:* A reliance index was also computed. The index was composed of two measures. Respondents were asked to assess their level of attention paid to Al Jazeera television in the past three days and to assess their level of reliance on Al Jazeera television for information. Response categories ranged from "a lot," "considerable," "some," "little," and "not at all."
- *Political Variables:* Measures of political activity and political interest were also employed. Respondents were asked to rate their level of political activity and their level of political interest on a scale of 0 to 10. Also, respondents were asked to report whether they politically viewed themselves as "very liberal," "liberal," "independent," "conservative," or "very conservative."
- *Demographic Variables:* A set of background questions was included for descriptive purposes: gender, age, English-language proficiency, education, and income. English-language proficiency was measured with a five-point scale from "not at all proficient" to "very proficient."

The data were analyzed in three stages. First, frequencies were run for measures of support for press freedom in the Arab world. Second, t-tests compared the perceived level of press freedom and media reliance among high and low Al Jazeera users. Finally, partial correlation examined the relationship between reliance on Al Jazeera and attitudes toward press freedom after partialing out the effects of political ideology and demographic variables.

## RESULTS

### Respondents: Demographics and Characteristics

A total of 638 usable responses were analyzed for this study. Nearly all (97 percent) respondents reported that they watch Al Jazeera TV. These respondents who watched the channel were attentive to, and relied on, Al Jazeera network for news. The mean scores were between the "a lot" and the "considerable" response categories.

Although respondents completed the survey from 53 different countries, 98 percent of the respondents indicated backgrounds from 20 Arab countries and two non-Arab Muslim countries (Afghanistan and Pakistan)[41]. Therefore, although this is an international audience, nearly all of the respondents originated from Arab nations.[42]

Overall, the respondents represented an international and highly educated elite group. Two-thirds (68.2 percent) reported having lived outside their native country, and 55.7 percent indicated living at least one year abroad. Twenty percent had visited the United States and the vast majority (82.2 percent) were at least somewhat proficient with the English language, with 63.6 percent reporting they were proficient or very proficient. Half of the respondents (51.1 percent) said they had at least a university degree and an additional 30 percent reported they had graduate degrees.

Respondents ranged in age from 18 to 70 years, with a mean of 32.4. Responses from participants below age 18 (a total of eight responses) were removed from the data set. Males greatly outnumbered females (89 percent to 11 percent). Nearly all those who responded (95 percent) reported they were Muslims, 3 percent reported they were Christians, and less than 1 percent reported they were Jewish. In terms of income, 55.4 percent reported an annual income that ranged between $1,001 and $25,000. Almost one-fifth (18.3 percent) indicated an annual income of less than $1,000. Few of the respondents (3.6 percent) indicated an annual income more than $100,000.

*Perceptions of Press Freedom*

The first research question explored how viewers of Al Jazeera TV judge the level of press freedom in the Arab world. Respondents indicated they believed the Arab press suffered under censorship and argued that the press should be free. Nearly 80 percent strongly agreed that the Arab media should be allowed to freely criticize their government and another 16 percent agreed. Less than 3 percent "disagreed" or "strongly disagreed." Respondents also strongly believed that the Arab media should be allowed to publish free from government control (64.4 percent) and almost a quarter of the respondents agreed with the statement. Overall, results showed that viewers in this survey believe that the Arab media are controlled, explaining that these media are just tools to deliver what "leaders" want their people to know and that journalism in Arab countries is nothing but an "accessory to those in power." As one viewer explained, "The media in the Arab world are instruments of the Arab regimes." Another one wrote,

> Journalists in Arab countries don't have the opportunity to express themselves and to reflect the reality because they are afraid of the governments that might take action against them . . . look at the number of arrests of journalists in Arab countries. Anyone saying or writing against the leaders is taken to jail. In some places, the only acceptable view is the one coming from the mouth of the leader. Anything else is wrong or even a crime against the nation.

Results also showed that almost 8 in 10 believed that Al Jazeera TV has led to an increase in press freedom in the Arab world. (See table 5.1 for frequencies and means.) One viewer explained,

> In the Arab World the liberty of the press is starting to be felt despite the fact we are far away from the ideal situation. *Al-Jazeera* and *Al-Arabya* are good examples of the development of the "other" media.

The second research question examined how viewers of Al Jazeera TV compare the level of press freedom in the Arab world to the level of press freedom in the United States. Results show that the freedom of the press in the United States, although average, is perceived to be higher than the freedom of the press in the Arab world. Respondents were significantly more likely to rate the level of press freedom higher for the United States than in Arab countries overall. On a scale of 1 to 10 wherein 10 indicates the culture enjoys a high level of press

**Table 5.1**  Percentages and Means of Responses Showing How Viewers of Al Jazeera Assess the Level of Press Freedom in the Arab World (N = 638)

|  | Mean | S. D. | Percent Reporting Agree and Strongly Agree | Percent Reporting Disagree and Strongly Disagree |
|---|---|---|---|---|
| The Arab media shouldbe allowed to freely criticize their governments | 4.73 | .68 | 94.4 | 2.7 |
| The Arab media should be allowed to publish free from government control | 4.51 | .92 | 88.2 | 6.7 |
| Al Jazeera TV has led to an increase in press freedom in the Arab world | 4.07 | 1.12 | 78.1 | 11.1 |

*Note*: 1 = strongly disagree; 2 = disagree; 3 = Neutral; 4 = agree; 5 = strongly agree

freedom, respondents scored Arab media low on freedom of the press (mean = 2.83) and rated the freedom of the press in the United States as only average (mean = 5.35). One respondent explained,

> It seems like American media are free, but actually they are not. For example, many reports were ignored by all mainstream media, which would have lowered Bush's chances to win and consequently would have affected election results. There is a definite agreement to support Israel's causes no matter what . . . This unconditional support is limiting the free media and makes it, rather, a manipulating media.

The third research question examined whether heavier viewers of Al Jazeera TV perceive more press freedom in the Arab world than lighter viewers do. As shown in table 5.2, reliance on Al Jazeera network positively relates to statements on whether the Arab media should be allowed to freely criticize their governments, and to publish free from government control. In other words, the more viewers relied on the TV network for news, the more likely they were to support free press in the Arab world. Further, results indicate that the more respondents relied on Al Jazeera, the more they were likely to rate the level of press freedom significantly higher in the Arab world on the 10-point freedom scale (mean 2.10 vs. 2.83).

The fourth and final research question examined whether reliance on Al Jazeera TV network correlated with attitudes toward press freedom

**Table 5.2** Comparing Means of Responses Regarding Reliance on Al Jazeera Network and Perceived Press Freedom in the Arab World (N = 638)

| | Light Viewers (mean) | Heavy Viewers (mean) | T-Score |
|---|---|---|---|
| Press Freedom Index | 3.94 | 4.65 | 155.46* |
| The Arab media should be allowed to freely criticize their governments | 3.80 | 4.76 | 113.95* |
| The Arab media should be allowed to publish free from government control | 3.78 | 4.52 | 162.29* |

*Note:* 1 = strongly disagree; 2 = disagree; 3 = Neutral; 4 = agree; 5 = strongly agree
Respondents that moderately rely on Al Jazeera network were coded as missing
*p < .001

after partialing out the effects of political ideology and demographic variables. A one-tail test indicates that reliance on Al Jazeera network has no significant correlation with statements regarding press freedom after controlling for political activity, political interest, and respondents' age, education, gender, English-language proficiency, and income. In other words, how heavily respondents relied on the network for news and information showed no relationship with how they assessed freedom of the press in the Arab world, after accounting for other factors.

## DISCUSSION

Because the broadcasting and political scenes are still evolving in the Middle East, it is difficult to assess whether satellite television networks have created a public opinion favorable to political democratization in the region. Studies do suggest that Al Jazeera has played a major role in ushering in a period of increased freedom of speech in the Arab world,[43] but authors debate whether this has loosened the reins of government censorship. Overall, however, results of this study suggest the emergence of Al Jazeera television as a possible contributor toward freedom of the press, one that has encouraged a more independent role of the media by supporting the lifting of government controls on the press. As one respondent wrote,

> Watching all of the new Arab channels I see that journalistic liberty has increased in recent years. Thanks to *Al-Jazeera* that showed that Arab journalism can be at the vanguard . . . Few media have already started to liberate themselves from their umbilical ties to the governments.

Clearly, this study found nearly eight in ten supported more press freedom. More importantly, respondents indicated that they believed the Arab press suffered under censorship and criticized the governments for limited press rights. Typically, respondents criticized media laws in the Arab world that explicitly restrict and limit freedom the press. As one viewer explained,

> The Arab media are a mouthpiece of the ruling party, or the government in their respective country. The Arab media are free ONLY when it comes to demonizing /criticizing Israel. Many of the honest journalists CANNOT publish any article that criticizes the government, because of the fear of imprisonment, or some form of punishment.

While, media systems vary somewhat from country to country in the Middle East, results of this study support past literature that those in predominantly Muslim countries place a high priority on having the right to criticize the government and on having a press that operated without government censorship[44]. That said, however, respondents in this study ranked freedom of the press in the United States as only average. They do not perceive the U.S. press as free, explaining they are controlled by multinational corporations. One respondent commented,

> American news media are in the hands of a few companies and it's in their best interest to keep the truth from the people. In some ways, some of them serve as an indirect mouthpiece of the system. The news is always short, and sanitized, and other points of view are not allowed. SELF-CENSORSHIP is a common practice, especially on TV. One always sees how the United States is glorified and the "others" are either demonized or ignored.

Further, for the concerned viewers and especially those who were critical of the U.S. media, ranking the freedom of the press as average could be seen as resulting from coverage of the recent wars in Afghanistan, Iraq, and Lebanon, and the Israeli/Palestinian conflict. Respondents were more critical of foreign reporting on events in the Middle East, Islam, Arabs/Muslims, and, more specifically, on the U.S. relationship with Israel. Respondents claimed that the U.S. coverage involves much more than the pursuit of journalistic objectivity. They reported that U.S. coverage of recent wars has demonstrated that the U.S. media are manipulated by the U.S. government. As one respondent explained,

> The media in the United States are ruled by multinational corporations that have certain objectives: Finding enemies to the United States to

gain more money and power. In the past it was communism, now it is the turn of Islam and Muslims.

This study also revealed that the more viewers relied on the TV network for news, the more likely they were to support free press in the Arab world. The more respondents relied on Al Jazeera, the more likely they were to support statements on whether the Arab media should be allowed to freely criticize their governments, and to publish free from government control. After controlling for political activity, political interest, and respondents' age, education, gender, English-language proficiency, and income, however, our findings revealed no direct connection between how heavily respondents relied on the network and how they assessed freedom of the press in the Arab world. One plausible reason is that media reliance and press freedom overall displayed very little variance. As table 5.1 shows, the standard deviations for the two items in the press freedom index were quite low. The only item with a standard deviation larger than 1.0 involved a statement that was not used in the index—whether Al Jazeera network has led to an increase in press freedom. Most of the respondents, then, showed clear homogeneous attitudes toward the level of press freedom in the Arab world.

Finally, a limitation of this study should be noted. The authors used an online survey posted on Al Jazeera's Web site. The purpose of this study was to examine how viewers of the television network perceive press freedom. In a largely oral society that for the most part restricts personal freedoms, it would be difficult to survey by traditional techniques. Careful use of purposive sampling generates results that might be representative of a specific subset of Internet users but might not be representative of the larger population.[45] Consequently, we consider this survey a pilot study designed to provide preliminary data on which to base further investigations. How viewers in the Arab world perceive Al Jazeera as a possible contributor toward attitudes and development of freedom of the press in the Middle East remains an evolving area of inquiry and this research represents a substantive effort to explore attitudes and perceptions of press freedom in the region. Further, the demographic profile of the users of Al Jazeera Arabic Web site who responded to this survey closely mirrors the characteristics found in earlier studies that posted surveys on the Al Jazeera Web site,[46] which suggests that this sample is representative of the population it surveyed. If democracy takes hold in most of the countries in the Middle East, it is hoped that future studies could employ a random sample to better understand how viewers of the Arab world perceive and rate freedom of the press worldwide. Future studies should attempt to post surveys on Web sites of other Arab media, to get a clearer sense of the Arab culture's view on press freedom.

## Notes

1. Anas M. Al-Rasheed, *Professional Values: A Survey of Working Journalists in the Kuwait Press* (Ph.D. diss., Southern Illinois University, 1998); Muhammad I. Ayish, "News Credibility During the Iraq War: A Survey of UAE Students," *Transnational Broadcasting Studies (TBS) Journal*, no. 12 (Spring 2004), available online at: <http://www.tbsjournal.com/ayish.htm>. Douglas A. Boyd, *Broadcasting in the Arab World: A Survey of Electronic Media in the Middle East* (Ames: Iowa State Press, 1999); Marvin Kalb and Jerome Socolovsky, "The Emboldened Arab Press," *Harvard International Journal of Press/Politics*, vol. 4 (Summer 1994): 1–4; William A. Rugh, *The Arab Press: News Media and Political Process in the Arab World* (New York: Syracuse University Press, 1987); William A. Rugh. *The Arab Press: News Media and Political Process in the Arab World* (West Port, CT: Praeger Publishers, 2004).

2. Hugh Miles, *Al-Jazeera: The Inside Story of the Arab News Channel that Is Challenging the West* (New York: Grove Press, 2005); Marc Lynch, *Voices of the New Arab Public* (New York: Columbia University Press, 2006); Noha Mellor, *The Making of Arab News* (Lanham, MD: Rowman & Littlefield, 2005); Mohammed El-Nawawy and Adel Iskandar, *Al-Jazeera: How the Free Arab News Network Scooped the World and Changed the Middle East* (Cambridge, MA: Westview Press, 2002); Safran S. Al-Makaty, Douglas A. Boyd, and G. Norman Van Tubergen, "Source Credibility During the Gulf War: A Q Study of Rural and Urban Saudi Arabian Citizens," *Journalism Quarterly*, vol. 71 (Spring 1994): 55–63; Ayish, "News Credibility during the Iraq War."

3. Ayish, "News Credibility during the Iraq War."

4. Miles, *Al-Jazeera*, p. 328.

5. Shahira Fahmy, "Egyptian Media: Into a New Millennium," in Art Silverblattt and Nikolai Zlobin (eds.), *International Communications: A Media Literacy Approach* (Westport, CT:Praeger, 2004), pp. 172–178; Naomi Sakr, "Seen and Starting to be Heard: Women and the Arab Media in a Decade of Change," *Social Research*, vol. 69 (Fall 2002): 821–850; Miles, *Al-Jazeera*; Ayish, "News Credibility during the Iraq War."

6. Sakr, "Seen and Starting to be Heard."

7. Freedom of the Press: Country Reports, available online at: <http://www.freedomhouse.org/>

8. The Pew Global Project, *Views of a Changing World*, available online at: <http://people-press.org/reports/display.php3?ReportID=185> (Accessed: December 15, 2004).

9. About *Al-Jazeera*, available online at: <http://www.aljazeera.net> (Accessed: August 10, 2004).
10. Delinda C. Hanley, "*Al-Jazeera* World Forum Takes a Hard Look at Freedom of the Press," *Washington Report on Middle East Affairs*, vol. 23 (October 2004): 14–15; Sam Cherribi, "From Baghdad to Paris: Al Jazeera and the Veil," *Harvard International Journal of Press/Politics*, vol. 11(Spring 2006): 121–138; Eric C. Nisbet, Matthew C. Nisbet, Dietram A. Scheufele, and James E. Shanahan, "Public Diplomacy, Television News, and Muslim Opinion," *Harvard International Journal of Press/Politics*, vol. 9 (Spring 2004): 11–37; el-Nawawy and Iskandar, *Al-Jazeera*.
11. Lynch, *Voices of the New Arab Public*, pp. 2–3.
12. Mohammed El-Nawawy. "Why Al-Jazeera Is the Most Popular Network in the Arab World" *Television Quarterly*, vol. 34 (Fall 2003): 10–15; Mellor, *The Making of Arab News*.
13. Neil Hickey, "Different Cultures, Different Coverage," *Columbia Journalism Review* (March/April 2002): 40–43; Miles, *Al-Jazeera*.
14. Faisal Al-Kasim, "Crossfire: The Arab Version," *Harvard International Journal of Press/Politics*, vol. 4 (Summer 1999): 93–97; el-Nawawy, "Why *Al-Jazeera* Is the Most popular"; Nisbet, Nisbet, Scheufele, and Shanahan, "Public Diplomacy."
15. Mark Lynch, "Watching al-Jazeera," *Wilson Quarterly*, vol. 29 (Summer 2005): 36–45; Lynch, *Voices of the New Arab Public*; Mellor, *Making of Arab News*.
16. Lynch, "Watching al-Jazeera."
17. Namdoo Kim and Seckjun Jang, "Reporting *Al-Jazeera's* Close Encounter with U.S. Militarism: A Comparative Content Analysis of American and British Newspapers' Post-9/11 Wartime Journalism," paper presented at the annual meeting of AEJMC, Toronto, Canada, August, 2004.
18. "Banning Bad News," *New York Times*, August 10, 2004, p. A1.
19. "The World Through their Eyes," available online at: <http://www.economist.com/displaystory.cfm?story_id=3690442>, February 24, 2005.
20. Michael I. Niman, "Yes, We Murder Journalists," *The Humanist* (March/April 2006), available online at: <http://www.thehumanist.org/humanist/MarApril06.html>; Peter C. Valenti, "Al-Jazeera in the Crosshairs: The Arab Media Scrutinize the Bush-Blair Memo," *Washington Report on Middle East Affairs* (January/February 2006): 30–31.
21. Julie L. Andsager, Robert O. Wyatt, and Ernest L. Martin, *Free Expression and Five Democratic Publics: Support for Individual and Media Rights* (Cresskill, NJ: Hampton Press, 2004); Jack McLeod, Mira Sotirovic, Paul S. Voakes, Zhongshi Guo, and Kuang-Yu Haung, "A Model of Public Support for First Amendment Rights." *Communication Law and Policy*, vol. 3 (Autumn 1988): 479–514;

Robert O. Wyatt, *Free Expression and the American Public* (Washington, DC: American Society of Newspaper Editors, 1991).

22. For instance, see Steven J. Chaffee and Stacey Frank, "How Americans Get Political Information: Print Versus Broadcast News," *The Annals of the American Academy of Political and Social Science*, vol. 566 (July 1996): 48–58; Peter Clarke and Eric Fredlin, "Newspapers, Television and Political Reasoning," *Public Opinion Quarterly*, vol. 42 (Summer 1978): 143–160; John P. Robinson and Mark R. Levy, "News Media Use and the Informed Public: A 1990s Update," *Journal of Communication*, vol. 45 (Spring 1996): 129–135.

23. Fiona Chew, "The Relationship of Information Needs to Issue Relevance and Media Use," *Journalism Quarterly*, vol. 71 (Autumn 1994): 676–688; Hugh M. Culbertson and Guido H. Stempel III, "How Media Use and Reliance Affects Knowledge Level," *Communication Research* (October 1986): 579–602; Alexis S. Tan, "Mass Media Use, Issue Knowledge and Political Involvement," *Public Opinion Quarterly*, vol. 44 (Summer 1980): 241–248.

24. Erica Weintraub Austin and Qingwen Dong, "Source v. Content Effects on Judgments of News Believability," *Journalism Quarterly*, vol. 71 (Winter 1994–1995): 973–983; Wayne Wanta and Yu-Wei Hu, "The Effects of Credibility, Reliance, and Exposure on Media Agenda-Setting: A Path Analysis Model," *Journalism Quarterly*, vol. 71 (Spring 1994): 90–98; Johnson and Kaye, "Using Is Believing"; Johnson and Kaye, "Cruising Is Believing."

25. Cecilie Gaziano and Kristin McGrath, "Measuring the Concept of Credibility," *Journalism Quarterly*, vol. 63 (Autumn 1986): 451–462; Cecilie Gaziano, "How Credible Is the Credibility Crisis?" *Journalism Quarterly*, vol. 65 (Summer 1988): 267–278.

26. Kenneth R. Blake, "Has Newspaper Credibility Mattered? A Perspective on Media Credibility Debate," *Newspaper Research Journal*, vol. 23 (Winter 2002–2003): 73–76; Robert O. Wyatt, Kenneth Blake, Jill Edy, and Teresa Mastin, "How Support for Journalistic Rights Is Related to News Media Credibility, Confidence in Institutions, and Civic Tolerance," paper presented at the Midwest Association for Public Opinion Research, Chicago, November 1999.

27. Hussein Amin, "Watching the War in the Arab World," *Transnational Broadcasting Studies (TBS) Journal*, no.10, available online at: <http://www.tbsjournal.com/archives/Spring03/amin.html/>; Ayish, "News Credibility during the Iraq War"; Masoud A. Abdulrahim, *Newspaper Readership and Credibility in Kuwait: An Analysis of Uses and Gratifications Theory* (Ph.D. diss., Southern Illinois University, 1999).

28. Thomas J. Johnson and Shahira Fahmy, "See no Evil, Hear no Evil, Judge as Evil? Examining the Degree to Which Users of Al-Jazeera English-language Website Transfer Credibility Views to its Satellite Network Counterpart," unpublished manuscript; Thomas J. Johnson

and Shahira Fahmy, "The CNN of the Arab World or a Shill for Terrorists?: How Support for Press Freedom and Political Ideology Predict Credibility of Al-Jazeera Among its Audience," paper presented at the ICA annual conference. New York City, May 2005; Philip Auter, Mohamed M. Arafa, and Khalid Al-Jaber, "News Credibility in the Arab World: An Analysis of Arabic People's Usage Patterns of Al-Jazeera after September 11, 2001 and Before the Iraq War," paper presented at the annual conference of Global Fusion, St. Louis, MO, 2004.

29. Johnson and Fahmy, "The CNN of the Arab World or a Shill for Terrorists?"

30. Shahira Fahmy and Thomas J. Johnson, "Show the Truth and Let the Audience Decide: A Web-based Survey Showing Support for Use of Graphic Imagery Among Viewers of Al-Jazeera," *Journal of Broadcasting & Electronic Media*, Vol. 51, No. 2 (2007), in press.

31. Thomas J. Johnson, "Exploring Media Credibility: How Media and Non-Media Workers Judged Media Performance in Iran/Contra," *Journalism Quarterly*, vol. 70 (Spring 1993): 87–97; Cecilie Gaziano, "News People's Ideology and the Credibility Debate," *Newspaper Research Journal*, vol. 9 (Fall 1987): 1–18.

32. Auter et al., "News Credibility in the Arab World"; Johnson and Fahmy, "The CNN of the Arab World or a Shill for Terrorists?"

33. Johnson and Fahmy, "The CNN of the Arab World or a Shill for Terrorists?"

34. Andsager, Wyatt, and Martin, *Free Expression and Five Democratic Publics*; McLeod, Sotirovic, Voakes, Guo, and Haung, "A Model of Public Support for First Amendment Rights"; Wyatt, *Free Expression and the American Public*.

35. Philip Auter, Mohamed M. Arafa, and Khalid Al-Jaber, "Identifying with Arabic Journalists: How *Al-Jazeera* Tapped Parasocial Interaction Gratifications in the Arab World," *Gazette*, vol. 67 (April 2005): 189–204; Khalid Al-Jaber, *The Credibility of Arab Broadcasting: The Case of Al-Jazeera* (Doha, Qatar: Qatar National Council for Culture, Arts and Heritage, 2004); Philip Auter, Mohamed M. Arafa, and Khalid Al-Jaber, "Who Is *Al-Jazeera*'s Audience? Deconstructing the Demographics and Psychographics of an Arab Satellite News Network," *Transnational Broadcasting Studies (TBS) Journal*, no. 12, available online at: <http://www.tbsjournal.com/html12.auter.htm>; Auter, Arafa, and Al-Jaber, "News Credibility in the Arab World."

36. Auter, Arafa, and Al-Jaber, "Identifying with Arabic Journalists," Auter, Arafa, and Al-Jaber, "Who Is *Al-Jazeera*'s Audience?"

37. Fahmy and Johnson, "Show the Truth and Let the Audience Decide."

38. Muhammad I. Ayish. "Political Communication on Arab World Television: Evolving Patterns," *Political Communication*, vol. 19 (April 2002): 137–154; Boyd, *Broadcasting in the Arab World*;

Kalb and Socolovsky, "Emboldened Arab Press"; Rugh, *Arab Press.*

39. J. Michael Dennis, Cindy Chatt, Motta-Stanko Li, Alicia Rick, and Paul Pulliam. "Data Collection Mode Effects Controlling for Sample Origins in a Panel Survey: Telephone and Internet," paper presented at the American Association for Public Opinion Research annual meeting, Miami, Florida, 2005.

40. Don A. Dillman. *Mail and Internet Surveys: The Tailored Design Method* (New York: John Wiley & Sons, Inc, 2000).

41. Because the sample was heavily skewed toward Arab respondents residing in Arab and Muslim countries, efforts to find if those in the United States or the West had different attitudes toward graphic media than Arab citizens failed. Therefore, this study did not explore geographic reasons for differences.

42. It would be an oversimplification to consider all Arab nations uniform in their characteristics and socio/political structures. The Arab world currently does not constitute a single society. In fact, the presence of various national trends, undermining the establishment of genuine Arab unity within the *Umma* (Muslim community), encouraged scholars to examine the relationship between the Arab personality verses regional differences. Attempting a normative conclusion, however, the Egyptian sociologist El-Sayyid Yassin writes that the Arab personality constitutes the primary personality pattern, while regional personalities constitute the secondary pattern. Indeed, scholars explain the great majority of the citizens of Arab countries view themselves, and are viewed by others, as Arabs. Halim Barakat (Halim Barakat. *The Arab world: Society, culture and state* (Berkley, CA: University of California Press, 1993), for example, argues that Arabs can belong together without being the same. In other words, their sense of Arab identity is based on what they have in common, namely language, culture, sociopolitical experiences, economic interests and a collective memory of their place and role in history (Barakat, *The Arab world).*

43. Hanley, "*Al-Jazeera* World Forum"; Cherribi, "From Baghdad to Paris"; Nisbet, Nisbet, Scheufele, and Shanahan, "Public Diplomacy, Television News, and Muslim Opinion"; el-Nawawy and Iskandar, *Al-Jazeera*; Lynch, *Voices of the New Arab Public.*

44. The Pew Global Project. *Views of a Changing World.*

45. Earl Babbie, *Survey Research Methods* (Belmont, CA: Wadsworth, 2001).

46. Auter, Arafa, and Al-Jaber, "Who Is *Al-Jazeera*'s Audience?"

# CHAPTER 6

# Arab Arguments: Talk Shows
# and the New Arab Public Sphere

*Marc Lynch*

Since Al Jazeera exploded on the Arab scene in the late 1990s, its talk shows have ushered in a culture of contentious public debate, a culture that has fundamentally shattered unitary Arab nationalist discourse.[1] They shattered decades of tight Arab state control over the public agenda that imposed a stifling silence on real political debate. Al Jazeera's talk shows helped to bring into being a new Arab public oriented toward contentious public argument about issues of interest to a shared Arab identity. This new public already has a deeply ingrained expectation of public disagreement and dissent that was almost unthinkable only a short time ago. Do Arab talk shows constitute a new Arab public sphere?

Many observers have raised serious concerns about the political effects of these talk shows. Some fear that it is driving a culture of talk rather than a culture of action, transforming Arabs into a "media phenomenon."[2] On the brink of the American invasion of Iraq, Al Jazeera presenter Faisal al-Qassem lamented, "why does nothing remain in the Arab arena except for some croaking media personalities? Why does a loud television clamor suffice as an alternative to effective action?"[3] Others despair at the perceived low quality of discussion that inclines to "the superficial and the sensational . . . [lacking] focused dialogue . . . and dominated by accusations and the settling of scores."[4] For Abdullah Schleifer, "all too often these talk shows degenerated into unproductive shouting matches in which abuse replaced dialogue and analysis . . . these talk shows are too often a vehicle for the collective venting of emotion rather than an exercise in critical thinking."[5] Others worry that the artificial staging of the debates leads to an exacerbation of differences and the elision of the vital center, degrading the political culture by driving argument to the extremes. [6] For Jon Alterman, "much of the debate in Arab media is a false debate, either between two ludicrous extremes, or between a guest espousing a 'proper' view and his heretical opponent. . . . Arab debates often resemble nothing so much as professional wrestling, where the outcome is clear before the adversaries even step into the ring."[7]

Arab talk shows have therefore generated considerable controversy. But due to the absence of serious research on either the content of the talk shows or on their impact, such arguments remain largely anecdotal and speculative.[8] Is Al Jazeera driving sectarian conflict in Iraq through its choice of guests on its talk shows? Is it fomenting anti-Americanism by constructing its talk shows in ways that ensure America cannot win? This chapter offers some empirical evidence to begin evaluating these arguments, first by offering an overview of the content of Al Jazeera's talk shows over a five-year period and then by looking in detail at a single "dialogue moment," the debates over a 2004 American reform initiative. I argue that much of the discussion of these talk shows has been slanted by an overemphasis on a particular type of talk show, exemplified by Faisal al-Qassem's *The Opposite Direction*, and by a failure to recognize the difference between "mobilizational moments" and "dialogue moments" in Arab politics.

## Talk Shows and Politics

*You are hurting America . . . stop, stop, stop, stop hurting America.*

—*Jon Stewart, to Tucker Carlson, host of CNN's* Crossfire.[9]

Talk shows have not generally been seen as a progressive political force. In his analysis of American daytime talk shows, Joshua Gamson noted the widespread concern about "the damage these shows do to democracy by posing as democratic public fora but gutting themselves of almost everything but ratings-driven exhibitions . . . [exposing] a liberal public sphere severely eroded and impoverished by its central driver, commercial television, where quick emotion displaces rational deliberation."[10] Echoes of such denunciations resound in the debates about Arab talk shows. But the Arab context is fundamentally different: rather than representing a degeneration of a once rational or sophisticated public sphere, these talk shows filled a gaping void in the Arab political arena.[11] Prior to Al Jazeera's emergence, an enforced silence about contentious issues—combined with loud but unanimous demands on issues such as Palestine—produced an Arab public in which dissent and argument (rare novelty acts, at the time) were quickly silenced.

Al Jazeera attracted unprecedented mass audiences with its pioneering coverage of the Iraqi crisis in the late 1990s and the Palestinian-Israeli fighting beginning in 2000. While Al Jazeera has faced mounting competition, it remains the one station watched by virtually everyone, making its programs the "common knowledge" of Arab politics, which all Arabs can reasonably assume that others have seen and are prepared to discuss.[12] Rather than limit debate to approved areas, Al Jazeera's programs delighted in shattering taboos and in provoking sharp debates. Broadcast live, these programs danced at the edge of chaos, tantalizing viewers with the possibility of transgression.

Some of its most sensational programs over the years have become iconic in discussions of the Arab media—the debate between Sadeq Jalal al-Azm and Yusuf al-Qaradawi over secularism; the time that the American academic Asaad Abu Khalil provoked a diplomatic crisis by mocking Jordan's King Hussein; the time that Toujan Faisal drove a spluttering Islamic conservative to stomp off the set; the time that the American-based feminist Wafa Sultan needled an Egyptian Islamic conservative about Islam's failures. This focus on exemplary moments can actually conceal what is most important about Al Jazeera's programs: the way their relentless return to critiques of the Arab status quo cumulatively reshaped the entire Arab public agenda.

Al Jazeera's prioritization of public argument is what transformed the satellite television form into a potentially revolutionary forum. The "public sphere" qualities of Al Jazeera resided in its live, unpredictable character, with public argument oriented toward an imagined audience conceptualized as incorporating all Arabs. Participation, through phone calls and faxes and internet voting created at least the illusion that this public was open to all members of this Arab identity, and that their Arab identity was made manifest through the act of expressing an opinion in public. These talk shows offered perhaps the first real opportunity for Arabs to argue freely about issues of the day before a vast audience of those who share an identity and concerns. In contrast to the demands for conformity in Gamal Abd al-Nasser's pan-Arabism, Al Jazeera celebrated difference and argument within the bounds of a shared identity. Few participants in these programs disagree with the core shared commitments that define the new Arab public: questions of reform, Israel, Iraq, and of Arab identity in the face of American power. But within those parameters, they disagree—often vehemently—about what should be done or about what conclusions to draw from events. Even on something as central to Arab identity as the Palestinian *Intifada*, it could air a debate on whether it was a waste of time.

Al Jazeera was not the first Arab TV station to offer talk shows. In the 1990s, Emad Al-Dib pioneered the call-in format with Istifta Ala al-Hawa on the pay-station Orbit, while various talk shows appeared and disappeared on other stations over the years. But most of these programs were crippled by the omnipresent red lines inhibiting free debate. Generally prerecorded to give censors a chance to approve their contents, the shows and their guests demonstrated expert knowledge of which issues to leave alone.

Few Arab television stations have dared copy the public sphere aspects of Al Jazeera's talk shows, even when they have imitated the forms. Al-Arabiya, for instance, for all its high-tech sheen has largely stuck to prerecorded programs, in explicit repudiation of Al Jazeera's commitment to live, uncensored and unscripted presentation of political argument. Abd al-Rahman al-Rashed, director of al-Arabiya, has frequently argued that Arab television should focus more on the objective, professional presentation of news than on opinion and argument. This can be seen as an attempt to purge the Arab media of precisely the qualities that made Al Jazeera into a public sphere. Such a trend can be seen even on Al Jazeera. *Behind the News*, the signature, nightly, prime-time program introduced during a revamp of Al Jazeera's programming in the summer of 2005, represents an important departure from the "public sphere" conception. Its topics are selected by the editorial team, not by the host; it lasts only half an hour, dramatically reducing the time for give and take and for the in-depth exploration of issues; its dialogue tends to flow through the host, with little give and take among the guests; and there are no phone callers or audience participation. In short, it is more controlled from the top down and less open to unscripted, revelatory moments.

## THE ARAB CONVERSATION: WHAT DO THESE TALK SHOWS TALK ABOUT?

Talk shows can be seen both as a window into Arab political discussions and as framing those debates. While it is risky to infer public opinion from these debates, they provide a unique entrance into Arab political arguments—not just public opinion as measured in surveys, but also the dynamic and fluid processes of arguments through which those opinions take shape. Al Jazeera's talk shows shaped the Arab political agenda, placing events within what I have called the "Al Jazeera narrative." Most of the guests came from civil society, political parties, or journalism, and many of the programs featured opportunities for viewers to call in or otherwise participate. Whether by choice or by necessity, Al Jazeera hosted far fewer Arab heads of state or cabinet members than was common for Arab television.

Looking at 1039 episodes of the five most prominent general-interest political talk shows reveals some important trends.[13] First, the Arab debate on Al Jazeera focused almost exclusively on Arab or Islamic issues. Barely a handful dealt with issues outside the immediate purview of the Arab world—and even those would be discussed in the context of how they affected Arabs. This was neither accidental nor insignificant: Al Jazeera self-consciously constructed itself as an Arab forum focused on Arab issues.

Four broad issues dominated Al Jazeera's agenda: Palestine, Iraq, reform, and America. Over a five-year period, Palestine and reform each made up about 26 percent of all programs, while Iraq and the United States each made up about 22 percent, with interesting variations over time. Palestine dominated the agenda from 1998 through 2002, while Iraq drove out virtually all other issues in 2003. Reform was a constant issue of concern, rising at some points and declining at others but always present. Finally, the United States became an increasingly central concern over the years, in line with its manifestly increased presence in the region after 9/11, the invasion of Iraq, and the adoption of a democratization agenda. Indeed, table 6.1 undercounts the American presence, as the United States increasingly intruded on and shaped discussion of all issues.

**Table 6.1** Al Jazeera Talk Show Topics [Number (percent of total)]

|       | Palestine | Iraq      | Reform   | America  | Total |
|-------|-----------|-----------|----------|----------|-------|
| 1999  | 33 (24)   | 13 (9)    | 51 (37)  | 14 (10)  | 138   |
| 2000  | 39 (27)   | 14 (10)   | 46 (32)  | 12 (8)   | 142   |
| 2001  | 56 (36)   | 14 (9)    | 42 (27)  | 37 (24)  | 157   |
| 2002  | 66 (39)   | 33 (19)   | 31 (18)  | 49 (29)  | 170   |
| 2003  | 31 (17)   | 104 (57)  | 42 (23)  | 66 (36)  | 184   |
| 2004  | 48 (19)   | 51 (21)   | 57 (23)  | 54 (22)  | 248   |
| Total | 273 (26)  | 229 (22)  | 269 (26) | 232 (22) | 1039  |

*Note*: "America" programs are those in which words such as "America," "United States," or some obvious referent appears in the *title*; as almost every program about Iraq could be considered "about America," this method undercounts American presence. "Reform" programs are those that dealt with social, economic, intellectual, or domestic political issues

These concerns were not treated as discrete issues, but rather cohered in a discernible Al Jazeera narrative, defined not by consensus on all points but on a shared basic storyline within which points of disagreement made sense. Iraq passed from an area of near consensus to one of deep contention. From Al Jazeera's launch to the fall of Baghdad, this public took the suffering of the Iraqi people under sanctions—and the perfidy of the United States and Arab rulers in enforcing those sanctions—as a key marker of the shared narrative. After the war, however, this public was stunned to discover considerable hostility among Iraqis who believed that they had given support to Saddam—a dissonance that triggered a fascinating and important debate.[14] It is telling that Al Jazeera responded to the fall of Baghdad by shelving its regular talk shows for six weeks in favor of *Minbar al-Jazeera*, a live call-in show that allowed ordinary Arabs to argue about the bewildering new world with relatively little editorial control or oversight.

In 1999 and 2000, Al Jazeera hosted—in addition to regular discussions of elections or significant political events—frequent discussions of big questions such as the impact of generational change on Arab hopes for democracy (March 5, 1999), democracy in the Arab world (March 29, 1999), the Arab economic situation (May 12, 1999), the use of states of emergency (August 31, 1999), human rights (October 5, 1999; May 2, 2000), how to unleash freedom of thought (November 8, 1999), unemployment (December 8, 1999), honor crimes (February 22, 2000), youth problems (May 17, 2000), the new Arab wealthy (June 27, 2000), and women's rights (July 19, 2000).

After the outbreak of the Palestinian *al-Aqsa Intifada* in September 2000, Al Jazeera greatly increased its focus on Palestinian issues, with those topics taking up 36 percent of all shows in 2001 and 39 percent in 2002. Still, Al Jazeera continued to air programs on issues such as secularist-Islamist conflicts over freedom of expression (December 11, 2000), civil society (April 10, 2001), obstacles to investment (May 2, 2001), freedom of expression in the Arab media (June 30, 2001), Islamism and democracy (July 28, 2001), and "security mentalities" in the Arab world (August 25, 2001).

September 11 dominated the agenda for months afterward, leading to a sharp increase in attention to the United States, Islam, and the war on terror. As early as November, programs were beginning to speculate about an American war on Iraq (November 28, 2001). Reform discussions also continued, particularly with an eye toward the effects of the war on terror on political freedoms: the future of human rights (December 25, 2001), the lost role of Arab parliaments (January 8, 2002), the crisis of Arab culture (January 30, 2002), a mocking look at 99.99 percent electoral victories (June 11, 2002), and considerable discussion of the 2002 Arab Human Development Report (August 13, 2002; August 7, 2002). But such reform talk was increasingly lost within angry arguments about Israel (especially toward the spring, when Israel reoccupied the West Bank), sullen defensiveness about external pressures, loud fury at incompetent and unresponsive regimes, and a growing, hostile focus on the United States—particularly after President Bush's "Axis of Evil" speech in early 2002 and the growing talk of war with Iraq.

Iraq absolutely dominated the first half of 2003, driving out almost all other issues. But in the second half of 2003, Al Jazeera returned to its reform agenda, with greater focus on the shortcomings of Arab regimes and more sustained debates about a possible American role in promoting reform. The tone of many of these programs about reform was defensive: responding to American pressure rather than working through Arab issues on their own terms. As early as May 2003, programs considered the possibilities of reform after the Iraq earthquake (HM May 17, 2003), with defensiveness and anti-American skepticism doing battle with desperate frustration and hopes for some kind of a change. By early 2004, reform debates were in full swing, even as Iraq continued to shape much of the discursive arena. Darfur emerged as a surprisingly central issue over the course of 2004, with at least eight programs devoted to Sudan in this period.

## AGAINST FAISAL-CENTRISM

Most discussion of Arab talk shows has focused on one very distinctive and important model: *The Opposite Direction*, hosted by Faisal al-Qassem. *The Opposite Direction* typically pitted two diametrically opposed individuals against one another, with a provocatively worded question and with Qassem baiting them and spurring them on into argumentative frenzy. *The Opposite Direction* was the most popular and controversial Al Jazeera program, but there was no single Al Jazeera style. Recognizing this diversity is important, because overreliance on this one format has colored much of the research on Arab talk shows, highlighting their polarizing and sensationalizing qualities. For instance, Mohamed Ayish studied ten episodes of *The Opposite Direction* to show how each tended to follow a consistent rhythm and flow, pushing toward a predictable outcome.[15] Mohamed al-Nawawy and Adel Iskander's chapter on Al Jazeera's talk shows, titled "Boxing Rings," primarily draws its examples from Qassem's program.[16] Mamoun Fandy's negative portrayal of Al Jazeera's talk shows as a reinvention of Nasser's Voice of the Arabs was limited to two episodes of *The Opposite Direction*.[17] For that matter, a significant portion of the formal complaints received by Al Jazeera or the Qatari government pertained to Qassem's program.[18]

But realizing that this "Faisal-centric" view of the talk shows captures only a very thin slice of the new Arab media can allow for a more nuanced understanding of how these programs are changing Arab politics.[19] As discussed below, Al Jazeera alone offered a wide variety of talk show formats. Other stations offered even more. Al-Arabiya recruited a number of talented talk show hosts, including Giselle Khoury, Montaha al-Rahmi, Hisham Milhem, Hussein Shobakshi, and Turki al-Dakhil. Most tended to favor more controlled formats and drew guests from the Arab ruling elite. No contrast could be starker than the comparison between each station's signature one-on-one interview program: almost two-thirds of all guests on Giselle Khoury's popular *Bil-Arabi* program on al-Arabiya were current or former high-ranking Arab government officials, while Ahmed Mansour's *No Limits* drew predominantly on independent, Arab nationalist and Islamist writers and activists. Popular programs on LBC, Abu Dhabi TV, and many others offer a wide spectrum of formats—each of which encouraged different kinds of debate and presumably pushed toward different kinds of outcomes. Even religious stations such as Iqra and Risala offered talk shows, as did entertainment-oriented stations.[20] Had programs on other stations been included in the discussion to follow, it would only have increased the finding of diversity in forums and approaches—a diversity that can already be seen within Al Jazeera's offerings.

## A DIALOGUE MOMENT: THE GREATER MIDDLE EAST INITIATIVE

Al Jazeera's talk shows look very different during what I call its "dialogue moments" and its "mobilizational moments." During intense conflicts and moments of crisis, such as the Israeli reoccupation of the West Bank in 2002, the American invasion of Iraq in March 2003, or the Israeli-Lebanese war of 2006, Al Jazeera tends to subordinate debate and discussion to traditional news coverage and to mobilizational interviews. These mobilizational moments are offset by "dialogue moments" in which even highly emotional and contentious issues are put up to sustained and focused debate.

In order to illustrate the diversity of these programs and the different ways in which they construct arenas for public discourse, one key "dialogue moment" has been selected: the 2004 American Greater

**Table 6.2**  Talk Shows about the GMEI

| Date | Show | Topic |
| --- | --- | --- |
| February 20 | More than One Opinion | The Greater Middle East Project |
| February 28 | Open Dialogue | Calls for change in the Arab world |
| March 13 | Open Dialogue | The Tunis Arab Summit |
| March 16 | Opposite Direction | The Middle East project |
| March 29 | *Minbar al-Jazeera* | Reasons for postponing the Arab summit |
| April 2 | Akthar Min Rai | Postponement of Arab summit |
| April 5 | *Minbar al-Jazeera* | Reform projects and the Arab position |
| March 30 | Opposite Direction | The Arab summit and reforms in the Arab world |
| May 25 | Opposite Direction | Future of reform project |
| June 10 | From Washington | The results of the G-8 Summit |
| June 14 | *Minbar al-Jazeera* | The results of the G-8 Summit |

Middle East Initiative (GMEI) for reform. Leaked to al-Hayat in February 2004, the GMEI represented an early draft of an American agenda for promoting reform in the Arab world. Arab governments unleashed a blistering campaign against it, branding it as a form of imperialism, hoping to harness the anti-American portion of the Al Jazeera consensus against the pro-reform portion. Over the next few months, this agenda became the subject of an intense and remarkably wide-open public debate about the desirability of reform and American credibility (see table 6.2). This section looks at 11 Al Jazeera talk shows devoted to the topics. By way of comparison, it was found that only three talk shows dealt with this topic on al-Arabiya: a May 23 episode of *Bil-Mursad*, hosted by the former Al Jazeera anchor Muntaha al-Rahmi; a June 8 episode of *Under the Lights*, hosted by Talib Kana'an; and a June 11 episode of Hisham Milhem's *Across the Sea*.[21]

## The Opposite Direction

As noted above, Faisal al-Qassem's *The Opposite Direction* presents a highly contentious, binary conception of debate. Qassem's March 16 program on "the Middle East project" exemplifies this approach. With head of the Arab Lawyers Union Abd al-Azim al-Maghrabi pitted against American-based neoconservative Shakir Nabulsi, Qassem ensured fireworks before the program even began. Qassem's introduction, as always, aimed to heighten the contradictions and to draw the sharpest possible argument. No reasonable middle ground, here: Qassem first ridiculed Arab opponents of the Greater Middle East Project, wondering what they were so afraid of, while lacerating the hypocrisy of the Arab regimes pretending to take reform seriously. Then a 180-degree pivot: but on the other side, he asked, who wanted outsiders intervening in their affairs? What did Palestine really have to do with the reforms Arabs so desperately needed? Nabulsi, with the twin disadvantages of holding an unpopular position and being off-site rather than in the studio, got to speak first. Qassem, who obviously disagreed with Nabulsi, began by agreeing with almost everything he said before ambushing him with the online voting results showing only 18.6 percent agreeing with his position and then turning the discussion over to the other guest. Maghrebi savaged the UN Human Development Report, usually taken as gospel on Al Jazeera, before wandering into an extended rant against America, Ahmed Chalabi, corruption, and CIA payments to Arab regimes. He left Nabulsi to hopelessly ask that he stick to the subject. Halfway in, the shouting and cross talk had begun. When Qassem went to the phones, it was not ordinary citizens who came on the line but carefully selected participants— including the Egyptian radical Talaat Ramih, who proceeded to insult Nabulsi's family and denounce America, and the America-based Egyptian Magdi Khalil, who generally sympathized with Nabulsi.

Two other episodes of *The Opposite Direction* dealing with this question followed a similar course. One, aired on March 30, focused on the Arab summit and reforms in the Arab world. Qassem's guests were of a high caliber: the Arab League's ambassador in France Nasif Hitti and the leading Paris-based Syrian intellectual Burhan Ghalyoun. Qassem's framing revolved around popular frustration with summits, balanced against calls for realism in the face of Arab weakness. Hitti went first, the turn usually reserved for the target of Qassem's disdain. Hitti expressed his understanding for Arab frustration, but he defended the Arab League's efforts under difficult conditions. Ghalyoun then calmly dissected the Arab summit, the failure of which was preordained as it had no real agenda and could never have one as the system was designed to fail. Even with such luminaries, the structure of the arena drove the debate: words such as "treason" flew around, while Qassem at one point derisively challenged Hitti to explain whether he was speaking as an intellectual or as an ambassador. A May 25 episode on the future of reform projects, featuring the Palestinian Hamdan Hamdan and the Washington-based Ali Ramadan Abu Zakouk, went the same way.

## More Than One Opinion

Sami Haddad's London-based *More Than One Opinion* was actually the first Al Jazeera program to deal with the GMEI question. This program usually hosted three or four guests selected on the basis of their potential contributions to the topic rather than on the basis of their extreme positions. On February 20, Haddad focused on the draft of the GMEI just published in *al-Hayat*. He invited four guests: Patrick Clawson, an American close to the Bush administration; Muta Safadi, a columnist for *al-Quds al-Arabi*; Haitham Manaa, spokesman for the Arab Committee on Human Rights; and Abd al-Wahab Affendi, a prominent moderate Islamist intellectual. Haddad framed the discussion by pointing out that the proposal came from the American security perspective, without consultation with Arabs, and wondered whether there would be a European alternative. On the other hand, he pointed out that the GMEI draft took the Arab Human Development Reports as a key reference, which suggested that it responded to Arab as well as American imperatives. Clawson was invited to speak first and put forward a positive vision of a Bush committed to Arab reform and democracy, and a long series of consultations that had gone into the draft. He pointed to Bush's admission that America had erred in the past by tolerating Arab dictatorships and said that he expected different reactions from around the Arab world. Haddad then turned to Safadi, who dismissed Clawson's remarks as nothing new, shrugging off the initiative as answering none of the Arab world's doubts about American intentions. Haddad pointed out that Bush had been the first American president to endorse the idea of a Palestinian state, to which Safadi responded with scornful derision. The program moved on to Affendi, who expressed outrage at Bush's (mis)use of the Arab Human Development Report (of which he had been a coauthor). Manaa argued that Bush himself was the biggest problem with the initiative. Two-thirds of the way through, Haddad took three phone calls, while the guests argued among themselves. Overall, the tone of the program was critical but relatively calm, with all the guests getting time to speak and little cross talk. Haddad challenged all the guests and did not seem to be overtly favoring any particular position. The one point of consensus was on the need for reform and the oppressive nature of the Arab regimes, although three of the four guests voiced deep skepticism or opposition to an American role.

When the preparations for the Arab summit collapsed shortly after Qassem's show, Haddad hosted an April 2 discussion with Abd al-Bari Atwan (editor of *al-Quds al-Arabi*), Jihad al-Khazen (editor of *al-Hayat*), Tunisian writer Burhan Bassis, and Egyptian parliamentarian Mustafa al-Fiqi. Haddad's introduction asked whether Bernard Lewis had been right to dismiss Arab states as tribes with flags. Since its creation, Haddad intoned, the Arab League had always failed at every-thing it touched—why should the Arab street even care anymore? Khazen, speaking first, hoped that at least it had not been an American decision to cancel the summit, but he did not sound convinced. Bassis argued that most Arab leaders preferred to kill the idea of reform, with Haddad pressing him to specifically include Tunisia's president in that roster. Then frequent guest Atwan came on, calmly indicting the entire Arab order for their hostility to reform. Finally Fiqi, after complaining about the marginalization of the guest not in the studio, attempted to defend the honor of the Arab League, to the evident displeasure of the other guests and the host—until Atwan firmly interrupted him to speak on behalf of the Arab street. Fast-paced, intense conversation ensued, with little screaming and few pyrotechnics—and only one caller, who was quickly dismissed.

## Open Dialogue

Ghassan bin Jidu's program offers a dramatically different kind of forum, one oriented more around audience participation than around pyrotechnics among the guests. On February 28, bin Jidu hosted a program on the "calls for change in the Arab world." The guests included Tunisian politician Ahmed al-Qadidi, Egyptian Parliament-arian Hamdayn Sabahi, and Layth Kubba, an Iraqi-American official of the National Endowment for Democracy. Bin Jidu framed the dis-cussion around the despotism and democratic deficiency in the Arab world. But bin Jidu highlighted three major critiques: the Bush administration's ethical and democratic failings, that the call for democracy was just another way for Bush to try to rule the world, and that some were happy with things as they are. The questions, as he posed it, were whether democracy under American patronage was realistic and possible and how the regimes would respond. Just as Haddad had given the first word to Clawson, bin Jidu gave the first word to Kubba, who defended at length the American efforts. Sabahi then expressed his doubts that America really wanted change or real democracy. Bin Jidu pushed Sabahi: as much of the Arab political class disliked the Arab regimes and said they wanted democracy, what was so wrong about accepting American help? Sabahi responded that America only wanted to strip Arabs of their ability to resist its hege-mony. Qadidi, finally, pointed out that the same America that said it wanted change had been the main support for the despotic regimes it now claimed to oppose. Bin Jidu intervened to suggest that America was capable of changing, pointing to the democracy in Iraq. Qadidi was unconvinced, leading to an extended exchange with Kubba. At that point, members of the studio audience began to participate. One participant demurred from Kubba's defense of American intentions by pointing out that it was America's interests that concerned him, not its intentions. Another asked about the role of youth in change, another about the role of protests—all told, eight studio guests participated. The tone of the discussion was civil and thoughtful throughout, with the studio participation giving a feel of spontaneity and unpredictability.

Bin Jidu's next program on the topic aired on March 13, dealing with the Tunis Arab summit. Rather than guests, bin Jidu assembled studio audiences in Beirut, Baghdad, and Cairo. He framed the discussion around the frustration felt by at least some parts of the Arab people at the recurrent failures of the Arab League to do anything productive. The show was presented as an opportunity for the assembled Arab citizens to give voice to their hopes and concerns. Bin Jidu began with a member of the Baghdad group member, who expected only frustration from the summit. An Egyptian journalist argued that the legitimacy of Arab leaders should not be questioned, but that Arabs could legitimately demand that they formulate a serious agenda. A Lebanese speaker expressed doubts that Arab leaders could possibly live up to the hopes of the Arab masses, because every Arab summit ended by frustrating the hopes of the people. The conversation bounced from city to city, with some 24 different speakers weighing in over the course of the hour.

## Minbar Al Jazeera

*Minbar Al Jazeera* was built around phone calls, with host Jumana al-Namour sitting at a desk taking calls with no time delay or pre-screening. In a March 29 episode on the postponement of the Arab summit, guest Hamdan Subayhi of the Egyptian Parliament demanded reform, denouncing Arab regimes and rejecting American credibility in promoting it. Most callers agreed. In the April 5 episode, with studio guest Ma'ataz Midani of the Lebanese newspaper *al-Safir*, the program focused on Arab attitudes toward reform projects. Namour's short preamble framed the discussion around the American desire for reform and the attitudes expressed by the Arab states. After Midani described the frustrations of the Arab people with the official Arab order's shortcomings, Namour took twenty callers. Most of the callers agreed with the need for reform—who does not want reform, asked one—and most expressed frustration with the failed Arab summit. Iraq was not a model, American tanks could not create democracy, the Arab leaders were corrupt despots, America did not really want reform—these were common formulations. One expressed hope that Bush would succeed in overthrowing Arab leaders, the more the better. Namour at times had trouble keeping callers on topic, but she maintained a level of civil discourse and prevented loquacious guests from monopolizing the air. A June 14 program on the G-8 Summit went much the same way, with Namour gracefully handling twenty different callers expressing diverse opinions, often going back and forth several times with each before ending the exchange.

### From Washington

On June 10, Hafez Mirazi hosted a program from Washington DC on the results of the G-8 Summit , with guests Robert Malley, Layth Kubba, and Magdi Khalil. Mirazi tends to eschew the confrontational tactics of other talk show hosts, preferring a calm, analytical style in which the guests have the chance to develop ideas, and does not take phone calls. All of his guests supported an American role in reform, in marked contrast to the other programs. Mirazi framed the program around the sincerity of the American initiative and the means adopted, and whether the official Arab order and its media onslaught would succeed in containing this initiative. The ensuing discussion was restrained and informative, with most of the contention revolving around American sincerity and whether its intentions could be good in light of its support for Israel and the invasion of Iraq. Viewers would come away from this program with a good sense of the current Washington debates.

### Summary and Analysis

Looking at the guests, callers, and frames in these 11 shows reveals much about Al Jazeera's dialogue moments. The sheer volume of the attention Al Jazeera paid to the American proposals in and of itself helped to place the reform question on the Arab public agenda, at a time when Arab regimes might have preferred to ignore it.

As the views of the invited guests were presumably reasonably well-known to the producers, this can be in some sense taken as a reflection of how they intended to construct the terms of debate. Some hosts might try for representativeness, bringing in as accurate as possible a sample of the spectrum of opinion; some might try for polarization, bringing in the most dramatically opposed views on the topic no matter how unrepresentative such views might be; some might aim for particular types of personalities, regardless of the issue; and some might prefer to construct panels in line with an ideological agenda or a particular state's interest.

In this dialogue moment, Al Jazeera hosted 22 guests across 11 programs. Seven of the guests (counting Kubba twice) spoke in favor of an American role in promoting reform, 15 spoke in favor of reform but against an American role, and none spoke out against reform (even if some might have done so in a different setting). Their debates revolved around the preferred *means* to reform, not the *goal* of reform. The active debates were about whether Arab regimes were capable of or interested in reforming, and how to assess the American initiative—turning many of the debates into referendums on America, not on reform. A healthy number of pro-American speakers appeared, though no Bush administration policymakers did.[22] The role of these guests varied markedly depending on how the arena had been constructed, however. On Qassem's show, the pro-American guest was usually a sacrificial lamb, a punching bag to serve as a foil for the host's agenda—although in some cases, a quick-witted or effective guest could subvert this agenda (often to Qassem's evident delight). On almost all of the other shows, however, the pro-American guest was part of a panel rather than being on his own, and had the chance to make his case.

What about the callers and studio guests whose role in the programs is to stand in for "public opinion"?[23] As callers are live and unscreened, and not fully under the control of the producers (even if they are self-selected and influenced by what they have seen), they offer some independent feedback. There were 120 callers or studio audience participants on these 13 programs. Neither Haddad's nor Mirazi's show relied heavily on callers. Qassem prearranges his phone calls, inviting particular personalities to participate—making them better coded as guests than as callers. The 13 callers to the three episodes of Qassem's show tended to appear at defined times in the program, functioning as a break for the guests; often they are well-known, rather than ordinary citizens, and are usually selected to roughly mirror the guests. Thirty three studio guests participated in bin Jidu's two programs. These guests are not randomly selected—in some cases, the audiences were carefully constructed—but they still represent a wide distribution of views. On *Minbar al-Jazeera*, the most unscreened of all, some of the 71 callers to three programs had the unfortunate habit of unleashing torrents of obscenities, or reciting horribly bad poetry, but many offered succinct and well-thought-out arguments about the issue at hand.

The way the reform debate was framed favored reformers against regimes, but it was deeply suspicious of America. This offered the regimes an opportunity to play their regular game of mobilizing fears of external intervention to protect themselves against the demands for reform. Even if very few regime representatives were invited to make their case on Al Jazeera, their campaign certainly helped to frame the terms of Al Jazeera debate as well. This played out differently on Al Jazeera than in the regime-controlled media, however. Few of the Al Jazeera debates gave credence . to their claims to be reforming at their own pace, with most remaining scathingly critical of those regimes and contemptuous of their initiatives. Some pushed beyond denunciation. As bin Jidu put it, if change from within is absurd and change from without rejected, then what did Arab reformers expect to happen? The real debate revolved around the relative distaste for Arab regimes and for America—making events in Palestine or Iraq, Guantanamo or Abu Ghraib, directly relevant.

Although many factors go into the formation of political attitudes, survey research shows that mass attitudes did largely reflect this Al Jazeera consensus. In May 2004, Shibley Telhami found that less than 10 percent of respondents in four Arab countries thought that promoting democracy had been an important American motivation for invading Iraq; in October 2005, Telhami found only 6 percent in six countries who agreed that democracy promotion had been an important objective that would make a difference.[24]

## A New Public Sphere

This close look at the 'dialogue moment' surrounding the American GMEI offers partial support to both sides of the "Arab public sphere" debate. Some of the programs fit Alterman's "professional wrestling" mold, with populism and sensationalism swamping reasoned analysis. But many others did not. From Mirazi's calm presentation of the Washington perspective, to Haddad's lively panel discussions, to bin Jidu's two very differently constructed audience participation programs, to Namour's hosted forum for callers, Al Jazeera offered a diverse array of forums, each privileging very different kinds of participation and debate. Dissenting views and reasoned analysis could be heard, albeit within a generally accepted identity framework. These debates produced a consensus that was hostile not only to the American project, but also to the perspective of the Arab regimes eager to stifle reform. Ultimately, what matters most in the long term is the opportunity for the new Arab public to argue these issues openly, cultivating pluralism and a culture of contention.

## NOTES

1. Marc Lynch, *Voices of the New Arab Public: Al-Jazeera, Iraq, and Middle East Politics Today* (New York: Columbia University Press, 2006).
2. Yusuf al-Awadh, *al-Quds al-Arabi*, June 3, 1999.
3. Faisal al-Qassem, *The Opposite Direction*, March 7, 2003.
4. Quoted by Ibrahim al-Ghurayba on *al-Jazeera*, August 24, 2003.
5. Abdullah Schleifer, "The Impact of Arab Satellite Television on Prospects for Democracy in the Arab World" *Transnational Broadcasting Studies (TBS) Journal*, no. 15 (2005).
6. Abdel Moneim Saeed, "The Arab Satellites-Some Necessary Observations!" *Transnational Broadcasting Studies (TBS) Journal*, no. 11 (2003).
7. Jon Alterman, "Slouching toward Ramullah," *Wall Street Journal*, November 21, 2002.
8. Kai Hafez, "Arab Satellite Broadcasting: Democracy without Political Parties?" *Transnational Broadcasting Studies (TBS) Journal*, no. 15 (2005).
9. Available online at: <http://transcripts.cnn.com/TRANSCRIPTS/0410/15/cf.01.html>
10. Joshua Gamson, "The Talk Show Challenge." *Constellations*, vol. 6, no. 2 (1999): 190–205.
11. Marc Lynch, "Assessing the Democratizing Power of Satellite TV," *Transnational Broadcasting Studies (TBS) Journal*, no. 14 (Spring 2005).
12. In an October 2005 survey—a period in which many observers considered Al Jazeera to be fading a bit from its preeminent position, Shibley Telhami found that only 10% of Arab respondents in six countries claimed to "never watch" Al Jazeera.
13. This data set includes all episodes of *The Opposite Direction, More Than One Opinion, No Limits, Minbar al-Jazeera*, and *Open Dialogue* for which transcripts appear on www.aljazeera.net
14. See Lynch, *Voices of the New Arab Public*, chapters 4–6, for details.
15. Ayish, in "The Al-Jazeera Phenomenon" (2005)
16. Mohamed Nawawy and Adel Iskander, *Al-Jazeera* (Boulder, CO: Westview Press, 2002), chapter 5.
17. Mamoun Fandy, "Information Technology, Trust, and Social Change in the Arab World," *Middle East Journal*, vol. 54, no. 3 (2000): 378–394; see 387–388.
18. Hugh Miles, *Al-Jazeera* (New York: Grove Press, 2005), p. 58
19. Personal interviews, Faisal al-Qassem, Ahmed Mansour, Jumana Namour.

20. Carla Power, "Look Who's Talking," *Newsweek International*, August 8, 2005.
21. According to the archives maintained at <www.alarabiya.net>
22. The Bush administration maintained an unwritten but real boycott of Al Jazeera from late 2001 until 2005.
23. Paolo Carpignano, Robin Andersen, Stanley Aronowitz, and William Difazio, "Chatter in the Age of Electronic Reproduction: Talk Television and the Public Mind," *Social Text* 25/26 (1990): 33–55, quote at 45.
24. Surveys done by Zogby International in conjunction with Shibley Telhami available online at: <http://www.bsos.umd.edu/SADAT>. See Mark Tessler and Eleanor Gao, "Gauging Arab Support for Democracy." *Journal of Democracy*, vol. 16, no. 3 (2005): 83–97.

# CHAPTER 7

# U.S. Public Diplomacy and the News Credibility of Radio Sawa and Television Al Hurra in the Arab World*

*Mohammed el-Nawawy*

## INTRODUCTION

In the aftermath of the September 11 attacks on the Pentagon and the World Trade Center, the U.S. government launched a series of multi-million-dollar programs designed under a wide-scale public diplomacy plan to improve America's image in the Middle East and win the hearts and minds of the Arab people. Two such programs, Radio Sawa and Al Hurra satellite television, were supervised by the Broadcasting Board of Governors (BBG), the federal body responsible for all U.S. international broadcasting. The target audience for Radio Sawa and Television Al Hurra is the younger Arab generation, who will be tomorrow's decision-makers.

* The researcher would like to express his gratitude for Dr. Leonard Teel, the Director of the Center for International Media Education at Georgia State University's Department of Communication, for establishing most of the connections that helped with distributing the questionnaires for this study to college students in the Middle East; and to Qing Tian, a doctoral student at Georgia State University's Department of Communication, for helping with the data entry and statistical analysis for this study. A version of this study was published in *Global Media and Communication*, vol. 2, no. 2 (2006): 185–205.

The main objective of Radio Sawa and Television Al Hurra, is to help explain various aspects of American foreign policy and "to provide information about basic characteristics of American society that are important for Arab and Muslim audiences to know and understand."[1] This information is regarded as critical at a time when there is increasing Arab dissatisfaction with the U.S. presence in Iraq and its handling of the Palestinian-Israeli conflict.

## PURPOSE OF THE STUDY

This study surveyed college students at Arab universities in five Arab countries (Kuwait, United Arab Emirates, Jordan, Palestine, and Morocco) regarding their perceptions of the news credibility of Radio Sawa and Television Al Hurra, and how far these perceptions were correlated to the frequency of using these channels. The students were asked to use a twelve-item credibility scale developed by Gaziano and McGrath (1986).[2] The study also investigated whether the students' attitudes toward U.S. foreign policy had changed since they started tuning in to Radio Sawa and Television Al Hurra. And finally the study asked students their suggestions for improving U.S. public diplomacy efforts in the Arab Middle East.

## SIGNIFICANCE OF THE STUDY

Understanding how the young or, as the U.S. Department of State likes to call it, the "successor" generation in the Arab world perceives news on Radio Sawa and Television Al Hurra should be of considerable interest to Washington decision-makers as they evaluate their current diplomacy efforts in the Middle East. Recent polls have shown that Arab opinion of U.S. foreign policy is overwhelmingly negative. A 2004 poll conducted by Zogby International in six Arab countries showed that Arabs, while not strongly opposed to American culture, detest U.S. foreign policy.[3] When asked in the poll, "What is the worst thought that comes to mind when you hear about America?," foreign policy issues were noted in almost 80 percent of the responses across the board in all six countries. The most frequently cited were "unfair Middle East policy," U.S. responsibility for Arabs' suffering (particularly in Iraq and Palestine), and what was perceived as "the U.S. preoccupation with Arab oil."[4]

Another poll conducted by the Pew Research Center for the People and the Press in March 2004 showed that majorities in some Muslim countries such as Jordan and Turkey believed that "America pays little or no attention to their [countries'] interests in making its foreign policy decisions."[5]

In many cases, it is difficult to determine the size and nature of audiences tuned in to foreign broadcasting because of methodological difficulties, language barriers, and foreign government bureaucracies.[6] These challenges are commonly experienced by researchers interested in Arab public opinion. "Because of the challenge of political sensitivities, or the reluctance to disclose [certain] information . . . ascertaining reliable data is difficult at best, and often impossible."[7] Yet accurate and reliable audience research is essential to assess the impact of international broadcasting. Public opinion research may play a critical role in designing foreign relations strategies and in enhancing mutual understanding between nations[8].

## LITERATURE REVIEW

### U.S. Image in the Arab World

The United States currently faces serious challenges as a result of its deteriorating image in the Arab Middle East. As mentioned above, recent polls show that the overwhelming majority of Arab opinion responds favorably to American values, but it is critical of U.S. foreign policy. Andrew Kohut, director of the Pew Research Center for the People and the Press, is cited in Seib (2004) as saying that "the most serious problem facing the United States abroad is its very poor public image in the Muslim world, especially in the Middle East/Conflict Area."[9]

Several polls have shown that a major source for anti-Americanism in the Middle East is the Arab perception of U.S. bias in favor of Israel. A 2001 poll of people from Saudi Arabia, Kuwait, UAE, Egypt, and Lebanon concluded that 60 percent of the respondents in those countries cited the Palestinian conflict as the "single most important issue" that negatively affected their perception of U.S. foreign policy.[10]

University of Maryland's Anwar Sadat professor of Peace, and Shibley Telhami, as cited in Meyer (2003), argues that the issue of Arabs' opinions of America "is not about the objective reality of where the blame lies; it is about entrenched perceptions. The public in the Middle East blames the powers that be, and sees Israel as . . . an occupier of Arab lands, and the United States as the anchor of that order."[11]

Telhami does not believe that the media play a major role in shaping Arabs' negative perceptions of the United States. In his April 2004 testimony before the U.S. Senate's Committee on Foreign Relations, Telhami argued that it is overall foreign policy on the ground, not the media, that contributes the most to anti-Americanism. "There are many people in the Middle East that do not have satellite television. They express just as much anti-Americanism as those who do."[12]

In his testimony in the same hearing (April 2004), Edmund Ghareeb, a Middle East expert, cited the U.S. invasion of Iraq as a further source of anti-Americanism in the Arab world. "They [Arabs] look at Iraq and ask if this is a war of freedom and democracy or a fight for oil and hegemony."[13]

William Rugh, an expert on Middle East politics, argued that Arabs' immediate reaction to the 9/11 events "was sympathy for Americans as victims."[14] According to Rugh, many Arabs even saw some justification in the U.S. war against the Taliban and al Qaeda. However, as the U.S. government "expanded the definition of 'the enemy' beyond Al-Qaeda, Arabs and Muslims concluded that [U.S. president] Bush's perception of the problem, and of the enemy, differed substantially from theirs."[15]

However, despite strong evidence pointing to alternative conclusions, the negative image of U.S. policies in the Arab world actually prompted U.S. officials to intensify their public diplomacy efforts in the Arab Middle East.

### Public Diplomacy

The term "public diplomacy" characterizes activities once described as propaganda. Malone (1988) argued that public diplomacy is the process of "communicating directly with the people of other countries . . . to affect their thinking . . . The objective, in most cases, is to influence the behavior of a foreign government by influencing the attitudes of its citizens."[16]

Public diplomacy utilizes a variety of techniques such as academic exchange programs, participation in international exhibitions and festivals, setting up cultural centers in foreign countries, and using international broadcasting.[17] Boyd (1997) identified four reasons as to why countries broadcast across national borders: "to enhance national prestige; to promote national interests; to attempt religious or political indoctrination; and to foster cultural ties."[18]

Gilboa (2000) cited another reason as to why a country broadcasts across its national borders: to create among foreign audiences a favorable perception of its policies. This is especially important in public diplomacy, where perceptions may sometimes be more important than reality. "If people believe something to be true, it is frequently the same, in political terms, as if it were true."[19]

Modern diplomats argue that the "actual consequences of a given policy initiative" depend upon the way "both the domestic and the foreign publics perceive the issues and the policy offered. This understanding depends partly, of course, on the way in which the communications media—formal and informal—present the picture. But it depends more profoundly on the complex of [peoples'] knowledge, attitudes, and prejudices."[20]

Ross (2002) argued that diplomats must realize that "it is not what one says, but it is what the other hears that ultimately matters most."[21] Furthermore, what people hear, and the way they hear it, is often determined to a large extent by their perceptions of the message's source. It is therefore of the utmost relevance that Radio Sawa and Television Al Hurra have been an integral part of recent U.S. public diplomacy efforts in the Middle East.

### Radio Sawa

Radio Sawa's official name is the Middle East Radio Network. *Sawa* is Arabic for "together." According to its official Web site, Radio Sawa is a twenty-four-hour, seven-day-a-week Arabic-language radio network that began broadcasting on March 23, 2002. It seeks "to effectively communicate with the youthful population of Arabic-speakers in the Middle East by providing up-to-date news, information and entertainment on FM and medium wave radio stations throughout the region."[22]

With a US$35 million budget, Radio Sawa set up offices in Kuwait, Qatar, the United Arab Emirates, and Jordan. Its regional broadcast center is located in Dubai, UAE.[23] To attract young Arab listeners (under thirty), the content is mostly music. Every hour, for about 53 minutes it broadcasts Arabic and Western pop songs alternately, the rest of the time being divided between a short news bulletin at quarter to each hour, and a longer one at quarter past each hour.[24]

The initiator of the Radio Sawa idea is Norman Pattiz, an American media entrepreneur who believes that regional Arab media contribute to the deterioration of the U.S. image in the Arab world. Pattiz, who also chairs the BBG's Middle East Committee, said, "There's a media war going on [in the Arab world], with incitement, hate broadcasting, disinformation, government censorship and self-censorship, and America is not in the race . . . You don't have to be a rocket scientist to understand that this isn't the way we want to be presented in the Arab world."[25]

Radio Sawa has been subject to criticism by several media observers. For example, Ali Abunimah (2002) argues that Radio Sawa is "a quick fix solution to a deep and worsening problem that will ultimately prove disappointing to its creators."[26] According to Abunimah, Radio Sawa would have a hard time establishing itself as a go-to news source in the Middle East, where there is information saturation from a myriad satellite channels.

Similarly, in his description of an environment where there are many sources of information that compete for audiences' attention, Joseph Nye (2004) coined the expression "paradox of the plenty." According to Nye, "attention rather than information becomes the scarce resource" in such an environment.[27] Radio Sawa would have to compete fiercely for Arab audiences' attention, divided among many other news outlets.

William Rugh (2004) goes further and argues that Radio Sawa drastically reduces the effectiveness of the U.S. public diplomacy efforts. "Although Radio Sawa may be useful in some ways, it does not replace more serious broadcasts."[28] el-Nawawy and Iskandar (2002) also argue that Arabs might likely be suspicious of the intentions of Radio Sawa in the Middle East. "There is a strong likelihood that [Radio Sawa] will be seen as a way to sell Americanism through entertainment rather than tackle issues that plague the [Arab] region."[29]

In an October 2003 report to the Committee on Appropriations of the U.S. House of Representatives, Ambassador Edward Djerejian, who led the U.S. Advisory Commission on Public Diplomacy for the Arab and Muslim World, adopted a modified position. He proposed that creating a large following in the Arab world should not be Radio Sawa's main goal. His commission report stated that Radio Sawa should prove its ability to change Arab audiences' negative attitudes toward U.S. policy and "move the needle" toward what the U.S. Department of State, in its public diplomacy mission statement, calls "influence."[30]

However, it is hard to see how Radio Sawa may be able to "influence" Arab public opinion if its listeners do not pay attention to the news it broadcasts. According to a recent editorial in the Egyptian newspaper *Al-Ahram Weekly*, as cited in el-Nawawy and Iskandar (2003), there is a big chance that "the Arab youth will split the strategy [regarding Radio Sawa]: take the U.S. sound and discard the U.S. agenda."[31]

The Djerejian report (2003) also reviewed the results of an ACNielsen survey conducted in five Arab countries between July and August 2003. The survey showed that Radio Sawa had an average listenership of 31.6 percent among the general population 15 years and older (BBG Web site). The Djerejian report highlighted the weakness of the survey, which had only one question on attitudes toward the United States. It asked, "How favorably or unfavorably inclined are you personally toward the USA?" and yielded more positive views from Radio Sawa listeners than from its nonlisteners. "This result was to be expected since any listener to a U.S.-sponsored station is likely to be favorably disposed to the United States. A better question would be whether Sawa had changed a listener's attitudes toward America."[32]

## TV Al Hurra

According to its official Web site, Al Hurra (Arabic for "The Free One") is a commercial-free Arabic-language satellite television network, devoted to news and information. Al Hurra, whose official name is Middle East Television Network, was launched on February 14, 2004 with a US$62 million budget. It is designed to counteract the impact of the Arab world's popular news channels such as Al Jazeera and Al-Arabiya (Seib, 2004). Norman Pattiz, who spearheaded the launching of Al Hurra, said, "Alhurra will present fresh perspectives for viewers in the Middle East that we believe will create more cultural understanding and respect"[33]

In his testimony before the U.S. Senate's Committee on Foreign Relations in April 2004, Mouafac Harb, Al Hurra's news director, highlighted what he considered Al Hurra's objective approach in covering news. He said, "Al Hurra has brought a new idea to journalism in the Middle East—telling the truth. We do our work the way it is supposed to be done. We play it straight and we behave like news professionals because that is what we are."[34]

However, several media experts question Al Hurra's success in changing Arabs' negative opinions toward U.S. policy, especially in a highly competitive media environment where some Arab satellite channels have gained Arabs' trust. Shibley Telhami, in his April 2004 testimony before the U.S. Senate's Committee on Foreign Relations, argued that Al Hurra's "detached objectivity" may not appeal to Arab audiences, especially when it comes to covering highly sensitive issues such as the Palestinian-Israeli conflict[35]

Telhami said, "[Al Hurra's] aim is to be precisely dispassionate while facing a passionate audience." To illustrate his point, Telhami referred to Al Hurra's coverage of Israel's assassination of Hamas leader Sheikh Ahmed Yassin in March 2004. Despite overwhelming Arab concern about this incident, "Alhurra ran a short story as the news [about the assassination] broke, then went back to its normal programming, which focused on an episode in American history."[36] This may be one reason why many Arab viewers would rather watch indigenous Arab satellite channels that reflect their convictions in a way that Al Hurra does not.

Kim Elliott, a veteran audience researcher at Voice of America, expressed his doubts too, in an interview with Sefsaf (2004), that satellite networks with strong ties to the U.S. government can gain mass appeal. He argued that the Arab people will always look at Al Hurra as a propaganda station that publicizes the ideas of the U.S. government.[37]

Several U.S. policymakers argue a different position, that channels such as Al Hurra should be utilized to enhance foreign audiences' understanding of the U.S. position, but not necessarily in the expectation that it will make them embrace it. In his testimony during the hearing on Public Diplomacy and International Free Press, before the U.S. Senate's Committee on Foreign Relations in February 2004, Senator Joseph Biden of Delaware said, "we tend to think of public diplomacy in terms of, we're going to convince people that they have to, or should, adopt our views, our values, our system. And I think that may be a bridge too far."[38] In Biden's view, it would be good enough if Muslims understand the motives behind the U.S. policies, even if they do not accept them.

### *The Pivotal Issue of Credibility*

Much credibility research began in the 1950s and focused on defining the dimensions of the source, or communicator, that receivers perceive as credible. Infante (1980) defined source credibility as "a set of attitudes toward a source that influence how receivers behave toward the source."[39] The well-known postwar American researcher Hovland and his associates (1963) specified source credibility by identifying two dimensions that can be used to measure it: expertness and trustworthiness. According to them, receivers' awareness of a source's intention or motives to persuade others in a way that would benefit him would negatively affect the source's trustworthiness. If the receivers have unfavorable attitudes toward the communicator, they will either be inattentive to the message or will not go out of their way to understand its content.[40]

Hovland and Weiss (1951) also, however, coined the term "sleeper effect," which they described as the possibility that the passage of time would make receivers more accepting of messages presented by an untrustworthy source. Nonetheless, this effect, they argued, would not take place if "the communicator and his stand [on issues] are so intimately associated that one spontaneously recalls the source when he thinks about the issue."[41]

Writing some twenty years later, Berlo et al. (1969) argued that credibility is not a unidimensional, dichotomous (either high or low) concept, but rather a more complex, multidimensional, and relational variable that is defined in terms of the receivers' changing perceptions rather than the source's static and objective characteristics. "The 'image' of the source," Berlo, et al. argue "is dynamic in that it both influences and is influenced by the communication event."[42]

Building on this latter approach, Gunther (1992) proposed that a person's perception of a source's credibility is a "situational response" governed by the stake that person has in the issue at hand, as well as how controversial the issue itself is. According to Gunther, the higher the audiences' personal stake in an issue and the more controversial it is, the less their trust in a source's treatment of that issue, especially if that treatment goes against the audiences' beliefs.[43]

One of the most widely used credibility scales was the twelve-item credibility index developed by Gaziano and McGrath in their 1986 study of newspaper and television credibility. Their study, conducted for the American Society of Newspaper Editors (ASNE), included items that asked whether television and newspaper news was fair, told the whole story, was unbiased, was accurate, respected people's privacy, watched out for audiences' interests, could be trusted, was factual, separated fact and opinion, was concerned with community well-being, had well-trained reporters, and was concerned with the public interest.[44] Rimmer and Weaver (1987) reported a .90 Cronbach alpha for the internal reliability of Gaziano and McGrath's scale.[45] Statistically, a reliability level as high as this is a very strong index that the items on the scale measure identical and are not dissimilar characteristics.

### Media Use and Perceived Credibility

Several studies have shown a positive correlation between the frequency of media use and the audience's perception of media credibility. Shaw (1973) stated that "it is as plausible to hold that an individual would tend to consume more of the products of a medium perceived more believable, as it is to suggest that an individual on special occasions, such as an interview or survey situation, would tend to declare in favor of a medium he uses the most."[46]

In a study that compared "television-believers" (i.e., those who had trust in television) with "newspaper-believers," Schweiger (2000) concluded that there was a significant correlation between the perceived credibility of a medium and its amount of usage.[47] Rimmer and Weaver (1987) argued that attitudinal, preference, or affective measures that involve choice of media show more correlation with credibility levels than behavioral measures that ask for the frequency of media use.[48]

# Research Questions

This study attempts to address the following research questions:

RQ1. Will the students' frequency of use of Radio Sawa and/or Television Al Hurra be positively correlated to the perceived news credibility of both channels in general?

RQ2. Have students' attitudes toward U.S. foreign policy improved since their exposure to Radio Sawa and/or Television Al Hurra?

RQ3. Is there a correlation between the students' use of Arab twenty-four-hour satellite news channels and their perception of Television Al Hurra's news credibility?

RQ4. Would travel to the United States make a difference in the students' perception of Radio Sawa's and/or Television Al Hurra's news credibility?

# Method

### Survey and Sample

This study relied on a cross-sectional survey method to collect data from a nonprobability convenience sample of readily accessible college students majoring in Communication at Arab universities in five Arab countries (Kuwait, the UAE, Jordan, Palestine, and Morocco). Although convenience samples contain unknown quantities of error and generate results that cannot be reliably generalized to the population as they lack external validity, they are still helpful in collecting exploratory information and can produce useful data.[49]

Given the challenges and complications that researchers in the Arab world often face, a convenience sample—such as political sensitivities and reluctance born of fear to participate in a survey—was the most appropriate for this study. In the end, however, 394 students filled out questionnaires for this survey. Collecting data from such a relatively large sample about an issue of high political sensitivity such as the issue at hand is difficult at best in the Arab world, and often impossible.

### Instrument and Procedure

The survey utilized a paper questionnaire that included a news credibility scale adapted from Gaziano and McGrath (1986). The semantic-differential scale had 12 items, which respondents were asked to rate using a series of five-point scales anchored by bipolar adjectives. The items in the scale are listed above in the summary of Gaziano and

McGrath's study. A summated mean was computed for the scale. The questionnaire included other Likert-type, closed-ended questions. It also included open-ended questions that yielded more detailed information regarding the students' perceptions of Radio Sawa and Television Al Hurra, and their assessment of the U.S. public diplomacy efforts in the Arab world.

The questionnaire was devised in English, but translated into Arabic by the researcher, who is a native Arabic speaker. The researcher contacted five Arab Communication instructors at five Arab universities in the five countries mentioned above. The five universities are Kuwait University, Yarmouk University in Jordan, Sharjah University in the United Arab Emirates, Al-Najah National University in Palestine, and the Institut Supérieur d'Information et de la Communication in Morocco.

In contacting the instructors, the researcher used a network of Arab Communication professors, which has been formed through the Arab-U.S. Association for Communication Educators (AUSACE), an organization consisting of educators, media professionals, and students in the Middle East, Europe, and the United States. The questionnaires were faxed to five Arab professors who are members of AUSACE. The professors then distributed the questionnaires to their students and mailed back the completed questionnaires to the researcher in the United States.

## RESULTS

### *Summary Statistics*

Of the 394 students who filled out questionnaires for this study, 46 were from Morocco; 59 from Kuwait; 99 from Jordan; 172 from Palestine; and 18 from United Arab Emirates. Of this sample, 40.6 percent were male and 59.4 percent were female. Of the total, 277 (70.3 percent) reported listening to Radio Sawa for either news or music, while 147 (37.3 percent) reported watching news or other programs on Television Al Hurra. Of the students who listened to Radio Sawa, 43.1 percent reported listening to the station for music "often" or "very often," while 13.5 percent reported listening to it for news "often" or "very often." Of those who watched Television Al Hurra, 10.9 percent reported watching it for news "often" or "very often," and the same percentage reported watching it for other programs "often" or "very often."

Descriptive statistics of the students' responses to Gaziano and McGrath's news credibility scale, which ranged from 1 (the lowest M) to 5 (the highest M), yielded overall credibility means of 2.73 and 2.68

**Table 7.1** Countries' News Credibility Means for Radio Sawa and Television Al Hurra

| Country | Radio Sawa News Credibility | | TV Al Hurra News Credibility | |
|---------|------|----------------------|------|----------------------|
| | Mean | Standard Deviation | Mean | Standard Deviation |
| Morocco | 2.17 | .618 | 2.46 | .757 |
| Kuwait | 3.29 | .586 | 3.14 | .552 |
| Jordan | 2.68 | .612 | 2.66 | .783 |
| Palestine | 2.71 | .776 | 2.62 | .829 |
| UAE | 3.08 | .192 | 3.00 | — |

for Radio Sawa and Television Al Hurra respectively. Respondents from Kuwait displayed the highest news credibility means for both Radio Sawa and Television Al Hurra, while respondents from Morocco displayed the lowest for both stations. See table 7.1 for countries' news credibility means for Radio Sawa and Television Al Hurra (1 is the lowest mean and 5 is the highest).

## RESEARCH QUESTIONS

RQ1. Will the students' frequency of use of Radio Sawa and/or Television Al Hurra be positively correlated to the perceived news credibility of both channels in general?

The students' frequency of use was measured by a question asking for the average number of hours per day spent listening to Radio Sawa, and the same question regarding Al Hurra. Pearson correlation analysis showed no significant relationship between students' frequency of listening to Radio Sawa and their perception of Radio Sawa news as credible. However, a weak positive linear relationship was revealed by Pearson correlation analysis between students' frequency of watching Television Al Hurra and their perception of its news as credible in general ($r = .21, p < .05$).

RQ2. Have students' attitudes toward U.S. foreign policy improved since their exposure to Radio Sawa and/or Television Al Hurra?

To measure whether students' attitudes toward U.S. foreign policy have improved since their exposure to Radio Sawa, students were given a scale of 1 to 7 (where 1 meant "much worse" and 7 meant "much improved"), and asked to rank their attitude toward U.S.

foreign policy, compared to their attitude before they started listening to it. The same question was posed regarding Television Al Hurra. Results showed that the students' attitudes toward the U.S. foreign policy had *worsened* slightly since they had started listening to Radio Sawa and watching Television Al Hurra. The means for students' answers on this scale were: $M = 3.35$ ($SD = 1.66$) for Radio Sawa, and $M = 3.19$ ($SD = 1.68$) for Television Al Hurra.

RQ3. Is there a correlation between the students' use of Arab twenty-four-hour satellite news channels and their perception of Television Al Hurra's news credibility?

The Pearson correlation test revealed that students' perception of Television Al Hurra news as credible also held a small negative correlation with their use of Arab twenty-four-hour satellite news ($r = -.15$, $p < .05$). Students who watched Arab twenty-four-hour satellite television news more frequently had a lower tendency to perceive Television Al Hurra news as credible.

RQ4. Would travel to the U.S. make a difference in the students' perception of Radio Sawa's and/or Television Al Hurra's news credibility?

One-way analysis of variance showed a difference between those respondents who reported traveling to the United States and those who did not, regarding their perception of Radio Sawa's news credibility ($F = 4.78$, $p < .05$). Students who reported traveling to the United States had a higher tendency to perceive Radio Sawa news as credible than those who did not report traveling to the United States. It is important to acknowledge, however, that only 30 respondents of the total sample reported traveling to the United States. One-way analysis of variance, however, showed no significant difference in perception of Television Al Hurra's news credibility between those respondents who reported traveling to the United States and those who did not.

## DISCUSSION

Data from this study partially support the literature on media credibility that suggests a positive correlation between the frequency of media use and the audience's perception of media credibility. This was the case with Television Al Hurra, whose news was believed to be more credible by the respondents who reported watching it more frequently. However, as this study showed, the respondents' perception of Radio Sawa's news credibility was not correlated with how frequently they listened to its programming. The explanation for this result is that most respondents in this study's sample reported listening more frequently to Radio Sawa's music, not its news. Even answers to an open-ended question that asked students about what they liked the most about Radio Sawa showed that it was music that attracted them the most. The question here is: If music is what attracts young people the most to Radio Sawa, how can it be expected to improve their perceptions of U.S. foreign policy?

The relatively low news-credibility means for Radio Sawa and Television Al Hurra shown in the results of this study confirm the findings of Hovland et al. back in 1963 that receivers' awareness of a source's intention to persuade others in a way that would benefit him would negatively affect the source's credibility. Because many Arab media users today are intensely aware of the U.S. administration's motives in trying to win Arab hearts and minds and to improve its image in the Arab world, they have a tendency not to trust news broadcast on Radio Sawa or Television Al Hurra. In assessing the way both networks are perceived in the Arab world, one has to consider that they are still relatively new, especially Television Al Hurra, which has been around for less than two years. A further question here is whether frequency of use over time might make Al Hurra and Radio Sawa news any more credible in the eyes of Arab audiences—the phenomenon described by Hovland and Weiss (1951) as the "sleeper effect." Further studies should be conducted to ascertain this.

One significant finding in this study is that respondents' attitudes toward the U.S. foreign policy have worsened slightly since their exposure to Radio Sawa and Television Al Hurra. In their answers to an open-ended question about what they liked or disliked about Sawa and Al Hurra, most respondents noted that the U.S. administration was trying to manipulate Arab opinion through networks such as Sawa and Al Hurra.

A Jordanian respondent wrote that "Radio Sawa serves U.S. interests and helps it spread its control over the world and to serve Zionist interests." A Palestinian respondent wrote that the U.S. administration "[spreads] lies and fabricates news" through Television Al Hurra.

Many respondents expressed a strong dissatisfaction with U.S. policies toward the Middle East. In this context, a Moroccan respondent stated that "the U.S. deceives Arabs while acting as a peace leader." In their answers to another open-ended question about what the United States needs to do to win the Arabs' hearts and minds, several respondents mentioned that the United States should get out of Iraq and stop taking Israel's side at the expense of the Palestinians. It is the U.S. stand on these two highly sensitive issues—the situation in Iraq and the Palestinian-Israeli conflict—that contributes most to its severely deteriorating image in the Arab world. And that spills over into the way many Arabs perceive the credibility of Sawa and Al Hurra. These networks may be completely unable to change opinions on these two issues, on which Arab audiences have a very strong stand. In this context, it maybe useful to draw on Gunther's (1992) concept of "situational response," which he used to explain that the higher the audience's personal stakes in an issue, the less their trust in the source's treatment of that issue.

The U.S. administration may need to face this reality and realize that launching channels such as Sawa and Al Hurra must go hand in hand with changing and/or modifying its policies on the ground. This researcher wholeheartedly believes that actions speak louder than words. It is only when the Arabs see a U.S. policy that reflects their own interests that they will trust the American-sponsored channels or any other form of public diplomacy. In this very context, Philip Seib (2005) argues too that "public opinion is ultimately shaped more by the substance of the policy [on the ground] than by how policy is sold."[50]

Another important finding in this study was that the respondents who watched Arab twenty-four-hour satellite television news more frequently were less inclined to perceive news on Television Al Hurra as credible. This strongly indicates that Arabs trust their indigenous "Arab" satellite news media more than they trust the U.S.-sponsored "Arabized" networks. Before the start of the 1990s, Arab audiences did not trust their own news media and used to seek out Western media outlets for news about what was happening in their own countries. But with the explosion of Arab satellite television and the appearance of Arab twenty-four-hour independent news networks such as Al Jazeera and Al-Arabiya, Arabs today feel that they have their own reliable news sources which they can trust.

Through this study, one can make a case that, for Arab-American understanding to be successful, there is a need—along with urgently needed changes in U.S. foreign policy—for a continuous dialogue between the United States and the Arab world on official, intellectual, and popular levels. In order for this dialogue to be successful, there have to be direct, face-to-face interactions between the two sides. This study suggests that respondents who travel to the United States might have a higher tendency to perceive Radio Sawa news as credible even under current conditions, than those without this experience. This reflects the need for cultural exchange programs to bring young Arab students and scholars to the United States to learn its various cultural and social aspects firsthand, and for the reverse movement to take place on a very large scale from the United States to Arab countries.

## NOTES

1. William Rugh, Fixing Public Diplomacy for Arab and Muslim Audiences, in S.A. Garfinkle (ed.), *A Practical Guide to Winning the War on Terrorism* (California: Hoover Press, 2004), p. 154.
2. Cecilie Gaziano and Kristin McGrath, "Measuring the Concept of Credibility," *Journalism Quarterly*, vol. 63, no. 3 (Autumn 1986): 451–462.
3. Zogby International, *Impressions of America 2004: How Arabs View America; How Arabs Learn About America.* A Six-Nation Survey Commissioned by The Arab American Institute, June 2004.
4. Zogby International, *Impressions of America 2004*, p. 7.
5. The Pew Research Center for the People and the Press, "A Year After the Iraq War: Mistrust of America in Europe Ever Higher, Muslim Anger Persists," 2004, available online at: <http://www.people-press.org>, 6.
6. Robert Fortner, Public Diplomacy and International Politics: The Symbolic Constructs of Summits and International Radio News (Westport, CT: Praeger, 1994).
7. Leo Gher and Hussein Amin, "New and Old Media Access and Ownership in the Arab World," *Gazette*, vol. 61, no. 1 (1999): 61.
8. L. Free, Public Opinion Research, in Arthur Hoffman (ed.), *International Communication and the New Diplomacy* (Bloomington: Indiana University Press, 1968).
9. Philip Seib, *Public and Media Diplomacy: The U.S. Concept.* Lecture delivered at University of Ljubljana, Slovenia, October 15, 2004, 3.
10. Brent Talbot, "The Arab Perception and Consensus Problems: Implications for U.S. Policy in the Middle East," 2003, available online at: <http://www.usafa.af.mil/inss/ocp/ocp48p/pdf>
11. Michael Meyer, "Arab Perceptions toward U.S. Foreign Policy: Why Perceptions Matter and what can be done to Improve America's Image in the Arab World," 2003, available online at: <http://www.usafa.af.mil/inss/ocp/ocp48p2/pdf>, 42.
12. Shebly Telhami, "U.S. Senate Foreign Relations Committee Hearing on Finding the Right Media for the Message in the Middle East," April 29, 2004, 2005, available online at: <http://www.access.gpo.gov/congress/senate>, 47.
13. Edmund Ghareeb, "U.S. Senate Foreign Relations Committee Hearing on Finding the Right Media for the Message in the Middle

East," April 29, 2004, available online at: <http://www.access.gpo. gov/congress/sentate>

14. William Rugh, "Fixing Public Diplomacy for Arab and Muslim Audiences," in S.A. Garfinkle (ed.), *A Practical Guide to Winning the War on Terrorism* (California: Hoover Press, 2004), p. 147.
15. Rugh, Fixing Public Diplomacy, p. 147.
16. Gifford Malone, *Organizing the Nation's Public Diplomacy* (Lanham, MD: University Press of America, 1988).
17. Eyton Gilboa, "Mass Communication and Diplomacy: A Theoretical Framework," *Communication Theory*, vol. 10, no. 3 (August 2000).
18. Douglas Boyd, "International Radio Broadcasting in Arabic: A Survey of Broadcasters and Audiences," *Gazette*, vol. 59, no. 6 (1997).
19. Hans Tuch, *Communicating with the World: U.S. Public Diplomacy Overseas* (New York: St. Martin's Press, 1990).
20. Glen Fisher, *Public Diplomacy and the Behavioral Sciences* (Bloomington: Indiana University Press, 1972).
21. Christopher Ross, "Public Diplomacy Comes of Age," *The Washington Quarterly*, vol. 25, no. 2 (Spring 2002): 77.
22. Radio Sawa Web site, available online at: <http://www.radiosawa. com>
23. George Gedda, "Radio Sawa: Music as a Tool," *Foreign Service Journal* (November 2002): 53–56.
24. Natan Guttman, "Good Morning Baghdad, this Is Washington Calling." *Haaretz, The Marker* supplement (December 2004), available online at: <http://www.haaretzdaily.com/hasen/pages/ShArt. jhtml?itemNo=219301>
25. Guttman, "Good Morning Baghdad," para. 10.
26. Ali Abunimah, "Radio Sawa: All Dressed Up with Nowhere to Go," August 2002, available online at: <http:// www.electronicintifada. net/features/articles/020820ali.shtml>, para. 16.
27. Joseph Nye, *Power in the Global Information Age: From Realism to Globalization* (London: Routledge, 2004), p. 89.
28. William Rugh, "U.S. Senate Foreign Relations Committee Hearing on Finding the Right Media for the Message in the Middle East," April 29, 2004, available online at: <http://www.access.gpo.gov/ congress/sentate>, 159.
29. Mohammed el-Nawawy and Adel Iskandar, *Al-Jazeera: How the Free Arab News Network Scooped the World and Changed the Middle East* (Boulder, CO: Westview Press, 2002), p. 195.
30. Edward Djerejian, *Changing Minds, Winning Peace: A New Strategic Direction for U.S. Public Diplomacy in the Arab and Muslim World.* Report of the U.S. Advisory Group on Public Diplomacy for the Arab and Muslim World, 2003, 30.
31. Mohammed el-Nawawy and Adel Iskandar, *Al-Jazeera: The Story of the Network that Is Rattling Governments and Redefining Modern Journalism* (Boulder, CO: Westview Press, 2003), p. 213.

32. Djerejian, *Changing Minds, Winning Peace*, p. 31.
33. Broadcasting Board of Governors, available online at: <http://www.bbg.gov/bbg_plan.cfm>
34. Mouafac Harb, "U.S. Senate Foreign Relations Committee Hearing on Finding the Right Media for the Message in the Middle East" April 29, 2004, available online at: <http://www.access.gpo.gov/congress/sentate>, 21.
35. Shebly Telhami, "U.S. Senate Foreign Relations Committee Hearing on Finding the Right Media for the Message in the Middle East," April 29, 2004, 2005, available online at: <http://www.access.gpo.gov/congress/senate>, 52.
36. Telhami, "U.S. Senate Foreign Relations Committee Hearing," 52.
37. Wendy Sefsaf, "U.S. International Broadcasting Strategies in the Arab World: An Analysis of the Broadcasting Board of Governors' Strategy from a Public Communication Standpoint," *Transnational Broadcasting Studies (TBS) Journal*, no. 13 (Fall 2004), available online at: <http://www.tbsjournal.com/Archives/Fall04/felizsefsaf.html>
38. Joseph Biden, "U.S. Senate Foreign Relations Committee Hearing on "Public Diplomacy and International Free Press," February 26, 2004, available online at: <http://www.access.gpo.gov/congress/senate>, 4.
39. Dominic Infante, "The Construct Validity of Semantic Differential Scales for the Measurement of Source Credibility," *Communication Quarterly*, vol. 28, no. 2 (1980): 21.
40. Carl Iver Hovland, Irving L. Janis, and Harold H. Kelley, *Communication and Persuasion: Psychological Studies of Opinion Change* (New Haven: Yale University Press, 1963).
41. Carl Hovland and Walter Weiss, "The Influence of Source Credibility on Communication Effectiveness," *The Public Opinion Quarterly*, vol. 15, no. 4 (1951): 649.
42. David Berlo, James B. Lemert, and Robert J. Mertz, "Dimensions for Evaluating the Acceptability of Message Sources," *The Public Opinion Quarterly*, vol. 33, no. 4 (1969): 576.
43. Albert Gunther, "Biased Press or Biased Public? Attitudes toward Media Coverage of Social Groups," *The Public Opinion Quarterly*, vol. 56 (1992): 147.
44. Cecilie Gaziano and Kristin McGrath, "Measuring the Concept of Credibility," *Journalism Quarterly*, vol. 63, no. 3 (Autumn 1986): 451–462.
45. Tony Rimmer and David Weaver, "Different Questions, Different Answers? Media Use and Media Credibility," *Journalism Quarterly*, vol. 64, no. 1 (1987): 28–36.
46. Eugene Shaw, "Media Credibility: Taking the Measure of a Measure," *Journalism Quarterly*, vol. 50, no. 2 (Summer 1973): 310.
47. Wolfgang Schweiger, Media Credibility—Experience or Image? *European Journal of Communication*, vol. 15, no. 1 (2000): 37–59.

48. Rimmer and Weaver, "Different Questions, Different Answers?" pp. 23–28.
49. Roger Wimmer and Joseph Dominick, *Mass Media Research: An Introduction* (Belmont, CA: Wadsworth Publishing Company, 1997).
50. Philip Seib, "The Fight for Air Time"; The Dallas Morning News, February 8, 2005, available online at: <http://dallasnews.com/s/dws/dn/opinion/viewpoints/stories/020905dnediseib.html>

# CHAPTER 8

# Women, Blogs, and Political Power in Kuwait

*Samar al-Roomi*

Recently in the Arab world, several institutional and legal changes have occurred, including, in May 2005, Kuwaiti women gaining the chance to vote and hold political office in the next parliamentary elections. Moreover, continued intellectual discourse regarding Middle East liberalization and democratization has taken place. Such developments can be attributed to internal and external factors, some of which are related to new media technologies such as, satellite television, cellular phones, and the Internet/blogging.

Kuwait has the longest existing democratically elected Arab legislature and has greater computer accessibility and Internet usage than the majority of the region. This raises a question: Do Kuwaiti women use the Internet/blogs as a tool of political activism? Logic would tell us that women's blog comments about political issues would be abundant and much recent blog commentary by women would be about political rights. Nevertheless, because of regional and gender-based facts, it is presupposed that female blogs focus on issues other than politics, such as entertainment or family.

This chapter examines blog literature and the essentials of Arab Internet and mass media use related to seven Kuwaiti women's blogs, between April and September 2005 (one month before women received their right to vote and five months after). The chapter sheds light on the realities of political activism reflected in Kuwaiti women's blogging.

## Blogs, Bloggers, and Blogging

A blog (a.k.a., a weblog) is a Web site containing periodic posts in reverse chronological order. Blog posts either share a particular theme, or group of authors that reside in what is commonly referred to as a blogosphere. Blogs appear in many shapes and sizes. A blog's design is at the author's discretion, much like a typical Web page. Many blog posts include photos and other multimedia content.

Bloggers (i.e., blog authors) can add new text to their sites easily and quickly, allowing them to become highly dynamic. The site's format can vary from a list of hyperlinks, to article summaries with user/reader-provided comments and ratings. Hyperlinks direct readers to "source Web sites" and serve as a "reference page" of sorts to see the sources and/or other blogs that support the authors' ideas. Blogs "cross-link" frequently to other blogs, commenting upon their information, analysis, and opinion, and exchanging information and ideas with one another.[1]

Blogs (along with text-messaging and satellite television) are at the fore of a media paradigm-shift toward a new interactive, participatory telecommunications model. Blogs are helping to erode the legitimacy of traditional authority, especially within authoritarian societies.[2] Blogs combine the immediacy of up-to-the-minute posts with a strong sense of the author's personality, passions, and point of view. Many blogs post commentary and invite interactive comment from readers. A blogs' "comments feature" (typically located at the end of a post) allows other users to directly leave feedback about the "write-up." The comments are viewable by everyone reading the blog, thus enabling a dialogue between bloggers and readers and increasing the blogs' conversational flow and information sharing. Since blogs are readable by anyone and anyone can leave feedback, they are, in turn, a way of allowing readers (who do not need to author their own blogs) to communicate with each other. Blog posts serve as discussion topics for readers, which potentially creates ties between them. "Comments" also help to increase a feeling of the presence of others. This enables bloggers to see which blogs are most popular, as well as which topics generate the most discussion.[3]

Blogging is about information sharing. The act of blogging makes information public; the public information is then available to anyone with Internet access. Blogs are not limited to use by professional researchers, but can also be used by laypeople conducting everyday research. Many bloggers (but not all) are experts within a particular field; they research a subject and use their blogs to publish and distribute their acquired knowledge about the subject area. This information is subsequently free to view by others. It is common for such bloggers to link to articles and papers supporting their claims, enabling readers to verify the sources. When blogs link to each other and comment on each others' content, multidimensional discussions and participatory journalism occur. Blogs concentrate on like-minded readers, not on geographical or ethnic groups as newspapers do. It is the blogosphere's diversity that plays a key role in allowing ideas to spread into new domains. The "links" created act as communication and collaboration channels, allowing various blogger groups to work toward common goals.[4]

Readers can return to a blog with the expectation of looking at new posts by the same author or group of authors, thus getting a sense of the identifying "voice(s)" behind the posts on the site. Authorship is central to blogs. Every word on a blog clearly and inescapably is associated with its author(s).

Bloggers have the option of publishing anonymously. Blogs allow people the opportunity to either conceal or reveal their identity. Bloggers (as well as readers) have full control over identity sharing. Blogs allow one to freely assert their own identity, without social stigma. For example, Persian and Arab women use blogs as an outlet for self-expression in their traditionally conservative societies.[5]

Regarding the gender makeup of bloggers, they are equitably distributed between men and women. Nevertheless, male bloggers have traditionally received most of the blogging attention, and this has unintentionally misguided others into believing that the blogosphere is male dominated. This is largely due to the fact that mainstream media have focused predominantly on a group of male bloggers who are interested in political commentary such as war and terrorism.

## BLOGGING IN THE ARAB WORLD

Although blogs have lead to a growth in participatory journalism worldwide, they have not taken off as quickly or critically in the Middle East. This is due to several reasons. First, the Middle East was late to blogging; it did not start until 2004. Prior to 2004, Arabs primarily relied on chat rooms to express their opinions.[6]

Moreover, Arab governments' willingness to block and or shut down sites has caused Arab bloggers—especially women in the case of Kuwait, as they were only recently granted their voting rights—to exercise greater care compared to their Western brethren, who may freely criticize their governments.

Though censorship remains an issue of great concern, Arab governments have not been able to silence dissent on the Internet or prevent their increasing use of technology to strengthen communication and coordination among opposition and civil society activities, as seen in the Cedar Revolution in Lebanon and the Pink Revolution for Kuwaiti women's rights. Banning access to certain sites does not keep people from communicating their dissent. Although the Kuwaiti press enjoys a certain degree of freedom, the government utilizes informal censorship by placing pressure on editors, writers, and bloggers who attack the government and Islam. This is reflected in the passage of the early 2006 press law that places exorbitant fines on editors and/or journalists who attack or lampoon Islam.[7]

Arab Internet users can be characterized as increasingly self-confident. They believe in their own potential and in enlarging their social circles. While becoming more self-assertive, Arab Internet users have also become more assertive about what they really want out of life. The Internet/blogs in tandem with other new communications technology (e.g., text messaging and satellite television) are bringing about a dynamic change, leading to the erosion of traditional authority structures in family, society, culture/religion, and nation-state. This has lead to increasing calls for political, social, and economic reform in the Arab world.

Arab bloggers write in Arabic, English, or a mixture of both languages. They are eager to set themselves apart from newspapers and Web columnists writing for established sites as well as for the hugely popular Islamic militant-leaning bulletin boards. There are now about 1,000 Gulf Arab bloggers, up five times from 2004, according to Haitham Sabbah, a Bahrain-based blogger and Middle East editor for *Global Voices*, a program that tracks and collects blogs worldwide, launched by the Berkman Center for Internet and Society at Harvard University.[8]

## BLOGS AND THEIR IMPACT ON OTHER MEDIA

A fundamental difference between blogs and traditional Web sites is that blogs are typically archive-oriented. Traditional Web sites are not. Instead of substituting new material for old, as is normally done on traditional Web sites, blogs add postings frequently, creating an ever-growing collection of posts. The ability to add new posts without erasing previous content makes blogs fundamentally different than traditional Web sites.

Blogs and newspapers both rely on timeliness to an extent. Nevertheless, it is not as significant for blogs as it is for a daily newspaper or television network. A blogger often writes about something that interests him or her that may be topical within any given day, but has no immediacy. Bloggers are often interested in unexpected stories that may not be time-sensitive. Sociocultural values do play a factor in the selection of blog information, but blogs consist of a community of intellectual interests, rather than group cultural similarities. This is unlike newspapers, which may publish stories about particular ethnic groups because of the large numbers of that population living in a geographic community. Clarity or lack of ambiguity plays an insignificant role in the blogosphere, while ongoing debate is more important for bloggers. The lack of clarity and a large dose of ambiguity—the opposite of what is important for gatekeepers—are at the heart of the blogging community.

Blogging has moved past media's traditional gatekeeping function, for better or worse—depending on whom you ask. Bloggers enlarge the national and international news agenda by finding and flagging ideas and events until traditional media cover them in greater depth. In this regard, they can be said to serve as watchdogs of the mainstream press. If enough bloggers find something important and blog it (expressing opinions and linking to others opinions), then the idea rapidly reaches an ever larger audience.

Nevertheless, many journalists in the mainstream media have a problem with what they call "pseudo-journalism" that harks back to the Penny Press days in the United States, before editorial standards were established and when the press mainly operated by publishing opinion and commentaries. Blogs' "bottom-up" approach to reporting, some believe, is akin to the American conservative talk radio style, which is not necessarily objective in its reporting. That is, listeners are influenced by the way the facts are represented, sometimes carrying a partisan bias that influences or engenders their audience, which tends to be of like mind.

Bloggers, on the other hand, point to blogs' merits, such as the ability to make instantaneous changes to stories, if facts are corrected at a later date. This is unlike newspapers, which often place such factual changes/corrections in the back pages of the succeeding days' paper. Another attribute they point to is "fisking," a method by which bloggers fact check articles, government documents, and speeches. They will take an entire document or a "chunk" of text and then comment on it, using links to informational sites that either disprove assertions put forth in the blocked text or refute their premise.

While bloggers and blog readers are critical of traditional media, they do not ignore them; Instapundit's founder notes that "to be a critic of the media means you must pay attention to it."[9] Because most bloggers are not independent news gatherers, they must rely heavily on the Web for their content, and much of that comes from traditional media.

Studies of mainstream media suggest that the more people rely on the Internet and thereby blogs for news and information, the more they will judge that information as credible. Similarly, people consider their preferred news source as the most credible. Many studies examining Web credibility also find that the more people go online the more credible they rate the information they find.

## BLOGS IMPACT ON KUWAIT MAINSTREAM MEDIA

The impact of blogs on the mainstream press and politics in Kuwait and the rest of the Arab world is uncertain. Printed editions of the local newspaper remain cheaper than online time, and the Internet penetration and IT sophistication of Kuwait's overall society are just not broad enough yet for most local groups to have an Internet presence. Moreover, Kuwaitis are more likely to trust inside voices than those from outside. Local newspapers hold far more credence with Kuwait readers about Kuwaiti events than do other Arab papers.

Kuwait's heavy reliance on tribal *Dywaniahs* (in which men meet regularly to talk about public and private concerns) plays a more significant role in determining Kuwait's communication process and news' validity than do Web pages/blogs, because readers may be uncertain about attributing their content. The Internet as compared to traditional media sources is not perceived as a neutral and credible medium, especially regarding local news. Most acceptance of Internet information in Kuwait is done through discussion with and mutual acceptance by friends. In Kuwait, interpersonal communication and networks are highly valued and indeed are more credible than mass communication. The society places an overwhelming importance on the *Dywaniahs*, in which opinion later reflected on the Internet is formed. *Dywaniahs* are unique because no other Arab country has such a daily social mechanism. The most likely activities that men engage in at *Dywaniahs* include discussions on politics, social issues, education, and entertainment According to Al-Khandari, during the earlier periods *Dywaniahs* served as communication centers aiding government policy distribution, understanding of global political developments, and formulation of ideas for educating children. The role of *Dywaniahs* was so important to the municipal communication process that every city had two or three. In recent years, most cities have between 15 and 30.[10]

Al-Khandari notes that *Dywaniahs* serve as an important forum for Kuwaitis to carry out various social functions. Seventy-six percent of Kuwaitis agree that *Dywaniahs* are essential. Sixty percent say they attend a *Dywaniah* one to three times a week. The role of *Dywaniahs* as a social institution for men has provided them with awareness of political, social, economic, and educational events in Kuwait and around the world.[11]

In Al-Rashidi's study about media and politics in Kuwait, he noted that *Dywaniahs* played a central role in understanding Kuwaiti politics and culture. He also noted that *Dywaniahs* help people share and expose each other to competing political views. *Dywaniahs* also help overcome the limitations of press freedoms.[12] Though Kuwait enjoys a great degree of press freedom, the government (as noted previously) imposes limits. *Dywaniahs* provide a forum for both verifying the credibility of news reports and probing news stories for greater details. It helps people gain access to unpublished information through inter-action with authentic sources, including National Assembly members, imams, and journalists. According to Al-Khandari, 85 percent of his survey sample believed that *Dywaniahs* provided such a fact-finding forum.[13]

*Dywaniahs* also help lay people understand the various angles and sides of a story. They also make news from different news sources avail-able to "functionally illiterate" and "motivationally-challenged" Kuwaiti readers. *Dywaniahs* serve as a portal for covering and disseminating information out to the broader masses.

Because of Kuwait's small, growingly insular, and Islamic nature, many fear that a mass medium such as the Internet can change their society. Some of these changes could impact Kuwaitis conceptions of the self, consciousness, religious forms, the experience of time and space, modes of self-expression, and social activism.

In Kuwait, as in other Arab countries, cultural and religious factors provide the greatest active challenge to Western culture and innova-tions. Religious influence causes many Muslims to fear the effects of Western media. Therefore, the main emphasis in these countries is on the loss of control over information flow that accompanies the greatly enlarged supply of information. The perceived threat from such new media is twofold. First, there is the ease with which "immoral" mate-rial, such as pornography, can enter the country via the Internet. There is also concern that the Internet is being used by young people for sex chats. Although this threat does not represent an active offensive directed against the country by any one party, it is perceived as though it was just as dangerous as a conscious attack by an enemy. Second, there is the threat of the new media being used to spread dissident political thoughts. This concern has increased because certain opposition groups have begun to use the Internet to spread propaganda.

When it comes to political mobilization, SMS text messages far overtake Internet/blogging in reach. Mobile phones are much more widespread than Internet use. SMS text messages played a role in forming protests against the 2003 U.S.-led invasion of Iraq, in motivating the 2005 Cedar and Pink Revolutions, and in fueling the 2006 dispute about the Danish caricatures of the Prophet Mohammed. Text messaging has helped Arabs to gather and protest against oppressive government practices and/or regimes. In fact, text messaging played a major role in gathering Kuwaiti women together to fight for their God-given rights in 2005, as well as in bringing the Lebanese people together to protest against their Syrian de facto rulers.[14]

## Reasons for Blogging

Although we mostly hear about blogs that threaten mainstream media, bloggers create and use blogs for several reasons. And personal blogs in the blogosphere outnumber political or journalistic ones.[15] People blog to document their lives. Blogs are used by many as a record to inform and update others about their activities and whereabouts, often including photos. Depending on the audience and content, a blog could be a public journal or a photo album. What draws writers and readers to blogs instead of homepages are the communication frequency and reverse chronological blog format. A writer could put up something short and sweet, anticipating that his/her audience would be checking in regularly. Readers know that in the blog they are likely to get fresh news of friends, family, and colleagues.

People blog because it is easy to do. Part of the allure of blogs is the easy way bloggers can move between personal and profound topics. To some people, blogging is an outlet for thoughts and feelings. Blogs support authors' venting of issues that they are passionate about. Blogs in this regard served as a catharsis for bloggers' pent-up feelings that they might not otherwise be able to express through other means.

Some people blog to create and find a group of like-minded people with whom they can share their ideas, opinions, dreams, and expressions. Blogs that gain the most attention, though, are the ones that critique mainstream media and politics (i.e., political blogs).

Personal and political bloggers have very different social interaction goals. The blog is well-suited for both types of "authors." For political-expression, a blog is a means for quickly conveying late-breaking news. Not only can blog writers post information from any news source quickly, but also any reader can contribute news immediately through email. Political blogs can be especially valuable for people who feel alienated from the dominant culture and feel that there are scarce channels to express themselves.[16]

Through self-expression in a blog, people can align themselves with like-minded people, even though their local community may express contrary views. Writing or contributing to blogs enables one to broadcast a message to the world in a relatively effortless way. Political bloggers intend to influence others through information or opinions, while personal bloggers intend to express and get reactions to their ideas.[17]

At a political level, bloggers are motivated by the belief that what they are doing is an important social phenomenon, with implications for the democratic processes and the media that report about politics. Political bloggers place a higher level of importance on activism, value their reputation, and are less likely to hide their identity than their personal blogger compatriots.

## KUWAITI FEMALE BLOGS

Discussion forums have always served as an important way for Arabs to express themselves. Forum participants have reflected all shades of political opinion. Frustrated with the uncivilized tone of discussion forums, the Arab world in 2005 turned to blogs in greater numbers. The first annual Best Arab Blog Awards were given in February 2005, and the press began to write about the phenomenon.[18]

Previous research has indicated that the key characteristic of Arabic/Kuwaiti Internet/blog use is that religion has a predominant weight. And Arab users are eager to engage in discussion, including discussion of taboo topics such as politics, religion, and sex.[19] According to a 1996 study on the adoption of the Internet by Kuwait University students, the strongest Internet gratification sought out by students was entertainment and social interaction, followed by surveillance. The most important gratification items were entertainment and fun, followed by killing spare time, personal communications, information gathering and exploring, and social relationships. This suggests that the bogs are used primarily as an entertainment tool for socializing.[20]

Internet usage by Arab women and children has outranked usage by Arab men. In Kuwait a majority of the highly educated citizens are women, and women find the most value in Internet/blog communication, because of the anonymity they enjoy on the Web. Nevertheless, not unlike Western women, a majority of Kuwaiti women's posts read like a diary, and not like a newspaper editorial page. This gives them lower recognition than men's blogs, which tend to consist of more editorial content, albeit considerably less than the material available on Western blogs.

Moreover, when talking about political commentary and exposure, lack of female leadership role models is discouraging to most Arab women. Women are expected to be attentive to family needs rather than to develop themselves as leaders, especially political leaders.

The seven Kuwaiti female blogs examined from April to August 2005 shared similar Internet/blog characteristics. The blogs tended to be used mainly for socializing purposes. They were used to empower female political leadership only on a limited basis. Although rare, in the event of such empowerment when women's political rights were discussed, they were examined more as an observation than a critique or inspiration.

Of the blogs that this study examined, the following observations were made:

1. The "Ultimate" blog had a total of 104 postings spanning the period of this study. Of the 104 postings, 36 posts (35 percent) were diary entries outlining her daily personal and family life, 18 posts (17 percent) were poems, 12 posts (11 percent) dealt with political commentary (2 of which involved women's political rights), 11 posts (10 percent) explored sexual exploration and love, 10 posts (9 percent) were about travel, 10 posts (9 percent) involved comments about attached pictures, and 7 posts (7 percent) involved showcasing her literary skills.[21]

2. "Snookie, the Maverick" blog had a total of 54 postings spanning the period of this study. Of the 54 postings, 20 posts (37 percent) were diary entries outlining her daily personal and family life, 9 posts (17 percent) were political commentary (2 of which involved women's political rights), 8 posts (15 percent) discussed popular culture, 5 posts (9 percent) discussed sports, 3 posts (6 percent) entries were poems, 1 post (2 percent) entry discussed local news events, and 1 post (2 percent) entry discussed love.[22]

3. The "Kuwaitism" blog had a total of 50 postings spanning the period of this study. Of the 50 postings, 21 posts (42 percent)

were diary entries outlining her daily personal family life, 7 posts (14 percent) involved popular culture, 7 posts (14 percent) were market demographic surveys, 7 posts (14 percent) dealt with political commentary (1 of which involved women's political activism), 6 posts (12 percent) discussed attached pictures, and 4 (8 percent) entries commented on local news events in the newspaper, 4 posts (8 percent) discussed sports, and 2 posts (4 percent) commented on dining experiences.[23]

4. "Dot in the Universe" blog had a total of 78 postings spanning the period of this study. Of the 78 postings, 62 posts (79 percent) were diary entries outlining her daily personal and family life, 4 posts (5 percent) were poems, 4 posts (5 percent) were about love, 3 posts (4 percent) entries demonstrated the bloggers literary writing abilities, 2 posts were about popular culture, and 2 posts (3 percent) were about women's political activism.[24]

5. The "Plushness" blog had a total of 66 postings spanning the period of this study. Of the 66 postings, 27 posts (41 percent) were reflections about her personal and family life in a diary format, 24 posts (36 percent) were about sexuality and dating, 6 posts (9 percent) displayed her literary writing skills in a romance novel, 4 posts (6 percent) were political commentaries, 3 posts (5 percent) discussed popular culture, 1 post (1.5 percent) was an inspirational quote, and 1 post (1.5 percent) discussed Kuwait women's political activism.[25]

6. The "Unskin" blog had a total of 20 postings spanning the period of this study. Of the 20 postings, 10 posts (50 percent) were poems or inspirational quotes, 7 posts (35 percent) were reflections about her personal and family life in a diary format, 2 posts (10 percent) displayed her literary writing skills, and 1 post (5 percent) discussed song lyrics.[26]

7. The "Jewaira's Boudoir" blog had a total of 107 postings spanning the period of this study. Of the 107 postings, 36 posts (34 percent) were reflections about her personal and family life in a diary format, 21 posts (20 percent) displayed her literary writing skills in a romance novel, 20 posts (19 percent) were about sexuality and relationships, 10 posts (9 percent) reported on local and international news stories, 9 posts (8 percent) were poems, 7 posts (7 percent) were in a Dear Abby "advice column" format, 2 posts (1.8 percent) were about women's political activism and empowerment, 1 post (1 percent) involved philosophical comments, and 1 post (1 percent) was about popular culture.[27]

The aforementioned blogs featured an assortment of uses, ranging from using it to record in a diary (48 percent), to demonstrate writing and literary skills (22 percent), to discuss sex, love, and dating (11 percent), to discuss popular culture (6 percent), discuss news and sports stories (5 percent), to make political commentary (3 percent), to discuss their travel experiences (3 percent), and to politically empower women (2 percent). Using a blog as a journal for her personal and family experiences is the most prevalent use of blogs, with discussion of taboo subjects such as dating and sexual exploration also ranking high. The Jewaira blog ranked highest in the discussion of taboo subjects. Kuwaiti women bloggers' use of blogs for women's political empowerment ranks as the lowest use. "Snookie the Maverick" blog ranked highest in the discussion of women's political commentary. Four blogs ranked highest in addressing women's political empowerment, with each having two postings.

Most of the blogs examined could not be strictly categorized as described in an earlier section "Reasons for Blogging." Rather, these seven blogs served as hodge-podge communication forums, encompassing a majority of the reasons people might blog. Perhaps this is due to the fact that Arab blogging is still in its early evolutionary stage, as Arab blogging did not really start until 2005. With more maturation, Kuwaiti women's blogging may feature more topical blogs, rather than ones that discuss everything under the sun. And with women's increased understanding of their political rights, more Kuwaiti female political activist blogs may crop up.

## BLOGGING'S DISADVANTAGES AND THEIR IMPACT IN THE ARAB WORLD

Blogs also have their disadvantages. Publishing spontaneity means that, at times, bloggers may impulsively publish ill-considered messages. Also, motives and identities of blog authors can be very murky, because there is no way to determine if bloggers are truly who they say they are. Therefore, blogs on the political side are a fertile opportunity for PSYOPS (psychological operations). On the corporate side, public relations companies can take advantage of the blogosphere to spread buzz and interest in their products and disinformation and scandalous rumors regarding their competitors' products. Not all bloggers are who they claim to be, thus lending credence to the vast majority of Arabs' belief in conspiracy theories.

The blogosphere also perpetuates a "bandwagon effect," which nurtures lies and half-truths, such as many extremist Arabs' contentions about, Jews, Christians, and the West in general. While adding to the richness of citizen voices, blogs exponentially expand this culture of assertion. It brings to it a philosophy of publish anything, especially points of view; the reporting and verification will occur afterward in the responses of fellow bloggers. Nevertheless, if readers never question the facts of bloggers, then mistruths can be perpetuated. Blogs in this case can create a serious obstacle to the creation of a "global commons"—something that a participatory journalistic style strives for—between different information communities operating within different national and cultural contexts. How, for instance, do you convince people in an Islamic country that Jews did not do something absurdly wild (such as attack the World Trade Center), considering that they are determined to believe it, as all their friends, local Web sites, and chat rooms insist upon it? If you cannot break through this basic barrier of mistrust, how can citizens get past the gorge of misinformation that even their national leaders have failed to bridge?

The digital divide in the Middle East (even though its depth as reported by the World Bank is questionable, due to how these numbers are statistically reported) poses another problem for the growth of the blogosphere's participatory-journalism and evolving democratic intent. Kuwaitis do have greater Internet access than other Arab countries through many Internet cafes and affordable Internet cards for home dial-up use. The home dial-up service is, however, extremely slow. The cost of Internet service through providers is expensive— around US$300 a month, which is not a cost-effective priority for most people. Regarding the Internet being used for political mobilization purposes, Arab extremists use it more effectively than do liberal and secular groups, as seen in their use of it to politically mobilize voters in Kuwait's May 2006 district reduction political row that resulted in the government sacking the National Assembly.[28]

## ANALYSES

Blogs serve as a means to communicate interactively in real-time. They foster participatory journalism that has disseminated power to the people. No longer can journalism be said to be a top-down form of communication. Blogging and the participatory journalism that it has spawned have transformed journalism and the dissemination of information into a "bottom-top" communication model. It has given power to the less powerful and has allowed people to exercise this newfound power without revealing their true identities.

Women worldwide have begun blogs with the same frequency as men. However, they tend to use them more for entertainment purposes, than for political purposes. Even though Kuwaiti women were ecstatic about gaining their political rights in 2005, they tended to use the Internet/blogs for entertainment purposes rather than political empowerment. Moreover, it was proven that Arab cultural factors further impede Kuwaiti women's ability and willingness to politically empower their Kuwaiti sisters via blogs.

The Internet is a fairly new medium in the Arab world to convey messages, news, and political commentary. In the Arab world (including Kuwait), because home Internet connectivity is expensive and slow, text messaging through mobile phones tends to be a more popular way of communicating in mass. It is far cheaper and faster than communicating through the Internet, and text messaging has been used effectively to rally Kuwaitis behind political issues, such as the 2005 women's rights movement.[29] The use of *Dywaniahs* and the heavy reliance upon the local press for shaping local opinion has also impeded blogs' development and cultural acceptance.

Most importantly, however, is the lack of peer leadership for women in Kuwait. Peer leadership and its by-products, such as networking and mentoring, are key factors in empowering women to become more effective advocates of women's political activism and community development. Kuwaiti women are currently mapping out their course on how to do so. And because women are exposed to much failure in mapping out such a course, there tends to be an early capitulation in their efforts. Many Kuwaiti women feel that they enjoy an easy and wealthy lifestyle, so they see little benefit in struggling with failure. More pioneers are needed to lead women into greater political activism.

Bloggers in Kuwait helped unleash a "virtual" campaign for election reform in April 2006, a campaign that spilled onto the streets in a Ukraine-type "orange" revolution. Three university student bloggers translated into a catchy campaign with a distinctive "5 for Kuwait" orange logo the call by pro-reform members of parliament to cut the country's electoral districts down to five in order to fight corruption. Bloggers spread the word online, and in a rare instance in the history of the oil-rich emirate, hundreds of young people waving orange banners demonstrated outside the seat of government on May 5.[30] The campaign escalated into further protests. A bitter standoff between Parliament and the government forced the country's emir, Sheikh Sabah al-Ahmed al-Sabah, to dissolve Parliament on May 21, setting new elections on June 29, 2006.[31]

Women's use of the Internet to stimulate the June 2006 elections was apparent, but such online discussions were led by and focused on male candidates opposing the government. Women bloggers served as opposition candidate message surrogates, rather than serving women's emancipation needs. In the Orange protest, Kuwaiti youth used the Internet to name candidates they alleged were corrupt or who oppose reform. Perhaps with the empowerment of the Orange movement (which took into consideration women and helped energize young women participants in the June 2006 National Assembly election), we will see a greater level of women's political empowerment.[32]

## FUTURE RESEARCH

More Kuwaiti female blogs should be examined for more accurate generalizability of data. Moreover, given that Kuwaiti men are not that politically active either, it is suggested that Kuwaiti women's blogs be cross-referenced by Kuwaiti men's blogs to see if gender-based differences in political commentary and empowerment exist.

Due to the recent blogging activity that Kuwaitis have shown during the June 2006 election (data that were not examined in this study), blog comments around the time of June 2006 election should be examined to see if there are any discernible changes in women bloggers' comments since May 2005, when women received their political rights. As blogs were used in the June 2006 election to compliment *Diwanyahs*, the use of blogs to compliment *Diwanyahs'* dissemination of policy ideas should be examined. Moreover, it is worth considering the prospects of blogs supplementing *Diwanyahs* or even replacing them to some extent in the future.

Since this study examines a limited number of blog comments prior to women receiving their political rights, analyzing more recent women's blog comments would allow more accurate definition of any significant changes in political activism. Moreover, since it has been determined that Kuwaiti women (like other women bloggers) talk less about political empowerment than about day-to-day events, a quantifiable analysis of Kuwaiti women bloggers' political comments and those of Western women bloggers might be useful. This would help us determine to what extent Kuwaiti women bloggers truly lag behind their Western blogging sisters.

Other Gulf women, such as Saudis, are active political bloggers. In fact, Saudi Arabia and the United Arab Emirates are the two largest Gulf blogging communities. Thus, the political commentary of Kuwait women bloggers might be compared with the commentary of women bloggers in Saudi Arabia, Bahrain, Qatar, United Arab Emirates, and Oman.

Moreover, the examination of Kuwaiti women blogs should be conducted in Arabic and English. Some Kuwaitis have grown up and have been educated abroad and thus feel more comfortable writing in English. For other Kuwaiti women, writing in English may be difficult and they may be less inclined to write on complex political issues in English. These women may be more inclined to write about such issues in Arabic. Such examination should be conducted for greater generalizability of data.

## Notes

1. Pew Internet and American Life Project [Online], available online at: <http://www.pewinternet.org/reports/pdfs/PIP_Content_Creation_Report.pdf> (Accessed: February 29, 2004).
2. T. Smith, "Weblogging" PBS Newshour with Jim Lehrer [Online Transcript], available online at: <http://www.pbs.org/newshour/bb/media/jan-june03/blog_04–28.html> (Accessed: April 28, 2003).
3. Ibid.
4. S.C. Herring, L.A. Scheidt, S. Bonus, and E. Wright. "Bridging the Gap: A Genre Analysis of Weblogs." *HICSS-37*, 2004, p. 40101b.
5. J.S. Donath, *Identity and Deception in the Virtual Community, In Communities in Cyberspace* (New York: Routledge, 1998), pp. 29–59.
6. A. Hofheinz, "The Internet in the Arab World: Playground for Political Liberalization," *Internationale Politik und Gesellschaft*, issue 3 (2005): 96–97.
7. A. Al-Jarallah, "Weakness of New Press Law," *Arab Times*, Wednesday, March 8, 2006, section 1, p. 1.
8. S. Dagher, "Middle East: Gulf Bloggers—a New Breed of Arab Activists," *South China Morning Post*, available online at: <http://www.asiamedia.ucla.edu/article.asp?parentid =47659> (Accessed: Thursday June 15, 2006).
9. S. Rosenberg, "Much Ado about Blogging," available online at: http://www.salon.com/tech (Accessed: February 12, 2003).
10. Y. Al-Khandri, "Al-Diwaniyah Al-Kuwaithya wa Al-Siyasiy" (Kuwait: Matabea Daar Al-Balaq, 2002), pp. 50–60.
11. Ibid., p. 59.
12. B. Al-Rashidi, "Alaalam wa Tanmiya Al-Siyasiyh fi Almetama Al-Kuwaiti," Doctoral Dissertation (Egypt: Al-Mansora University, 2002), p. 73.
13. Y. Al-Khandri, "Al-Diwaniyah Al-Kuwaithya wa Al-Siyasiy" (Kuwait: Matabea Daar Al-Balaq, 2002), p. 45.
14. S. Al-Roomi, "New Use of Tech-Ethics," *Arab Times*, Sunday, February 5, 2006, section 1, p. 1.

15. S.C. Herring, L.A. Scheidt, S. Bonus, and E. Wright. "Bridging the Gap: A Genre Analysis of Weblogs." *HICSS-37* (2004): 40101b.
16. Allan C. Elms. *Personality in Politics* (Harcourt Brace: Cartersville, GA, 1976), p. 135.
17. B. Nardi, D.J. Schiano, and M. Gumbrecht, "Blogging As Social Activity, or, Would You Let 900 Million People Read Your Diary?" *Proceedings of CSCW'2004* (2004): 222–231.
18. Al-Wa'y al-Misri, available online at: misrdigital.blogspirit.com (Accessed: February 2005).
19. J. Al-Menayess, "Television Viewing Patterns in the State of Kuwait After the Iraqi Invasion," *Gazette*, issue 57 (1996): 29–50.
20. Kuwait University College of Science Windows, available online at: <http://www.kuniv.edu.ku/public/html/kucswin/Feb96/int_conn.html> (Accessed: February 1996).
21. The Ultimate, available online at: <http://3asal.blogspot.com/> (Accessed: April–September 2005).
22. Snookie the Maverick, available online at: <http://www.kuwaitism.com/> (Accessed: April–September 2005).
23. Kuwaitism, available online at: http://snookie77.blogspot.com (Accessed: April–September 2005.
24. Dot in the Universe, available online at: <http://lilie.blogspot.com/> (Accessed: April–September 2005).
25. Plushness, available online at: <http://plushness.blogspot.com/> (Accessed: April–September 2005).
26. Unskin, available online at: <http://unskin.blogspot.com/> (Accessed: April–September 2005).
27. Jewaira's Boudoir, available online at: <http://jewairasboudoir.blogspot.com/> (Accessed: April–September 2005).
28. A. Al-Baghli, "Sneak Turns Fundamentalist," *Arab Times*, Thursday, June 29, 2006, section 1, p. 1.
29. S. Al-Roomi, "Text Messaging: The Good & Bad," *Arab Times*, Wednesday, January 25, 2006, section 1, p. 1.
30. S. Dagher, "Middle East: Gulf bloggers—a new breed of Arab activists," *South China Morning Post*, Thursday June 15, 2006, available online at: <http://www.asiamedia.ucla.edu/article.asp?parentid=47659>
31. S. Abdallah, "Arabs Eye Kuwait's Elections and Reforms," *Middle East Times*, Monday, July 3, 2006, available online at: <http://www.metimes.com/articles/normal.php?StoryID=20060703-054858-9185r>
32. S. Al-Roomi, "Children of Orange," *Arab Times*, Saturday, June 10, 2006, section 1, p. 1.

# CHAPTER 9

# Israel and the New Media

*Yehiel Limor*

## INTRODUCTION

The summer 2006 war in Lebanon, arguably the first war of the New Media Age, posed new and globally unfamiliar realities for an entire country: War waged largely on the civilian home front, with virtually live media coverage and online reporting via the Internet.

Essentially, the war was a kind of proving ground for a theoretical model of twenty-first century media and warfare. This model, first introduced in 2002 and refined after the 2003 war in Iraq, sketches the battlefield of the future in which media technologies and international media organizations play a key role[1] at an intensity and scope unprecedented in human history.

The current study examines the development of the new media in Israel at the end of the twentieth century and the beginning of the twenty-first, as well as the function they fulfilled during the war in Lebanon. The war—and the State of Israel itself—may serve as a case study for other countries and societies, especially at war or in states of emergency, demonstrating the new media's function under such circumstances.

## THEORETICAL BACKGROUND

Several theoretical points of departure apply to discussion of the new media in Israel. Classic mass media literature identifies four basic types of state/society-media relations: Authoritarian, Libertarian, Totalitarian, and Social Responsibility.[2]

The Authoritarian Model, that applies rigid supervision and censorship to the media, was typical of seventeenth to nineteenth century European regimes, the Libertarian Model is purely theoretical and was never fully realized, the Totalitarian Model, according to which the media are considered part of the state or the ruling party and consequently subject to strict control, was common to communist regimes, most of which disappeared in the last decade of the twentieth century, although some of its components are still applied in theocracies and some other countries. The fourth model, Social Responsibility, perceived as characteristic of democratic states, is effectively an unwritten compact between the state/society and the media. A fifth, later model, the Developmental Model,[3] seeks to explain relations between the state/government and the media in developing countries. All these models were subject to criticism from the outset and none were applicable to the late twentieth century[4] and *a fortiori* to the twenty-first. On the other hand, they cannot be discounted entirely, as they still constitute the theoretical basis for any discussion of relations between state/society and the mass media.

Other models may prove beneficial as well. Altschull,[5] for example, differentiates among three basic models of state-media relations: (1) Market—characteristic of the First World, (2) Marxist—that prevails in the Second World, and (3) Advanced—typical of the Third World.

Reliance on theories and/or models concerning state-media relations enables assessment of media development as a reflection of government policy that defines the rules of the game in the media market, including determination of its permissible boundaries, constraints on players, and the like. Governmental involvement is thus liable to limit and even prevent the development of new (and sometimes also old) media and place them in a strait jacket insofar as content is concerned. The constraints imposed by the Chinese government on the Internet constitute only one example of such control.

The Market Model is also connected to the second theoretical point of departure, a point that is anchored in political economics, or, more precisely, in bureaucratic procedures originating in neo-Marxist conceptions. According to this approach, the media are primarily viewed as businesses[6] whose owners strive to preserve the existing political and social situation because any change is liable to undermine economic stability. On the other hand, perhaps the media may not be assessed separately from the economic system in which they operate because the system's economic forces are directed at its directors, along with those of all other industries, imposing pressure and coercion accordingly.[7] Hence the development of the media is essentially only one facet of market economics and a practical reflection of a media industry that seeks to profit by adapting its products (both hardware and software) to its target audiences while applying a variety of sophisticated marketing techniques.

In the Israeli case, it may be said that the privatization and market economy policies adopted by governments since the 1990s[8] have also made their mark among the new media, wherein it is primarily the private companies that control Internet infrastructure service supply. Section 4 of the 1982 Telecommunications Law empowers the minister of communications to grant general licenses for telecommunications activity and service provision, including those issued to companies offering IP-based communications. The Law also empowers the minister to grant a "special license," that is, one "limited to a specific type of telecommunications activity or service." These were granted to companies and organizations that provide Internet access or switching services.

In 2006, the Israel minister of communications expressed the political-economic conception calling for minimal regulation of telecommunications activity: "In the new era," declared the minister, Mr. Ariel Atias, "regulators may intervene formidably when essential but must not do so otherwise." One example of such intervention was the ministry's order issued that year to all licensed Internet service providers throughout the country, calling on them not to cooperate with worldwide pirate service providers that unlawfully use VOIP technology over data lines.[9]

The third theoretical point of departure is anchored in the technological sphere. Technological determinism considers the medium to be the message,[10] claiming that what shape society are the media themselves, or technological innovations, and not the messages transmitted thereby. For example, we may offer a technological explanation in response to the question "What is the Internet?"[11]. Effectively, even the term "new media" itself may be considered a result of technology, as it defines emerging media that join their more veteran counterparts. Radio was a "new medium" in the early twentieth century, television in mid-century, and cable and satellite television, cell phones, personal computers, and the Internet thereafter.

Development of the new media—and especially their proliferation and reception by the public—is not only the result of market economics reflecting financial and business entrepreneurship and committing manufacturers to constant development of new products and improvement of old ones, but also evidence of the existence of target audiences, actual or potential, with needs to which the new media products are designed to provide an adequate response. Such development may also be informative regarding the financial ability of a given country/ society to invest in media technologies and infrastructures, as well as the population's financial capacity for media product acquisition and its ability to benefit from and to operate advanced media technologies. In this respect, the development of the new media and their rapid reception in the State of Israel are based on a tripartite infrastructure:

- **Technological**: reflecting that some of the world's most advanced development infrastructures (such that of all Israeli society, including the military) may be defined as technology saturated.
- **Economic**: resources originating in numerous external and domestic investments—the result of a flourishing economy that enjoys stable annual growth.
- **Literate**: based on an educated population that adopts modern media technologies regularly and applies them rapidly in response to a variety of needs.

## The New Media in Israel

The development of the new media in a given country may be assessed practically in three respects: (1) technological developmental; (2) mass media—press, radio, and advertising, and (3) personal—use of PCs and the Internet.

### (1) Technological

Since the 1990s, Israel has been positioned at the forefront of new media technological development. Israeli jargon includes frequent references to the "Israeli Silicon Valley" in the Haifa Bay area. Various international corporations (such as Intel) have set up major development centers in Israel at which technological developments, many of them produced by startup firms, focus on both infrastructures and applications for personal and/or office/organizational use. Numerous startup companies that concentrated on advanced and sophisticated developments, particularly in the software field, were acquired over the years by American and international corporations (among which the most outstanding, of course, is Mirabilis, the company that developed ICQ). At the same time, there were many transactions conducted for the acquisition of Israeli-developed knowledge and applications in computers, information security, and telephony. Over the years, know-how exporting (primarily to the United States) was accorded extensive coverage by the country's general and financial press.

### (2) Mass Media

Various Israeli Web sites began to appear as soon as the Internet hit the market in the latter half of the 1990s. As the technological sector conducted dynamic R&D, financial bodies closely examined the U.S. Internet market and hastened to adopt and apply many of its processes and developments. The problems typical of many Web sites in their early days—particularly the lack of a well-formed economic model to guarantee financial viability and long-term survival—did not spare Israeli Web sites. Indeed, many of the pioneer sites closed within a short time, while others merged with or were acquired by the successful ones.

In Israel, as in other Western countries, the major newspapers rapidly set up and developed Web sites, generally without developing any uniform financial and operational model. The English newspaper *The Jerusalem Post* was the first to break through to cyberspace and offer its editorial content, followed by Israel's most prestigious daily *Ha'aretz*, which established a portal with a different name that was not identified with the paper. Subsequently, however, *Ha'aretz* set up a home site at which printed paper content was offered gratis. The popular daily *Maariv* first set up a site with free newspaper content, but replaced it a few years later, with a comprehensive portal that demanded a considerable financial investment. It was the country's most popular daily *Yedioth Ahronoth*—which is the flagship of the biggest media conglomerate in Israel—that elected not to offer its content for free on the Internet, instead setting up a separate portal with press content produced by an editorial board different from that of the home paper, along with a series of services, including virtual community forums. The sites owned by two of the major dailies *Walla* (*Haaretz*) and YNet (*Yedioth Ahronoth*) enjoyed the most hits in 2006.

Four principal operating formats prevail in the online press in Israel:

1. Sites owned by printed papers that supply newspaper content gratis.
2. Sites owned by printed papers offering content only to those who pay subscription or usage fees.
3. Sites owned by printed papers and operated by separate editorial boards.
4. Independent news sites.

These categories allow differentiation between online newspapers and other "pure" news sites primarily or exclusively offering information and news and portals that provide a variety of services, among them information and news supply.

While the development and operation of the online press is not unique to Israel, and similar patterns can be now found in many countries, another online medium, Internet radio, merits special attention. In this case as well, four principal operating formats may be discerned:

1. *Sites operated by established conventional radio stations:* Their content is same as what is transmitted through the corresponding radio stations, either live or on demand. Israel's public radio network *Kol Israel* (The Voice of Israel) and Israel Defense Forces radio *Galei Zahal* (whose broadcasts are aimed at the general public), the two nationwide radio networks, have sites of this type, as do regional/local radio stations owned by private entrepreneurs.

2. *Sites operated by educational radio stations:* in 2006, there were about 30 such stations in Israel at institutions of higher learning and secondary schools, some of which also maintained Web sites. Common to them all are limited programming and relatively few hits.

3. *Amateur Internet radio sites:* It is difficult to pinpoint these sites and their activity because many operate irregularly and often have very brief life spans.

4. *Former pirate stations:* These went off the air due to government harassment and shifted their activity to cyberspace.

Pirate radio is of particular interest. The phenomenon was very popular in Western Europe during the 1960s and began proliferating rapidly in Israel in the 1990s. By 1998, there were about 140 active stations of this type.[12] Repeated raids by the authorities did not wipe out the illegal stations that continued operating throughout the country.[13] Those that were tired of playing cat and mouse with the authorities left the airwaves and took to the Internet, confirming Eric Rhoads's[14] observation that radio, like the phoenix, adapts itself to changing circumstances. In other words, the Internet did not render radio an obsolete and irrelevant medium but actually enabled it to position itself at the forefront of technological progress and thus increase its audience. The development of the Internet had a dual and conflicting influence on pirate radio in Israel, as in other countries in which illegal stations operate. On the one hand, it created a convenient alternative infrastructure for those who sought to refrain from circumventing the law, offering a new sphere of broadcasting activity and a means of acquiring new audiences. According to Yoder,[15] professionals consider the Internet a public relations tool that provides listeners with a taste of pirate radio and arouses their curiosity.

Only gradually did the Israeli advertising agencies discover the Internet in Israel, as did their counterparts in other countries. In 2000, the Internet accounted for only 0.3 percent of all advertising in Israel[16]; two years later, the percentage rose to 2 percent and to 4 percent the following year[17]. By 2005, online advertising came to some 7 percent of all advertising in Israel, nearly the same as radio but far behind the printed press (51 percent) and television (30 percent). The overall investment in Internet advertising in 2005 was 76 percent higher than it had been the previous year.[18] Internet advertising in Israel achieved a new record in summer 2006, when the number of online campaigns exceeded that of the printed press, placing the Internet in a position second only to television.[19]

### (3) Personal PCs and the Internet

A survey conducted in 2005 indicated that 73 percent of Israelis have computers at home and 59 percent surf the Internet.[20] Those who do not have PCs largely consist of people with low incomes, older adults (age 50 and up), ultraorthodox Jews, and new immigrants.

In 2001, Israel's Internet surfing rate (then about 20 percent of the population) was the world's twelfth highest.[21] Four years thereafter, in 2005, a survey by Israel's [National] Central Bureau of Statistics found that 51 percent of Israelis use computers and 43 percent surf the Internet. The same survey displayed a wide gap between computer users and surfers in the Jewish and Arab sectors (Arabs constitute about 15 percent of Israel's population), as only about a third of Arab households is connected to the Internet.[22] The percentage continued to rise in 2006, as 52 percent of Israelis aged 13 and up reported that they use the Internet. Another finding indicated that most Israeli users have a broadband Internet connection.[23] Between 2002 and 2005, the number of households with broadband capabilities increased sixfold from 210,000 to 1.2 million.[24] The Internet market in Israel appears to have achieved saturation; estimates show that any further increase in the number of broadband Internet surfers will occur only as a consequence of growth in the number of personal computers. A 2005 survey indicated that about 28 percent of Internet users in Israel are "power users," that is, those who surf the Internet at least four times every day.[25]

Cumulative data show that the digital gap among various population sectors in Israel is shrinking steadily and rapidly. Computers have become a common accessory at schools; colleges and universities have countless computer laboratories and rooms, and laptops are a common sight. The ultraorthodox sector, that functions primarily as a closed society within Israeli society, has also been adopting home computers gradually, partly because they enable women to work at home rather than at outside jobs that entail contact with the external, secular society.

## THE NEW MEDIA AND THE WAR IN LEBANON

The summer 2006 war in Lebanon was the first war on earth in which the Internet played an active role as an agent of information. Although the war was waged between the Israeli army and Hezbollah terrorists entrenched in Lebanon, its principal victim was the civilian hinterland. Over a period of several weeks, about 4,000 missiles and rockets were fired at cities and other civilian localities in northern Israel. The looming threat of missile attacks led tens of thousands of Israeli citizens to leave their homes for points south and move in with others, primarily relatives and friends.

The war was the world's first demonstration of the Open Space pattern characteristic of twenty-first century media, based on the assumption that contemporary wars are not only waged locally between two rival countries but also take place as part of the global, supranational system in which various political, economic and other factors may well be involved.[26] This assumption also posits that such wars will take place in a new and unfamiliar media environment, influenced by the presence of anational and supranational players, especially television networks and international news agencies, motivated by financial and professional interests, with no affinity or loyalty to any particular nation state.

Furthermore, the closed, state-supervised media space is no longer impenetrable. Modern technologies enable any of the warring parties to overcome technical and other obstacles that once blocked the free flow of information. The Internet offers a live alternative to the information transmitted via official, supervised state and military channels.

The Vietnam War took place in closed space over an extended period of time, during which the American public was not supplied with up-to-date information about the horrific events unfolding in Vietnam. In Iraq, the war was being waged in a distant arena where reporters' movements were limited. The civilian public had no media of its own and information originating at the battlefront was usually partial, delayed, and controlled.

Different realities obtained during the war in Lebanon. The war, at least on the Israeli side, was waged in the civilian hinterland that included large cities attacked by missiles fired from sites only a few dozen kilometers away. But even when local residents had to spend long hours in shelters, they were not cut off from the world around them, as they were accompanied by the computers and Internet access that had been household fixtures for some time. The old media (radio and television) and especially the new media (primarily the cell phone and Internet) created media ecology unknown in previous wars.

Essentially, the Internet fulfilled a fourfold function during the war:

1. An alternative information channel to the major media—the press, television, and radio—especially for civilians in shelters who had no radio or television access, partially because power lines were damaged in missile attacks. A survey conducted immediately after the war revealed that about a third of Israel's population relied on the Internet as a source of information about unfolding events, demonstrating that the Internet had become the third most important information source—behind television and radio but ahead of the printed press.[27] The built-in advantages of the Internet—instantaneous transmission of information, broad scope, and convenient access—accorded it an important place among civilian information options throughout the war and possibly promised it a role in the future as well.

2. Convenient transmission of information directly from a battle-front that essentially constituted the civilian hinterland. News of attacks and casualties also found its way to other media, bypassing spokespersons under official control (including those of the armed forces and police), and was dispatched to people throughout the country via email.

3. For the first time, the Internet—whether through email or blogs—developed a generation of "civil military correspondents." The role played by bloggers in reporting civilian disasters has been examined by John Schwartz of *The New York Times*, who stated that "for vivid reporting from the enormous zone of tsunami disaster, it was hard to beat the blogs."[28] The war in 2006 thus opened a new page for bloggers and "civil military reporters," possibly constituting a kind of milestone in coverage of wars or other belligerent incidents, such as mass terror

attacks. Built-in cameras in cell phones played a similar role and helped to create a new type of "war photographers."

4. The Internet inaugurated new spheres of activity in civil society and mapped out activities for the volunteer and nonprofit sectors, especially during periods of disaster, war, or other emergencies. The massive attack on the civilian home front disrupted everyday life, hindered the supply of food, electricity, and water, and exerted other effects that revealed the varied advantages of Internet innovations, including:

    i. Media formats (including forums) responding to groups or audiences with special needs, such as new immigrants who do not speak the language of the country, when "governments and major organizations usually have difficulty providing solutions to targeted needs of this type."[29]

    ii. Contact between "service providers" and "consumers," for example, matching people who wanted to leave their homes because of the bombings and sought a safe haven in a distant city with residents of distant localities who would be willing to take these refugees in.

    iii. Rapid flow of information and identification of ancillary forces for specific missions, using designated channels, well-defined forums, and the like.

## CONCLUSIONS

In many respects, including scope of penetration and differential use, the new media in Israel are no different from those in industrialized Western countries. A developed, hi-tech saturated industry, advanced research centers, extensive technological infrastructure, computer-intensive industries and services, and a literate society with a high average salary all combine as a fertile field conducive to rapid development, effortless reception, and extensive use of the new media.

Nevertheless, the Israeli case is likely to be a test case or at least an experimental field and a research laboratory in several respects concerning absorption of the new media and the various uses thereof, considering the prevailing sociogeopolitical conditions.

Israel's status as a country with a small and densely concentrated population (about seven million people in an area of about 20,000 square kilometers) facilitates the study of various types of media use by the authorities and the public. The findings of such studies will provide a comprehensive view of new media use in both the national and local spheres.

Furthermore, Israeli society is heterogeneous in nature, characterized by several marked schisms—between old-timers versus new immigrants, nonreligious versus religious/ultraorthodox, Jews versus Arabs,[30] and between other such disparate groups—exacerbated by the ethnic rift between Israeli Jews of European origin and those of Asian/African extraction (especially Jews from Arab countries, who make up more than a quarter of the population). Even if other small countries exhibit similar schisms and rifts, none is likely to match Israel in terms of number, prominence, and facility of discernment and diagnosis, thereby providing a potential area of research that focuses primarily on uses and gratifications of the new media as well as their reception.

The ongoing emergency situation in the State of Israel, originating primarily in threats by Muslim states and Muslim terrorism, also provides material for an extraordinary sphere of research activity. Disasters occur in many countries and terror incidents have become common throughout the world over the past decade, but it is doubtful whether there are other countries under constant threat of terror whose social-technological-economic portrait resembles that of Israel. In this respect as well, Israel is likely to be a test case of new media developments, reception, and differential use by a population in a state of emergency.

Moreover, the small, technology-saturated Israeli society may be studied to examine the functions and significance of the new media, especially the Internet, in a modern civil society and as a medium that aids in the functioning of organizations belonging to the third sector. The war in Lebanon only drives home the significance of the Internet as a communications medium, but at the same time also points to the need for organized research in this area.

Finally, the 2006 war in Lebanon may constitute a test case for new media functions and uses during wartime. No comprehensive research has been conducted on the topic to date and the findings of studies undertaken may serve as captivating source material for other states and cultures that find themselves in similar situations.

## Notes

1. Yehiel Limor and Hillel Nossek. "The Army and the Media in the 21st Century: Towards a New Model of Relationships." *Israel Affairs*, vol. 12, no. 3 (July 2006).
2. Fred Siebert, Theodore Peterson and Wilbur Schramm, *Four Theories of the Press* (Urbana: University of Illinois Press, 1956).

3. William Hachten, *The World News Prism: Changing Media, Changing Ideologies* (Ames, IA: Iowa State University Press, 1981).
4. John Nerone (ed.), *Last Rights: Revisiting Four Theories of the Press* (Urbana: University of Illinois Press, 1995); Denis McQuail, *McQuail's Mass Communication Theory*, 4th edition (London: Sage, 2000).
5. Herbert Altschull, *Agents of Power: The Role of News Media in Human Affairs* (New York: Longman, 1984).
6. Nicolas Garnham, "Contribution to a Political Economy of Mass-Communication," in Richard Collins(eds.), *Media, Culture & Society* (London: Sage, 1986), pp. 9–32; Edward Herman and Noam Chomsky, *Manufacturing Consent* (New York: Pantheon Books, 1988).
7. Robert Picard, *Media Economics* (Newbury Park, CA: Sage, 1989).
8. Yehiel Limor, "The Mass Media in Israel," in Ephraim Yaar and Zeev Shavit (eds.), *Trends in Israeli Society* (Tel Aviv, Israel: Open University, 2003), pp. 1017–1103.
9. See the June 29, 2006 notice published at the Ministry's Web site, available online at: <http://www.moc.gov.il/new/Hebrew/index.html> (Accessed: September 8, 2006).
10. Marshall M. McLuhan, *Understanding Media* (New York: McGraw-Hill, 1964).
11. Andrew Chadwick, *Internet Politics* (New York: Oxford University Press, 2006).
12. Yehiel Limor, *Pirate Radio in Israel* (Jerusalem: The Hebrew University, 1998); Yehiel Limor, "Stormy Waves: The Proliferation of Pirate Radio in Israel," paper presented at the ICA annual conference (Acapulco, Mexico, June 2000).
13. Yehiel Limor and Hanan Naveh, *Pirate Radio in Israel—2006* (Jerusalem: The Second Television and Radio Authority, 2006).
14. Eric B. Rhoads, "Looking Back at Radio's Future," in Pease, E. and E. Dennis (eds.), *Radio—The Forgotten Medium* (New Brunswick, NJ: Transaction, 1995), pp. 15–30.
15. Andrew Yoder, *Pirate Radio Stations* (New York: McGrawHill, 2002).
16. "Leaving the Recession," *Otot*, June 2000, p. 27 (Hebrew).
17. Ayala Zoref, "2004: A Shining Year for Internet and Television," *Haaretz, The Marker* supplement, December 15, 2004, p. C6 (Hebrew).
18. Ayala Zoref, "Internet Advertising en route to Third Place among the Leading Media," *Haaretz, The Marker* supplement, January 10, 2006, p. 18 (Hebrew).
19. Ayala Zoref, "More Campaigns Will Be Mounted on the Internet than in the Press this Summer," *Haaretz, The Marker* supplement, July 3, 2006, p. 17 (Hebrew).
20. Ido Keinan, "91% of surfers connected to fast [Internet]," *NRG Website*, September 28, 2005, available online at: <http://www.nrg.co.il/online/10/ART/989/511.html> (Hebrew) (Accessed: September 13, 2006).

21. Hanni Barabash, "1.3 million Israelis Surf the Internet," *Haaretz, The Marker* supplement, January 31, 2001, p. C7 (Hebrew).
22. Motti Bassok, "Central Bureau of Statistics: 51% of Israelis Use Computers, 43% Surf the Internet," *Haaretz, The Marker* supplement, August 15, 2005, p. 20 (Hebrew).
23. Ayala Zoref, "TIM survey: 3.7 million Internet users aged 13 and up; 94% of surfers have broadband connections," *Haaretz, The Marker* supplement, August 1, 2006, p. 19 (Hebrew).
24. Gil Klien, "Israelis taken over by fast Internet: 1.2 million families connected to the net," *Yedioth Ahronoth*, financial supplement, January 3, 2006, p. 1 (Hebrew).
25. Ibid.
26. Ibid., Limor, and Nossek.
27. Roni Koren-Dinar, "Government Advertising Agency survey: Most residents of the north keep up to date with the news on Channel 10, Radio Haifa and Ynet," *Haaretz, The Marker* supplement, August 15, 2006, p. 15 (Hebrew).
28. Jay Rosen, "Bloggers vs. Journalists Is Over," January 2005, available online at: <http://journalism.nyu.edu/pubzone/weblogs/pressthink/2005/01/15/berk_pprd.html> (Accessed: September 8, 2006)
29. Azi Lev-On, "The Internet Replaced the Government in War," *Haaretz, The Marker* supplement, September 14, 2006, p. 4 (Hebrew).
30. Ephraim Ya'ar and Ze'ev Shavit (eds.), *Trends in Israeli Society* (Tel-Aviv, Israel: The Open University, 2001–2003).

# CHAPTER 10

# The Palestinian-Israeli Web War

## Chanan Naveh

This chapter explores manifestation of the Israeli-Palestinian conflict in cyberspace and, in doing so, examines a field that has been scarcely studied—international-propaganda war in the Internet environment. Although other virtual international conflicts, such as wars in the Balkans or the war in Iraq, have been examined, the Israeli-Palestinian conflict on the Web has not been a subject of systematic study to date. The research reported here deals with a new unique phenomenon: the meeting between personal surfing on the Web and processes of international public communications in cyberspace and how this is transformed into transborder propaganda.

The study examined, principally, the hypothesis that appropriate use of the Web for purposes of international propaganda provides an additional dimension to international processes, adds new actors to the propaganda arena, and integrates them in a manner that was not possible in the actual-external environment.

This is examined during the period of the Second *Intifada* (2000–2005), one of the most recent stages in the prolonged Israeli-Palestinian conflict.

## THEORY

This study assumed that cyberspace is a complex global technological environment that integrates and unifies within it and its surroundings many different, varied aspects of human activity through the use of new telecommunication networks that connect users to a variety of content.[1] In terms of international politics, this environment is *anarchical* in nature since it is based on a technology of knowledge transmission that is not centrally controlled.[2] Additionally, this is a *global* environment that includes cross-border processes and yet in many respects is also borderless.[3]

We should also remember that we are dealing with an environment that is first and foremost technological, one that requires that all kinds of users have access to technological infrastructures. Such access creates a "digital divide"—between those who are connected to these processes and those who are not. The technology also allows for *interactive* activity, bilateral and even multilateral, rapid action, and across endless expanses.[4] It also creates a *spatial* sphere that demands adaptation to dimensions of time and place.[5] Here we are speaking of a very *dynamic* environment that changes and develops continuously and in which it is difficult to predict what will happen, even in the short run. This sphere includes varied processes of *convergence* and *synergy* that create *multimedia* systems that act, function, and appeal nearly simultaneously to nearly all of a person's senses.

This cyberspace is relatively *egalitarian* and, thus, a user who has overcome entry obstacles (that is, has crossed the *digital divide* and has access to the Net) is able to act within it nearly without ideological or other limitations. Due to these characteristics, the Internet environment is considered to be one of the most characteristic of public spheres in which to conduct communication processes.[6] These communication processes are complex; indeed, according to Seib,[7] "the Internet is much more than a news medium. It transcends borders, creating virtual communities and states through its informational and interactive capabilities."

This study examined the meeting between this international public sphere and the international political arena in which international actors are active at different levels[8]—as individuals, national forces (groups or communities), and actors at the level of the international system (such as international organizations, corporations, or diasporic communities[9]). The interactions in the public sphere can be undertaken simultaneously by different publics and even counterpublics,[10] and since the nature of the Net is unlimited and global these publics are defined as "transnational."[11] Here it should be noted that actors in the changing and virtual international arena are undergoing what Rosenau[12] referred to as *fragmegration* processes. (*Fragmegration* juxtaposes the processes of fragmentation and integration occurring within and among organizations, communities, countries, and transnational systems such that it is virtually impossible not to treat them as interactive and causally linked.) At the same time, international processes are taking place in nonterritorial spaces where due to virtuality distances are shortened and a new term coined—*distant proximities*.[13] More, some scholars think that this new environment changes the nature of international politics and instead of diplomacy that is based upon *Realpolitik*, we have what can be called *Netpolitik*:

> *Netpolitik* is a new style of diplomacy that seeks to exploit the powerful capabilities of the Internet to shape politics, culture, values, and personal identity. But unlike *Realpolitik*—which seeks to advance a nation's political interests through amoral coercion—*Netpolitik* traffics in "softer" issues such as moral legitimacy, cultural identity, societal values, and public perception.[14]

We should note that users of the Net in this environment can act violently and cause injuries and damage, as has been undertaken by terrorists, hacktivists, and hackers.[15]

International actors manage their activities in the international public sphere by means of different platforms that exist on the Net and exploit its nature: email, distribution lists, blogs,[16] chats, forums, media *talkback*, use of surveys conducted over the Net, Web site construction, and community organizing.[17] Studies that have examined these platforms (Internet tools) have applied different criteria, some derived from the technological-media arena and others from international politics. One of these criteria is the use of tools/platforms (for private or public use or at the international level[18]); another criterion relates to the manner in which information is transferred (direct or mediated[19]); and a third focuses on the degree of interactivity (passive or interactive). Additional criteria concern the outcomes and the influences of the Internet as a tool,[20] and others the type of interrelations that appear in the Internet (cooperation or confrontation[21]), while yet others are based on the duration of the conflict, its orientation (global or local in terms of geographical scope and extent of the issues),[22] or domains of media and political activity conducted by means of the Internet (e. g., use of Internet tools as hubs for information, connections and communication, contributions, or recruiting volunteers[23]).

Prior to completing this summary of theories, attention should be directed to those researchers who have been dealing with manifestations of international disputes in the Internet environment. Initially, we can note that "All of the cyberwars thus far have only been reactions to and repercussions of what has happened in the physical realm."[24]

Additionally, we should note that there is a need

> to differentiate between the terms "cyberwar" and "netwar." While cyberwar refers to a more "heavy" mode of new military conflict like

destruction of the enemy's infrastructure through information technology, the term netwar was devised to refer to information-age conflict at the less military, low intensity, more social end of the spectrum.[25]

It should be noted that in the violent domain of cyberwar, there is a variety of activities that include "website defacement; denial of service attacks; domain name service attacks; use of worms, viruses and Trojan horses; exploitation of inherent computer security loopholes and unauthorized intrusions into an opponent's computer systems and networks."[26]

Even though we are speaking of a virtual arena, it should be emphasized that the struggle with an opponent in this arena has great international repercussions because Internet conflict at a low level of strength could escalate through a number of stages of attacks,[27] and the Internet may also be used as a weapon in waging psychological warfare via the use of information.[28] The present study has not focused on violent types of battles in the Net, but rather on "softer" types of Internet activity taking place during conflicts, principally, those that have meaning for the media and that exploit the international public sphere during the period of the conflict (mainly through propaganda).

By *propaganda*, we mean the purposeful use of the mass media for influencing those whose intent is to shape, mold, and shift attitudes in the hope that this will bring about behavioral change that will advance the propagandists' aims and interests.[29] Akzin defined international propaganda as any activity that is intended to arouse or to strengthen support for any country, movement, or idea in another country.[30] According to Akzin, propaganda activity is not directed principally at the official bodies authorized to deal with the subject, but rather toward individuals and groups who have unofficial status or informal influence.

## INTEGRATION OF THEORIES

This study explores propaganda management exploiting the nature of cyberspace in an international conflict. In order to advance the research in a systematic manner, a matrix was developed using some of the criteria mentioned above. This matrix will facilitate the examination of various Internet platforms utilized for propaganda purposes during a conflict (graph 10.1). The horizontal axis examines the degree of interactivity of the platform (from passive to interactive), while the vertical axis examines the type of international actor making use of the platform (individual, group, state, community, global actor).

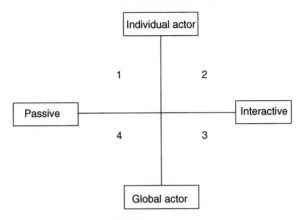

**Graph 10.1** Internet Propaganda

Thus, for example, use made of electronic mail for propaganda purposes in an international conflict is usually undertaken by individuals and is a tool that can be defined as active (the sender initiates its writing and transmission); accordingly, its matrix location will be between 1 and 2. In contrast, placement of new materials on the Internet site of diaspora communities is less active and will be located in the matrix at a place near point 4, while an attack such as defacement by a group of surfers will be located closer to 3. Accordingly, such analysis allows for mapping of Internet propaganda and indicates its nature.

## THE RESEARCH

The present study investigated the Second *Intifada*, the latest stage of the Israeli-Palestinian conflict, a period inclusive of the initiation of the violent events at the end of September 2000 through the final stage of the disengagement from Gaza in September 2005.[31]

During this period, the very intense Internet activity conducted by Israelis and Palestinians was a manifestation of the conflict between the two peoples, and various scholars have examined a wide variety of activities involved in this cyber struggle. Maoz, for example, studied the mediated dialogue between youth from both sides,[32] while Dahan examined discussions among Israeli and Palestinian adults involved in establishing a special "extraterritorial" public sphere for the Middle East.[33] Other studies compared Israeli sites during the state's jubilee celebrations (1998) with the Palestinian sites emphasizing the *Nakbah*, the disaster that befell them,[34] while others investigated the use of the

Web by both parties to disseminate information and to create extensive propaganda at the beginning of the Second *Intifada*.[35]

Other researchers sought to clarify whether the virtual struggle expanded beyond the Israeli-Palestinian arena directly into the international system. According to Jokisipilä,[36] no "electronic Islamic community" was created to manage part of the virtual struggle in support of the Palestinians against Israel. In his opinion, Palestinian society was incapable of organizing such a struggle because of its inferiority in this field, principally because it suffered from a "lack of cyberindependence" and did not have the capability to get to the *International Internet backbone* on its own.[37] In contrast, Allen and Demchak[38] claimed that there actually was international intervention that involved "hackers from Israel, Palestine, Lebanon, Germany, Saudi Arabia, Pakistan, Brazil, and the United States." One study of Hamas in the United States even found that they used Internet chat rooms and emails to coordinate their activities across Gaza, the West Bank, and Lebanon, making it difficult for Israeli security officials to trace their messages and decode their contents.[39] According to Karatzogianni, "what distinguishes this cyberconflict from past ones is that it moved beyond being a game controlled by a few highly specialized hackers into a full-scale action involving thousands of Israeli and Arab youngsters."[40]

Applying the analytical matrix to the past studies reveals that while a war broke out between the hackers, a propaganda struggle was initiated in parallel along with initial signs of dialogue between the sides. The present study seeks to map and to present the nature of the vast virtual propaganda arena that developed in the recent years within the framework of the Israeli-Palestinian conflict.

## THE FINDINGS

The Internet sphere was used by the Israelis and Palestinians as an arena for communication and primarily for propaganda. Tens of Internet sites and different materials transmitted over the Web during three events of the Second *Intifada* were examined: The Israeli Military *Operation Defense Shield* in the West Bank (April 2002); the imposition of a boycott on Israeli academics; and the international struggle vis-à-vis Israel's construction of the Fence/Wall. Several sources of materials were examined, mainly Web sites: Formal sites of the state of Israel or the Palestinian National Authority (PNA), and their institutions; sites of nongovernmental internal organizations (NGOs); sites of international NGOs; blog sites, and sites of petitions.

## Official Government Propaganda

The Web sites of the PNA did not function properly during the period under investigation, either because of changes in URL, technical failures related to the *Intifada*, or due to the activities of hackers.[41] Only the site of the presidency functioned throughout the entire research period with elements dedicated to the memory of President Yasser Arafat, while others presented information about the activities of his successor, Abu-Mazen,[42] but the site was not updated and was not effective for propaganda purposes.

In contrast, Israel maintained a series of official sites that included informational and propaganda materials such as the Web sites of the Office of the Prime Minister,[43] Ministry of Foreign Affairs (in both English[44] and Arabic),[45] and the Israeli Army.[46] With all of the sites interconnected through links that are prominently displayed, it creates the impression that the official network of the government of Israel enables it to present the state's official positions in an inclusive manner. The platforms of these sites present propaganda materials in different languages (particularly in the site of the Ministry of Foreign Affairs), biased news reports, documents, different types of data, propaganda presentations, photo galleries, video clips that present the Israeli perspective, and primarily materials that seek to condemn terror.

## Sites of Organizations and Institutions

According to the nature of the Internet environment, Palestinian activity in the NGO arena extends beyond the organizations' boundaries even if they are intra-Palestinian—as all become international organizations that can be accessed and activated from any place in the world. Thus, in practice, these different platforms create a virtual Palestinian community that includes sites dealing with different areas, all of whom are interconnected through a comprehensive cyber network.

The Palestinian Internet community includes a group of commemorative and nostalgic sites, some with an educational orientation while many are laden with propaganda materials that justify the Palestinian struggle. These sites focus on the *Nakbah*/the Palestinian disaster following the 1948 war[47] and include associated issues such as the Palestinian refugees "right of return"[48] to their homes in the areas of pre-1948 Palestine. Different groups of Palestinians constructed sites in this framework to commemorate villages destroyed following the 1948 war and whose residents fled or were banished.[49] Prominent use is made of photo galleries and of the refugees' personal stories[50]—all of which serve in practice as tools in the propaganda battle. The sites of Palestinian cities include testimonies and photos about the situation in these cities during the *Intifada*, and as such they too serve as propaganda sites against the Israeli occupation.[51]

The Palestinian community both within the domain of the PNA and in the diaspora activates a series of information sites that can serve as propaganda sites,[52] the most salient of which is *Electronic Intifada*.[53] These sites are linked to human rights sites that examined the Palestinian situation during the *Intifada*[54] or to sites that support the release of Palestinian prisoners, such as Marwan Barghouti.[55] In addition, Palestinian sites engaged in media watch activities checking whether the Palestinian story is being presented in the international media in a favorable manner and without any bias toward the Israeli framing.[56]

One of the most active Palestinian arenas—both within cyberspace and outside it—is the commercial struggle with Israel, whose most overt expression is advancing a boycott on products from Israel or the boycott of companies that are either engaged commercially with Israel or have enterprises there. The Internet was extensively used to advance these boycotts and the primary site for this activity is boycottisraeligoods.org.[57]

Most of the Palestinian sites are interconnected so that, in practice, there is a virtual community network created by means of lists of sites in linkages and icons that enable users to connect to sites active in regard to the same issue or to the entirety of the Palestinian struggle.[58]

Israeli and Palestinian cyberspaces are not significantly different, but in the case of Israel there is also a virtual community that includes groups and organizations that are entirely Israeli as well as worldwide Jewish communities and organizations that operate sites that present the Israeli position and practically serve as propaganda sites. Especially prominent in this environment are Internet sites of Israeli and Jewish organizations that seek to provide assistance to terrorist victims.[59] Ostensibly these sites provide services, but they also contain links and referrals to one of the primary content areas of Israeli sites— commemoration of victims of terror. So extensive is such activity as to claim that there is an international Israeli community that identifies with the victims.[60] Such commemorative sites consist primarily of multimedia materials that serve at the same time the propaganda needs of Israel in its struggle with terror.

During the Second *Intifada*, sites of individuals, groups, and organizations in Israel and in the world appeared and started advancing pro-Israel propaganda. The lobbying groups that work on Israel's behalf throughout the world act with their governments and parliaments, and the most prominent organization is the American Israel Public Affairs Committee (AIPAC), the American lobbying organization. Interestingly, this organization's Web site presents very little propaganda materials related to the Israeli-Palestinian conflict.[61] Some organizations active on Israel's behalf in the international arena have constructed Internet sites,[62] while others act exclusively in cyberspace.[63] Each of these sites takes advantage of the Net's multimedia capabilities and present photos, maps, documents, video clips, and other forms of presentation. Most of the sites have links and secondary connections that form part of the Web of the virtual community.

Like the Palestinian sites, sites supporting Israel include media watch activities that monitor how the international media report the narrative of the conflict. HonestReporting.com,[64] the most salient among these sites, also includes propaganda materials on behalf of Israel.

## INDIVIDUAL PROPAGANDA ACTIVITY ON THE INTERNET

Individuals who use the Internet to advance the struggle on behalf of their national actor do so because of a sense of deep involvement and for different motives, alongside frustration due to the difficulties facing their nation.[65] The activities in this arena are varied and individuals utilize different platforms: sending emails via mass online distribution lists,[66] signing petitions, participating in online surveys or media *talkback*, writing blogs, and constructing Web sites.

The primary innovation for both sides is the widespread use of the blog platform. The focus of the Israeli narrative in blogs is terror, while the Palestinian framing is primarily the Israeli occupation. Bloggers who write from a sense of deep involvement sought to relate their personal story within the framework of the larger national struggle. Employing all of the means available through the blog platform, these writers sought first and foremost to relate their personal experiences and stories, and to express their views. By making use of the platform's varied multimedia capabilities, they included translations of documents, photos, as well as both audio and video clips. Attached to their texts are many links and connections to other surfers and their blogs, as well as, to Internet sites with similar points of view, and this serves as another tool to develop a virtual supportive community.

Palestineblogs.com[67] is the salient blog in the Palestinian Internet arena that includes referrals and connections to more than 30 types of

Palestinian blogs. These include blogs by Palestinians living within the PNA,[68] others in the Palestinian diaspora,[69] and non-Palestinians who support the Palestinian cause.[70] A majority of the Israeli blogs in English can be accessed at the Blogspot-Blogger site, where Israelis and their supporters throughout the world describe the situation and the price paid due to the *Intifada*.[71] One important aspect of the struggle by individuals via the Internet is the fact that these individual bloggers do not sense that they are engaged in a personal struggle, because they are connected with one another and are part of an online community that takes advantages of the nature of the net and the specific tools available to bloggers.

Two international-political battles between Israelis and Palestinians were most prominent during the Second *Intifada*, in addition to the direct violent confrontation between the two sides. The first was the Internet confrontation in regard to the question of the Fence/Wall that Israel constructed between itself and Palestinian territories as part of its war on terror. The international political and legal struggle related to the Fence found its expression in cyberspace: propaganda from the Israeli side was posted primarily by representatives of the Israeli establishment—the Ministry of Defense[72] and the Ministry of Foreign Affairs,[73] alongside sites run by private groups explaining the Israeli position.[74] In contrast, Palestinian propaganda against the Wall appeared in nearly all of the sites involved in the struggle, for example, municipal sites in Bethlehem that enabled surfers to send electronic messages that eventually would be written on part of the Wall.[75] Most salient of all was the Web site Stopthewall.org that organized an extensive campaign that included news and reports about activities relating to the Wall: petitions, email addresses, documents, maps, video clips, and photo galleries.[76] The battle over the Wall also involved both sides of the online communities—Israel and its supporters on the one hand, with Palestinians and their supporters, on the other hand.

The second battle manifest widely over the Net was different in character—the boycott of Israeli scientists and academics. Here the Internet served the campaigns run by both sides of this confrontation, and the activities were widespread due to the excellent knowledge of the Net's capabilities among the forces involved. Within a short period of time, online communities constructed sites, distributed petitions, and sent chain letters via viral marketing.[77] British scientists initiated the boycott in April 2002[78] soon after the beginning of Operation Defensive Shield during which Israel Defense Forces (IDF) reoccupied Palestinian cities in the West Bank, following a most violent wave of terrorist activity. The initiative spread from England to universities in the United States and to other places[79] and rekindled a number of times over the last several years.[80] The battle against this campaign was conducted on two fronts within the Internet environment; on the one hand, by individual scientists in Israel and throughout the world who circulated petitions and constructed Internet sites,[81] and, on the other hand, by international scientific organizations.[82]

And to conclude on a positive note, in the midst of the Second *Intifada* while both sides were attacking one another violently, the Internet served as an arena for dialogue between the two opposing sides. A number of international and some local groups, agencies, and organizations conducted dialogue by taking advantage of the opportunities offered by the Internet to make contact from both distance and nearby. Such dialogue took place, for example, by means of the Internet site of the binational radio station—*All for Peace*—broadcasting from Palestinian town of Ramallah,[83] on sites that serve usually as the arena for academic communication,[84] or on sites of organizations that dedicate themselves to such matters,[85] the most prominent of which is *Seeds of Peace*—an international organization that arranges for meetings of youth from conflicted societies all over the world.[86]

## CONCLUSIONS

In previous studies of this phenomenon, it was observed that

> the use of the Internet in conflicts leads to a proliferation and diversification of voices by allowing a variety of actors to spread their views and opinions easily. Direct channels of communication and information distribution create wider communities of the like-minded than was previously possible.[87]

Undertaken as an additional step in the investigation of these developments, the systematic study reported here was aided by the analytical matrix presented in the earlier theoretical section (graph 10.1). In analyzing the findings by means of this matrix, it appears that both sides of the Israeli-Palestinian conflict took full advantage of the Internet environment during the Second *Intifada*. There were three types of activity along the *actor* axis: at the first point, a *national actor* located midway along the axis, the Israeli government is the primary factor while the PNA is barely active; at the second point, located at the extreme end of the axis, there was extensive activity by individuals via the Net in constructing Web sites, using electronic mail and, especially, blogging.

Further, it should be emphasized that the *actor* axis amalgamates the individuals' activity at a third point, located at the end of the axis—activity of the virtual community that creates actors involved in cross-border global activity.

The investigation along the second axis—activity—is more complex. A majority of the actors' conflict-related activities use interactive Internet platforms—such as Web sites and blogs, while a minority uses them for the transmission of materials. Here both presentation and access require that surfers and other interested parties initiate and actively seek such information. Furthermore, when a person who has not been involved attempts to find material about the conflict, she or he must obtain it by means of external search engines. Once there, it is possible to access and to use internal search systems as well as the connections and linkages that exist in different Web sites. At the same time, the Web sites can serve as banks for surfers who seek propaganda materials. Such materials that exist in cyberspace can be accessed (a passive act) and then distributed immediately (active act).

The analytical matrix enables us to identify propaganda innovations on the Internet. In this regard, it appears that during the years of the Second *Intifada* the Palestinian-Israeli activity on the Web advanced beyond what has been observed in this arena in other conflicts. In light of the development of Internet platforms, propaganda was concentrated in two domains of the matrix—the active-interactive of the individuals (fields 2 and 3 in graph 10.1). These activities of the individuals as propaganda initiators advanced significantly and they joined virtual-international communities that succeeded in utilizing the Internet in order to develop and to present their views throughout the world.

Given this development, we found that there is support for the hypothesis presented in the introduction—appropriate use of the Web for purposes of international propaganda provides an additional dimension to international processes, adds new actors to the propaganda arena, and integrates them in a manner that was not possible in the actual-external environment.

In addition, it should be noted that this study investigated, principally, the Web techniques, tools, and platforms that both sides of the conflict used for propaganda purposes, but did not explore the contents of this propaganda. It appears that the contents, the framing, and the narratives are those that have been used by the sides in the conflict for many years. From a cursory view, it appears that the Palestinians present, principally, the Israeli occupation and the opposition to it, while the Israelis believe that terror and the struggle against should be the focus. Both sides share motifs such as death, memory, and commemoration in their Web sites. It seems that the content domain is worthy of additional research that will investigate if entry into the environment of complex technological media brought not only adaptation of the contents to this arena but also development of new contents and a new view of the conflict, as in the case of the few Israeli-Palestinian dialogue sites.

## NOTES

1. John Pavlik, *New Media Technology*, 2nd edition (Needham Heights, MA: Allyn and Bacon, 1996); Sheizaf Rafaeli and Fay Sudweeks, "Networked Interactivity," *Journal of Computer-Mediated Communication*, vol. 2, no. 4 (March 1997); Hill and John Hughes, *Cyberpolitics* (Oxford: Rowman and Littllefield, 1998); Edward Downes and Sally MacMillan, "Defining Interactivity," *New Media and Society*, vol. 2, no. 2 (June 2000); Chanan Naveh, *National E-Image* (The Expression of National Identity in Governmental Web sites), paper presented at the Conference of the Israeli International Studies Association (Jerusalem: 2003) (Hebrew). Joseph Walther, Geri Gay, and Jeffrey Hancock, "How Do Communication and Technology Researchers Study the Internet," *Journal of Communication*, vol. 55, no. 3 (September 2005); Geoffrey Herrera, *Cyberspace and Sovereignty: Thoughts on Physical Space and Digital Space*, paper prepared for the 47th Annual International Studies Association Convention (San Diego, CA: 2006).
2. Sheizaf Rafaeli and John Newhagen. "Why Communication Researchers Should Study the Internet: A Dialogue," *Journal of Computer-Mediated Communication*, vol. 1, no. 4 (March 1996).
3. Peter Smith and Elizabeth Smythe, *Globalization, Citizenship and Technology: The MAI Meets the Internet*, paper presented at the 41st Annual Convention of the International Studies Association (Los Angeles, CA: 2000); Jacob Baal-Schem and Dov Shinar, "The Telepresence Era: Global Village or Media Slums," in Dov Shinar (ed.), *Internet: Communication, Society and Culture* (Tel Aviv, Israel: The Open University, 2001) (Hebrew).
4. Tanjev Schultz, "Mass Media and the Concept of Interactivity: An Exploratory Study of Online Forums and Reader Email," *Media, Culture & Society*, vol. 22, no. 2 (March 2000).
5. Rafaeli and Newhagen. "Why Communication Researchers."
6. Mark Poster, "Cyberdemocracy (The Internet and the Public Sphere)," in David Holmes (ed.), *Virtual Politics* (London: Sage, 1997); Phil Agre, "The Internet and Public Discourse," *First Monday*, vol. 3, no. 3 (March 1998), <http://www.firstmonday.org/issues/issue3_3/agre/> (Accessed: July 6, 2006); Wolfgang Truetzschler, "The Internet: A new Mass Medium," in Denis McQuail and Karen Siune (eds.),

*Media Policy* (Convergence, Concentration and Commerce) (London Sage: 1998); Peter Dahlgren, "The Internet, Public Spheres, and Political Communication: Dispersion and Deliberation," *Political Communication*, vol. 22, no. 2 (April–June 2005).

7. Philip Seib, "Weaving the Web: The Internet's Effect on International News Coverage and International Relations," *Millennium: Journal of International Studies*, vol. 32, no. 3 (December 2003).

8. Joel David Singer, "The Level of Analysis Problem in International Relations. *World Politics*, vol. 14, no. 1 (October 1961); Bruce Russett and Harvey Starr, *World Politics: The Menu for Choice*, 4th edition (San Francisco: Freeman 1992), pp. 26–36.

9. David Bollier, *The Rise of Netpolitics* (How the Internet Is Changing International Politics and Diplomacy) (Washington, DC: The Aspen Institute, 2003).

10. John Downey and Natalie Fenton, "New Media, Counter Publicity and the Public Sphere," *New Media & Society*, vol. 5, no. 2 (June 2003).

11. Thomas Olesen, "Transnational Publics: New Spaces of Social Movement Activism and the Problem of Global Long-Sightedness," *Current Sociology*, vol. 53, no. 3 (May 2005).

12. James Rosenau, *States, Sovereignty, and Diplomacy in the Information Age*, paper prepared for presentation at the annual meeting of the International Studies Association (Washington, DC: 1998), p. 4.

13. James Rosenau, *Distant Proximities (Dynamics beyond Globalization)* (New Jersey: Princeton University Press, 2003).

14. David Bollier, *The Rise of Netpolitics*, p. 2.

15. Dorothy Denning. *Activism, Hacktivism, and Cyberterrorism: The Internet as a Tool for Influencing Foreign Policy*, paper presented at a conference on "The Internet and International Systems: Information Technology and American Foreign Policy Decision Making" (San Francisco: The World Affairs Council, 1999). Michele Zanini and Sean Edwards, "The Networking of Terrorism in the Information Age," in John Arquilla and David Ronfeldt (eds.), *Networks and Netwars: The Future of Terror, Crime, and Militancy* (Santa Monica, CA: Rand, 2001); Gabi Weimann, *Terror on the Internet: The New Arena, The New Challenges* (Washington, DC: United States Institute of Peace, 2006).

16. Daniel Drezner and Henry Farrell. "Web of Influence." *Foreign Policy*. no. 145. (November–December 2004); Glenn Reynolds, "The Blogs of War: How the Internet Is Reshaping Foreign Policy," *The National Interest*, no. 75 (Spring 2004).

17. Sheryl Brown and Margarita Studemeister. "Virtual Diplomacy: Rethinking Foreign Policy Practice in the Information Age," *Information and Security*, vol. 7, no. 1 (2001); Alan Kluver, "The Logic of New Media in International Affairs," *New Media and Society*, vol. 4, no. 4 (December 2002): 512–513; Maria Bakardjieva, "Virtual

togetherness: An Everyday-life Perspective." *Media, Culture &* *Society*, vol. 25, no. 3 (May, 2003): 292; Chanan Naveh, *From the PC* *to the Global Arena (Private/International Propaganda on the Web)*, paper presented at the Conference of the Israeli Communication Association (Netanya: 2004) (Hebrew).

18. Myriam Dunn, "The Cyberspace Dimension in Armed Conflict: Approaching a Complex Issue with Assistance of the Morphological Method," *Information and Security*, vol. 7, no. 1 (2001).

19. Mario Diani, "Social Movement Networks: Virtual and Real," in Frank Webster (ed.), *Culture and Politics in the Information Age: A New Politics?* (London and New York: Routledge, 2001), cited by Thomas Olesen, "Transnational Publics: New Spaces of Social Movement Activism and the Problem of Global Long-Sightedness," *Current Sociology*, vol. 53, no. 3 (May 2005).

20. Myriam Dunn, "The Cyberspace Dimension in Armed Conflict."

21. Myriam Dunn, "The Cyberspace Dimension in Armed Conflict"; Adi Nizan-Zamir, *Online Peace and War: The Israeli Palestinian Conflict on the Web*, paper presented at the conference—Directions in Peace Journalism (Jerusalem: June 2006).

22. John Arquilla and David Ronfeldt, "The Advent of Netwar (Revisited)," in John Arquilla and David Ronfeldt (eds.), *Networks and Netwars: The Future of Terror, Crime, and Militancy* (Santa Monica, CA: Rand, 2001), pp. 17–18.

23. Chanan Naveh, "'No Secret Handouts'—International Aid in the Cyberspace (The Case of the 2004 Tsunami)," *Net Magazine* (The Israeli Internet Association, October 2005) (Hebrew).

24. John Arquilla and David Ronfeldt, "The Advent of Netwar," 11; Markku Jokisipilä, "Interfada: The Israeli-Palestinian Cyberconflict" (From Traditional Warfare to Cyberwar: Information War and Dissemination of Propaganda on the Internet in the Light of Israeli-Palestinian Conflict), paper presented at the 3rd conference of the War and Virtual War Project (Salzburg, Austria: 2004), p. 6.

25. John Arquilla and David Ronfeldt (2001) quoted in Athina Karatzogianni, "The Politics of 'Cyberconflict,'" *Politics*, vol. 24, no. 1 (February 2004).

26. Jokisipilä, "Interfada," p. 3.

27. Ibid., p. 6.

28. Karatzogianni, "The Politics of 'Cyberconflict,'" pp. 51–52.

29. Baruch Chazan, "The Operative Propaganda of the USSR in the Middle East Conflict," *State, Government and International Relations*, no. 6 (Fall 1974); Garth Jowett and Victoria O'Donnell, *Propaganda and Persuasion*, 2nd edition (Nebury Park, CA: Sage, 1992).

30. Benjamin Akzin, *The Basics of International Politics* (Jerusalem: Academon, 1984) (Hebrew).

31. Shai Feldman, "The Second Intifada: A 'Net Assessment,'" *Strategic Assessment*, vol. 4, no. 3 (Tel Aviv, The Jaffe Center for Strategic

Studies, Tel Aviv University, November 2001); Alan Dowty and Michelle Gawerc, "The Intifada: Revealing the Chasm," *Middle East Review of International Affairs*, vol. 5, no. 3 (September 2001); (2001); Amira Hass, "Israel's Closure Policy: An Ineffective Strategy of Containment and Repression," *Journal of Palestine Studies*, vol. 31, no. 3 (Spring 2002); Amos Harel and Avi Isacharoff, *The Seventh War* (Tel Aviv: Miskal/Yedioth Ahronoth Books and Hemed Books, 2004) (Hebrew). Peter Lagerquist, "Fencing the Last Sky: Excavating Palestine after Israel's 'Separation. Wall.'" *Journal of Palestine Studies*, vol. 33, no. 2 (Winter 2004–2005).

32. Yifat Maoz, Peace Building via the Internet: Computer Mediated Dialogues of Israeli and Palestinian Youth in the 2nd Intifada, paper presented at the Conference—Directions in Peace Journalism (Jerusalem: 2006).

33. Michael Dahan, "Between a Rock and a Hard Place: The Changing Public Sphere of Palestinian Israelis," *Journal of Computer-Mediated Communication*, vol. 8, no. 2 (January 2003).

34. Steve Niva, "Countering Israel's 50th on the Internet: Al-Nakba Websites Document Palestinian Dispossession," *Middle East Report*, no. 207 (1998).

35. Most prominent is the Palestinian site <http://www.electronicintifada.net/new.shtml> (Accessed: July 9, 2006); Philip Seib, "Weaving the Web"; Adam Hanieh, "The WWW in Palestine: An Informational and Organizing Tool," *Middle East Report*, no. 213 (Winter 1999–2000).

36. Jokisipilä, "Interfada."

37. Adam Hanieh, "The WWW in Palestine."

38. Patrick Allen and Chris Demchak, "The Palestinian Israel Cyber-War," *Military Review* (March–April 2003).

39. Athina Karatzogianni, "The Politics of 'Cyberconflict,'" 49.

40. Ibid., 50.

41. The Official site of the PNA <http://www.pna.gov.ps> Palestinian Information Ministry <http://www.minfo.gov.ps> only in Arabic (Accessed: July 21, 2006). Palestinian Ministry of Foreign Affairs, available online at: <http://www.mofa.gov.ps>, not active (Accessed: July 21, 2006).

42. Palestinian presidential site, available online at: <http://www.p-p-o.com> (Accessed: July 21, 2006).

43. <http://www.pmo.gov.il/PMOEng> (Accessed: July 21, 2006).

44. <http://www.mfa.gov.il/mfa> (Accessed: July 21, 2006).

45. <http://www.altawasul.net/MFAAr> (Accessed: July 21, 2006).

46. <http://www1.idf.il/DOVER/site/homepage.asp?clr=1&sl=EN&id=-8888&force=1> (Accessed: July 21, 2006).

47. Palestinian Nakba sites: <http://nakba-online.tripod.com> in Hebrew (Accessed: July 15, 2006).

48. <http://www.alnakba.org>(Accessed: July 15, 2006).
49. <http://www.al-awda.org/index.html> (Accessed: July 15, 2006).
50. <http://www.palestineremembered.com/index.html> (Accessed: July 15, 2006).
51. <http://www.deiryassin.org/> (Accessed: July 15, 2006). <http://www.openbethlehem.org/>; (Accessed: July 16, 2006) <http://www.ramallahonline.com/index.php> (Accessed: July 16, 2006). http://www.savethechildren.org.uk/eyetoeye/explore/ balata_bureij.html (Accessed: July 15, 2006); <http://www. dheisheh-ibdaa.net/home.htm> (Accessed: July 15, 2006).
52. <http://www.palestine-info.co.uk/am/publish/> (Accessed: July 16, 2006). <http://www.palestine-net.com/> (Accessed: July 18, 2006). Particularly interesting, for example, is online sale of Palestinian products on different sites—<http://www.sambarforpins.com/ palestine.htm> (Accessed: July 18, 2006).
53. <http://electronicintifada.net/new.shtml> (Accessed: July 16, 2006). <http://www.intifada.com/> (Accessed: July 18, 2006).
54. <http://www.pchrgaza.org/files/W_report/English/2006/ weekly2006.htm> (Accessed: July 15, 2006). The Palestine Children's Welfare Fund <http://www.pcwf.org/> (Accessed: July 16, 2006).
55. <http://www.freebarghouti.org/> (Accessed: July 16, 2006), or for 2 Palestinian women jailed in Israel <http://www.freesaj.org.uk/> (Accessed: July 16, 2006).
56. <http://www.pmwatch.org/pmw/index.asp> (Accessed: July 15, 2006).
57. <http://www.boycottisraeligoods.org/> (Accessed: July 16, 2006).
58. A few such sites serve as Palestinian portals <http://www. palestinemonitor.org/nueva_web/> (Accessed: July 16, 2006).
59. <http://www.natal.org.il/eng/eindex.aspx> (Accessed: July 21, 2006). see also: <http://www.navah.org.il/index.html> (Accessed: July 21, 2006); <http://www.onefamilyfund.org/default.aspx> (Accessed: July 21, 2006).
60. <http://www.israel-wat.com/parent_eng.htm> (Accessed: July 21, 2006); <http://www.forthem.up.co.il/> (Accessed: July 21, 2006).
61. <http://www.aipac.org/hamas/> (Accessed: July 21, 2006).
62. <http://www.israelatheart.org/> (Accessed: July 21, 2006); <http://www.bambili.com/> (Accessed: July 21, 2006); <http://rotter.net/israel/> (Accessed: July 21, 2006).
63. <http://www.all4israel.org/> (Accessed: July 21, 2006); <http:// www.pro-israel.org/> (Accessed: July 21, 2006); <http://www. projectonesoul.com/> (Accessed: July 21, 2006); <http://www. masada2000.org/> (Accessed: July 21, 2006); http://home.ca. inter.net/jason7770/humancost/report.html (Accessed: July 21, 2006).
64. <http://www.honestreporting.com/> (Accessed: July 21, 2006).

65. Chanan Naveh, *From the PC to the Global Arena.*
66. Christine Ogan, Filiz Çiçek, and Muzaffer Özakça, "Letters to Sarah: Analysis of email Responses to an Online Editorial," *New Media and Society,* vol. 7, no. 4 (2005). An example is an email written in April 2002 by the director of the company *Radix Israel* to a Danish business partner in protest of the latter's critique of Israel. This email was distributed throughout the world by Israelis and their supporters <http://hydepark.hevre.co.il/topicarc.asp?topic_id=104805> Accessed 25.3.2003.
67. <http://palestineblogs.com/> (Accessed: July 17, 2006).
68. <http://abuaardvark.typepad.com>, <http://bethlehemghetto. blogspot.com/>, <http://www.a-mother-from-gaza.blogspot. com/> (Accessed: July 16, 2006).
69. <http://lawrenceofcyberia.blogs.com/>, <http://angryarab. blogspot.com/>, <http://freckle.blogs.com/> (Accessed: July 16, 2006).
70. <http://angrywhitekid.blogs.com/weblog/> (Accessed: July 16, 2006).
71. <http://www.kicisrael.blogspot.com/> (Accessed: July 21, 2006); <http://members.cox.net/jenniewoolf/> (Accessed: July 21, 2006); <http://drybonesblog.blogspot.com/> (Accessed: July 21, 2006); <http://kiwijewpundit.blogspot.com/> (Accessed: July 21, 2006); <http://westbankblog.blogspot.com/>(Accessed: July 21, 2006); <http://www.jewishrefugees.blogspot.com/> (Accessed: July 21, 2006).
72. <http://www.securityfence.mod.gov.il/Pages/ENG/default.htm> (Accessed: July 21, 2006).
73. <http://www.mfa.gov.il/MFA/MFAArchive/2000_2009/2003/ 11/Saving+Lives-+Israel-s+Security+Fence.htm> (Accessed: July 21, 2006).
74. <http://www.aboutisrael.co.il/eng/site_intro.php?parent_id= 296> (Accessed: July 21, 2006); <http://www.hagader.com/ English/main.asp> (Accessed: July 21, 2006).
75. <http://www.openbethlehem.org/leave_your_message_on_the_ wall.asp> (Accessed: July 22, 20060).
76. <http://www.stopthewall.org/> (Accessed: July 17, 2006).
77. Richard Wilson, "Viral Marketing Techniques the Typical Business Website Can Deploy Now," *Web Marketing Today,* no. 71 (February 2000). <http://www.wilsonweb.com/wmt5/viral-deploy.htm> (Accessed: February 1, 2004); Michael Bloch, Viral Marketing & the Internet <http://www.tamingthebeast.net> (Accessed: February 1, 2004).
78. <http://umist.ac.uk/news/InquiryReport.pdf< (Accessed: December 25, 2002).
79. <http://www.ucdivest.org> (Accessed: December 12, 2002); <http://www.princetondivest.org> (Accessed: December 12, 2002);

<http://www.harvardmitdivest.org> (Accessed: December 12, 2002);
<http://www.petitiononline.com/mod_perl/signed.cgi?bin&251>
(Accessed: December 12, 2002); <http://www.pjpo.org> (Accessed:
December 12, 2002).

80. <http://www.mylinkspage.com/israel.html#ACA> (Accessed:
July 22, 2006); <http://www.monabaker.com/ontheboycott.htm>
(Accessed: July 22, 2006); <http://www.sue.be/pal/academic>
(Accessed: July 22, 2006); <http://www.pacbi.org> (Accessed:
July 22, 2006).

81. <http://www.anti-boycott-petition.org> (Accessed: December 25,
2002); <http://www.aaisc.net> (Accessed: December 25, 2002);
<http://euroisrael.huji.ac.il> (Accessed: December 25, 2002);
<http://www.notoboycottscience.net> (Accessed: December 25,
2002); <http://www.anti-boycott-petition.org> (Accessed:
December 25, 2002).

82. <http://nationalacademies.org/morenews/20060530.html>
(Accessed: August 25, 2002); <http://www.european-association.
org/> (Accessed: December 25, 2002); <http://contreleboycott.
free.fr/index.php3> (Accessed: December 25, 2002); <http://
www.princeton.edu/~aizenman/acci/IMUresolution.html>
(Accessed: December 25, 2002).

83. <http://www.allforpeace.org/> (Accessed: July 20, 2006).

84. <http://www.bitterlemons.org/index.html> (Accessed: July 16,
2006); <http://www.pij.org/> (Accessed: July 16, 2006).

85. <http://www.givathaviva.org.il/english/> (Accessed: July 16,
2006); <http://www.arikpeace.org/> (Accessed: July 16, 2006).

86. <http://www.seedsofpeace.org/site/PageServer> (Accessed: July 16,
2006).

87. Myriam Dunn, "The Cyberspace Dimension in Armed Conflict,"
p. 123; Ogan, Çiçek, and Özakça, "Letters to Sarah."

# CHAPTER 11

# New Palestinian Media and Democratization from Below

*Orayb Aref Najjar*

## INTRODUCTION

The fate of the newest song on the Jihad pop chart is indicative of the importance of new media in the Palestinian territories. Israeli soldiers tried to suppress a song praising Hasan Nasrallah, leader of Hezbollah of Lebanon,[1] after the Palestinian press reported that it was being played in coffee shops, taxis, at weddings, and as ring tones on cell phones. The Israeli army confiscated cassettes of the song from shops and checked for them in taxis "at checkpoints that sever the limbs of Palestinian regions and separate towns and villages from each other," as one writer put it.[2]

The description above sums up what one needs to know about new media in the West Bank: that technology is part of popular culture that spreads quickly despite physical barriers, that it is not just the elite who participate in its spread, that it is popular because it fulfills the population's needs, that it is a source of empowerment because it defies the Israeli occupation's physical restrictions on the movement of Palestinians in their own country; and finally, that Israelis fear new media because they understand there is a war over communication between them and Palestinians—a war that is played out daily in the occupied territories and in every medium of communication.

All those themes will be explored in this chapter that describes how and why Palestinian individuals and groups have resorted to the establishment of private radio and TV stations and to the use of the Internet for political communication more extensively than many other Arab countries. This chapter will trace the Palestinian attempts to use political communication from the poster to Internet radio. It will describe how cell phones and the Internet have extended the reach of Palestinians and broadened their horizons in politics, education, and human rights.

As Israel still occupies large parts of the Palestinian territory it occupied in 1967 and can and does enter the area at will, the story of Palestinian technology use is intimately related to their relations with Israel as an occupying power and is driven mostly by those relations.[3] Because European nations and the United States have a stake in Palestinian communication, this is also the story of the various political and religious actors who fund and try to influence Palestinian media decisions and content through direct aid or NGO funding.

This study will use Pierre Bourdieu's field theory, described below, to examine the different components of Palestinian communication. The study will further look at who is communicating, what is being communicated by different groups, and how those groups are funded. Finally, the chapter concludes with general observations on media use and with some predictions for the future of new Palestinian media.

## CONCEPTUAL FRAMEWORK

A field may be viewed as a microcosm that brings together the agents and institutions engaged in the production of whatever that particular field produces; for example, articles in the journalistic field, art in the artistic field. Members of a field both constitute it and are constituted by it. Professionals who share a field are constrained by the forces inscribed in it but are also able to act "in ways that are partially pre-constrained, but with a margin of freedom."[4] The essence of field theory in the social sciences is the explanation of regularities in individual action by using the position of an agent within a given field vis-à-vis other fields (e.g., the position of the journalistic field in relation to the political field).[5] "In analytic terms, a field may be defined as a network, or a configuration, of objective relations between positions."[6] Field theory provides perhaps the best defense against "media-centrism," helping situate journalism in its larger systemic environment. Against the fruitless question of whether the press is or is not "independent," research could help pinpoint the journalistic field's relative position vis-à-vis the range of other societal fields that compete to shape our vision of the social world.[7]

The journalistic field is important because it is seen as part of the field of power; that is, it tends to engage with powerful agents who possess high volumes of what Bourdieu calls "economic and cultural capital," both of which are important forms of power.[8] By economic capital, Bourdieu means money or assets that can be turned into money. Cultural capital includes educational credentials, technical expertise, general knowledge, verbal abilities, and artistic sensibilities. The social world is structured around the opposition between these two forms of power, with economic capital, on the whole, being more powerful.[9] Inside the journalistic field, economic capital is expressed via circulation, or advertising revenues, or audience ratings, whereas the "specific" cultural capital of the field takes the form of intelligent commentary, in-depth reporting,—the kind of journalistic practices rewarded each year by local and international journalistic prizes. Each field is thus structured around the opposition between the pole representing forces external to the field (primarily economic) and the "autonomous" pole representing the specific capital unique to that field (e.g., political or journalistic skills). Fields are arenas of struggle in which individuals and organizations compete to valorize those forms of capital that they possess.[10] Perhaps the most important quality of fields for this chapter is the interconvertability of capital. Since the structure of fields is characterized by the dynamic relationship between symbolic and economic assets, at any given moment some fields move closer to the economic end of the pole than do others; that is, the knowledge they produce is simply more convertible into material or political power than the products of other fields.[11]

Benson and Neveu suggest that in field theory, journalistic fields do *not* always reinforce the power status quo, but under certain conditions they may actually transform power relations in other fields.[12] Finally, Bourdieu's theory takes power dynamics seriously, both within and among fields. As a result, field analysis places greater emphasis on competition and distinctions *among journalists.*[13]

In this chapter, I try to pinpoint Palestinian media's position from various fields of economic and political power, both local and international. I also discuss how the economic field encroaches on the symbolic journalistic field. Finally, while doing so, I pay attention to how competition has affected the development of the media.

## FROM THE POSTER TO THE INTERNET

Palestinians understood the importance of visual communication and used it to introduce their cause to the outside world. Artist Dan Walsh got interested in posters about Palestine when he first encountered them in 1974 while working for the Peace Corps in Morocco. Walsh has since collected 3,500 posters with a Palestinian theme.[14] A man working for the American Israel Public Affairs Committee (AIPAC), a pro-Israel lobby, told Walsh as he was buying a copy of a particularly effective pro-Palestinian poster, "I want you to know that you and your posters have utterly destroyed 35 years of really sophisticated anti-Palestinian propaganda work on our part."[15] So while the PLO was making headway in its information campaigns in Europe and Asia, including those via posters, Palestinians under occupation had a harder time, both because borders separated them from the outside world and because the effective technology they used at a later date had not yet been invented.

## THE CULTURAL ISOLATION OF THE WEST BANK AND GAZA: THE EARLY YEARS

For 23 years starting in 1967, Palestinians under Israeli occupation could not phone or mail anyone in the Arab world because there was no phone connection between Israel and Arab countries. Even nearby Jordan was out of reach by phone. Political communication in the form of newspapers, magazines, and books from the Arab world was not available to them. The various Israeli military governors of the West Bank controlled who got a driver's license or phone connection, and who got to keep them. The Israeli authorities forbade the use of the telex machine from 1983 until 1986.[16] A June 1989 Israeli military order prohibited the use of phone lines to send faxes from the occupied territories in an effort to stop Palestinian contacts with the outside world during the first Uprising.[17]

Obtaining a phone connection from the Israeli company Bezeq, Palestinians' only choice, had a seven-year average waiting period. The Israeli telecommunications infrastructure was planned to make it possible for Israel to control all facets of communication by rerouting them through Israeli cities. The Oslo Accords between Israel and the Palestinian Liberation Organization (PLO) in 1993 canceled the prohibition on sending faxes and email and gave the Palestinians partial control over telephone lines in areas A and B. The next segment provides the regulatory context in which political communication operates, discusses the rise of the Internet, and then charts the growth of online news agencies that united existing radio and TV stations. The next segment discusses the advent of Internet radio, produced in Jordan, but broadcast from private stations in the West Bank, and then speculates on whether Palestinians will continue to enjoy government-free media.

## The Internet

The Internet proved to be the Palestinians' savior, although it took a while before Israel allowed Palestinians access to it. Israel connected to Education and Research Network (EARN), the European counterpart to Because It's Time Network (BITNET), in 1984, but the first Internet connection did not take place until 1990. The Inter-University Computer Center (IUCC) became the first provider of Internet services via a 9.6 Kbps line to the United States. Commercial ISPs began operation in 1992.[18] The Palestinian telecommunications sector was established in 1995 and privatized in 1996 when the Palestinian National Authority (PNA) awarded an exclusive license to the Palestine Telecommunications Company (PALTEL) to operate and develop telecommunications services in the West Bank and Gaza starting in January 1997. In 1998, PALTEL established the Palestine Cellular Communications, Ltd. JAWWAL. PALTEL provides a full range of services (telephone lines, payphones, digital leased lines, paging, and internet access).

When PALTEL was established, the telecom infrastructure of the West Bank and Gaza Strip had only 77,000 telephone lines for a population of 2.5 million and a waiting list of about 200,000. PALTEL has benefited from this pent up demand as demonstrated by the strong growth in subscriber numbers to 327,000 fixed phones in 2005 and 750,000 mobile-phone accounts.[19] JAWWAL cellular service has more than 300,000 subscribers. The other 400,000 are using cellular services provided by Israeli companies.[20]

Just when the Internet was beginning to take off, Israel at first denied email use to Palestinians of the West Bank and Gaza, with the exception of Jerusalem. Palestinians who lived in East Jerusalem, however, could hook up through Israeli service providers. To overcome the prohibition against hooking up to the Internet from Ramallah, PALNET used its ingenuity and leased a 128 KB line from Netvision to the Sami Ramis Arab neighborhood of East Jerusalem, creating a wireless network using microwave transmissions that linked all West Bank and Gaza Strip cities through digital microwave systems.[21] Internet and intensive use of email followed, starting with universities and research centers and then trickling down to refugee camps in several innovative projects. Scholars could now contact their counterparts for research as well as political support.[22]

The Palestinian Ministry of Telecommunications and Information Technology is responsible for regulating and monitoring the telecommunications sector. Some critics charge, however, that the ministry has given PALTEL too free a hand in developing the telecommunications sector. Sam Bahour, Palestinian-American businessman involved in the privatization of the telecom sector in Palestine and currently a business and technology consultant, charges that the ministry "is dangerously putting the sector in the hands of corporate interests."[23] Bahour decries the fact that the Internet market was a competitive one until January 1, 2006, when PALTEL bought out the competition and introduced subscription-free Internet via a monopolistic model.[24] On the other hand, he notes that Israeli companies also capitalize on the inability of the PNA to regulate its market by flooding the Palestinian marketplace with prepaid scratch cards to market their services. Faced with four operators working without licenses (illegal under Israeli-Palestinian agreements), the Palestinian operator competes against tremendous odds.[25]

Israeli-Palestinian adversarial relations initially delayed Palestinian use of the Internet but later spurred Palestinians to speed up their use of technology to break free of the constraints imposed on them by Israeli checkpoints and town closures.[26] Sam Bahour says that, "Given Israeli occupation constraints, the Internet has been used as a tool of necessity and not a tool of luxury in order to maintain connectivity amongst each other and with the outside world. Thus, this real life need has lowered our learning curve and increased internet penetration in the market place."[27] The example of Birzeit University's Ritaj portal is a case in point. Developed initially to increase the efficiency of admissions and registration, the portal was turned into a way to bypass the Ramallah-Birzeit road checkpoints that often forced the university to cancel classes. During the almost-one-month Israeli curfew, university technicians turned the house of one of the programmers into a primary work station. By the time the curfew was over, the system was able to provide materials online to Birzeit students and to facilitate their contacts with their professors. On discovering that 30 percent of students were not computer literate, the university set up computer literacy courses to enable all students to access the system.[28] A number of courses are now available online. Art S-p-a-c-e identifies itself as "an alternative online gallery for the visual arts in Palestine. The gallery will host a wide variety of exhibitions of Palestinian and international art. It will also support the creation of experimental and innovative internet art through an artist residency program."[29]

## THE INTERNET AND HUMAN RIGHTS

Because Israel prevented attempts at forming countrywide leadership in the West Bank and Gaza in the 1970s and 1980s, it inadvertently strengthened Palestinian nongovernmental organizations that took over the information-delivery functions of government. Furthermore, says Ali Jarbawi, director general of the Palestinian Independent Commission for Citizens' Rights, "Vocal human rights groups are unabashed in their criticism not only of any human rights abuses by Israel, but PNA abuses of power as well."[30] The PNGO network (pngo@palnet.com) brings together on the Internet the resources of 92 groups who provide information via the Internet to the international press, international NGOs, and diplomatic missions. One member, the Health, Development, Information and Policy Institute (HDIP), established in 1989, keeps track of the latest statistics on Palestinian dead, wounded, and maimed and makes them available to governments and the press.[31]

The Internet also allowed diaspora Palestinians to form communities online by forming Ramallah Online (www.ramallahonline.com), Jerusalemites (www.jerusalemites.org), and Jaffa (www.palestineremembered.com/Jaffa/Jaffa/index.html). The Nakba Oral History Video Podcast provides 195 oral history interviews with refugees.[32] Maps of Palestine during different historical periods are displayed on several Web sites, as are maps of Israeli settlements.[33] The Palestinian Christian Community promotes liberation theology and peaceful resistance to occupation on their Web sites.[34] Diaspora Palestinians have their favorite Web site Electronic *Intifada*, dubbed as "the Weapon of Mass Instruction" (http://electronicintifada.net/new.shtml).

Even though the Internet frees Palestinian journalists by allowing them to occupy jobs they would not otherwise have, jobs such as being the online correspondents for Al Jazeera, the continued Israeli occupation means that Internet journalists can be picked up by Israeli police—just like they would regular journalists, only this time, with their hard drives.[35]

Internet penetration in the West Bank and Gaza is 4.9 percent; higher than Syria's 4.2 percent, or Yemen's 1.1 percent, but not as high as Jordan's 22.8 percent, the United Arab Emirate's 35.8 percent, or Israel's 45 percent.[36] Palestinian critics contended that the development of PALTEL as a monopoly and the high cost of hookup constitute a burden in a country with a large refugee population. This disadvantage, however, is being lessened by universities. Under the auspices of Birzeit University (BZU), a Palestinian IT Special Interest Group (ITSIG), which consists of professionals in the IT field, was formed in 1997 to influence and promote the development of progressive IT policies in Palestine.[37] Across Borders Project (ABP) was launched in February 1999, under the umbrella of Birzeit University, with Oxfam funding to enhance educational and vocational training opportunities for camp residents and to link Palestinian refugees spread around the world. At present, eight computer centers are operational, two in Gaza, four in the West Bank, and two in Lebanon.[38] It is not the number of subscribers that make IT in Palestine unique, but the creative ways in which the Internet was handled.

## THE POLITICS OF FUNDING THE PALESTINIAN MEDIA

Perhaps the most relevant attribute in field theory for this study is the concept of the interconvertability of capital. The journalistic field tends to engage with powerful agents who possess high volumes of what Bourdieu calls "economic and cultural capital," both of which are important forms of power.[39] Since the structure of fields is characterized by the dynamic relationship between symbolic and economic assets, at any given moment, some fields move closer than others to the economic end of the pole. In other cases, interactions may be able to convert economic capital into political capital. Bourdieu viewed with alarm the commercialization of the French press, assuming that proximity to the economic field corrupts media content. Similarly, some Palestinians are worried that the demands of the economic and political fields are encroaching on Palestinian research practices and media funding.

Sociologist Salim Tamari notes that substantial amounts of money are available to people researching the hot topics of "Islamic fundamentalism, women's movements, Arab-Jewish dialogue, economic development and health." Tamari describes the rise of an entire network of "service centers" that includes "data centers, academic escort agencies, car rentals, and even research 'stores' (*dakkakin*) that market scholarship." The division of labor assigns Palestinian consultants the role of the proletariat, allowing "visiting scholars" to dictate the terms in which Palestinian discourse is packaged and presented.[40]

To a certain extent, the same is true of media funding by international sources. Foreign countries or NGOs fund hot topics such as democratization, election coverage, human rights, women's rights, children's rights, and above all, Israeli-Palestinian cooperation. Left to their own devices, most Palestinian news outlets would prioritize news about land confiscation and house demolition by Israel and reports of death and injury. International funding agencies, however, are interested in decreasing tension in the occupied territories short of ending the conflict. Funding goes to what one may call politico-developmental coverage (election reporting, women's rights, and children's rights) and peace-is-possible good news. Thus, Palestinians who accept Western funding walk a fine line between transmitting what they may want to communicate and what international agencies fund. The American government, the European Union, Canada, and Christian ecumenical groups are deeply involved in funding the media.

One example of funded projects, in addition to Ma'an News Agency (Ma'an means "together" in Arabic) and Palestine News Network (PNN), is Sesame Street (produced in Jordan, the West Bank, and Israel) in which Arab and Jewish puppets cooperate with each other. The project has eight underwriters, all American except for the European Union and the Canadian Kahanoff Foundation. The cost of producing 26 shows is US$7 million from each of the three partners.[41] Unfortunately, this cooperation did not do one of the three partners, al-Quds Educational TV, any good. When Israelis reoccupied Ramallah in 2002, they threw the station's TV equipment down from the fourth-floor balcony when they destroyed all the TV and radio stations they occupied.[42]

Nevertheless, funding opportunities have enabled Palestinians who are genuinely interested in developing their capabilities to buy equipment, attend training courses, and learn new skills. One recipient of funding that has benefited the community is Birzeit University's Internet radio station, OUTLOUD. The station, which was launched in 1998, is run by students for two hours every day. Some of the courses and the 92.1 MHz FM transmission are financed by the German Heinrich Boll Foundation, while the Internet section is broadcast from a studio financed by the Finnish government and Finnish Radio. The Finns trained student technicians.[43] Funding has encouraged coverage of issues some stations may not have placed at the top of their priorities (e.g., the handicapped). Thus, funding practices illustrate the convertibility of economic capital into technical expertise and political capital. On the other hand, economic assets of richer countries are converted into symbolic capital that becomes legitimate information when transmitted by Palestinian stations. But, says Ghada Karmi, such funding helps the Israeli occupier when Western donors relieve Israel of its obligations under international law to deliver services to the occupied. "Instead," she says, "international aid has rendered the occupation cost-free. It has even enriched Israel's economy . . . for every dollar produced in the occupied territories, 45 cents flows back to Israel."[44]

Conditional funding gives other nations the right to monitor Palestinian broadcasting. Israelis monitor the official Palestinian radio and TV stations and the American Israel Public Affairs Committee lobbies American legislators to control the content of Palestinian media by withholding funding from them.[45] Thus, negative monitoring involves keeping track of what Palestinians broadcast about Israel, but not of what independent radio stations run by Israeli settlers in the occupied territories broadcast about Palestinians.

Palestinians welcome the type of monitoring instituted by the European Union to ensure that candidates running for the January 2005 Palestinian elections are given equal time by broadcasters. The media monitoring is conducted by a team of Palestinian media monitors trained with the methodology normally used by the EU Election Observation Missions to measure the time, space, and tone devoted to the political parties, candidates, members of PLO, and PNA.[46]

## FRAGMENTATION AND CONSOLIDATION

The presence of a weak PNA, occupied by Israel and dependent for money on Western donors and expatriate capitalists, has both negative and positive consequences for the Palestinian media. Outside funding has removed communication from government bureaucracy and allowed it to develop quickly in a creative manner. As Benson and Neveu point out, the journalistic fields do *not* always reinforce the power status quo but may under certain conditions actually transform power relations in other fields. In this case, relations have been transformed in that the impetus for change has fallen on the private media.

An international foundation gave Daoud Kuttab a grant to create a Web site called Arabic Media Internet Network (AMIN)—www.amin.org—in 1996. He explained that,

> In the Arab world, the Arabic press is free and open on all Arab issues except the news of its own country. . . . With the Internet, my idea was to put all these Arabic newspapers on one site, so if you're a Palestinian or a Jordanian, you can read news about you just by looking at the Web site of Syrian or Iraqi or Gulf newspapers, and vice versa.[47]

AMIN also publishes articles by independent writers and cartoonists and provides links to the international press, radio, and TV.

Benson and Neveu note that Bourdieu's field theory places greater emphasis on competition and distinctions among *journalists*. It was competition with Israeli journalists over who has the right to tell the Palestinian story that spurred the development of independent Palestinian media. Kuttab got interested in training young Palestinians as journalists at the beginning of the *Intifada* (Uprising) when he saw foreign producers covering the West Bank and Gaza with Israeli camera people. He said, "I always commented that these young Israelis were shooting us with a camera 11 months a year. And because they have to do one month service in the army, in the twelfth month they come and shoot us with real guns." So he began to train 50 young Palestinian journalists who are now successfully working for the local as well as the international media.[48]

Thanks to Kuttab and others, most foreign news crews now employ Palestinian camera technicians. Satellite stations have also tapped Palestinian talent. Today, almost all of the West Bank and Gaza correspondents for major Arab satellite networks such as Al Jazeera, Abu-Dhabi, and al-Arabiyya are Palestinian, as are some on-air talent. Out of the 22 awards made to individuals and publishers in 2001, ten were awarded to women, five of them Palestinian. Four of the winners were working for Arab satellite television, the fifth, Omayya Juha, is the only female cartoonist in the Arab world. Juha publishes her cartoons in al-Quds daily newspaper in Jerusalem,[49] but the Internet gives her an edge. On her Web site, she publishes the cartoons Israelis censor.

The Internet has allowed Palestinians to form alliances with technophiles all over the world.[50] One can trace over the Internet the excitement generated by Daoud Kuttab as weblogs report on his news and invite him to speak at various universities such as the Berkman Center of Harvard Law School. Ethan Zuckerman opines, "I have seen the future of radio, and it is AmmanNet," in reference to the radio station Kuttab had established in 2000.[51] Bloggers like the fact that Kuttab hired young reporters who use the Internet, supplied eight of them with mini–disc recorders and computer workstations, and trained them to become professional reporters. The young staff transformed coverage of the Jordanian parliament by archiving debates, transcribing interviews, and publishing voting records. Kuttab is extending radio to high schools.

Private radio stations were banned in Jordan prior to the introduction of the Audiovisual Media Law and the Audiovisual Commission in 2002. The law eliminated public sector domination of the radio and TV sector, opening the door for private entrepreneurs such as Kuttab, who got UNESCO and the Greater Amman Municipality to sponsor the Internet radio AmmanNet. Kuttab, a Palestinian, married a woman who lives in Jordan and found frequent commuting difficult, so he started AmmanNet. His West Bank connections, however, allowed him to arrange for those programs to be transmitted on

Palestinian FM terrestrial radio stations that are heard in Jordan.[52] This type of innovative thinking enabled Kuttab "to do something illegal—radio broadcasting—in a legal manner—Internet," before he got a license that allowed him to broadcast on FM in Jordan.

AmmanNet has a section called Palestine News and a program called *Eye on the Media*, which critiques media performance in Jordan, Palestine, Egypt, and Lebanon.[53] In July 2005, AmmanNet began broadcasting to the residents of Amman on 92.4 FM.[54] The station monitors Jordanian parliamentary activities through a weekly FM radio program, regular news reports, and updates to its Web site, all of which profile members of parliament and their voting records.[55]

## THE DEVELOPMENT AND CONSOLIDATION OF PRIVATE TV STATIONS

When Yasser Arafat entered the West Bank and Gaza on July 1, 1995, he brought with him people who had worked for various PLO radio stations around the Arab world.[56] In contrast, Palestinians in the West Bank and Gaza had no experience with TV. The Palestinian Broadcasting Corporation (PBC) was established in 1994 with financial backing from the European Union, France, Germany, and other donors.[57] Even though most funding was awarded to the Palestinian government, some was given to private institutions. The Ford Foundation, the Open Society Institute of George Soros, and the Palestinian Welfare Association funded al-Quds Institute for Modern Media, modeled on America's Public Broadcasting Service (PBS).[58] So despite the presence of the government-run PBC, the real impact on Palestinian media practices came from private TV and radio, literally "broadcasting from below."

Starting in 1994, many stations were established in the north and south of the country in areas that were underserved by the Palestinian print press because checkpoints made distribution difficult and subscriptions impossible.[59] No private TV stations operated in Gaza in those early years, in contrast to the West Bank, where 22 TV and 11 private radio stations were operating by 2000.[60] This number is unique in the Arab world. Only Lebanon at that time allowed independent broadcasting, even though it restricted the number of stations allowed. Jordan and Egypt have only recently allowed independent broadcasting and most of these new stations are broadcasting entertainment.[61] Several Palestinian citizens who had never worked in TV established radio or TV stations.[62] Many of these private stations were small "mom and pop" operations located in apartments and sometimes run by husband-wife teams. Later, those stations became the backbone of independent TV networks.

The Palestinian Ministry of Information has given permits to 32 local TV and 38 local radio stations over the decade, most in the West Bank. Hamas lagged in establishing radio and TV stations because permission for them was hard to obtain from the Israelis as well as from the ruling party, Fateh. There is only one local Hamas TV station operating in Gaza, Al-Aqsa Radio is owned by Hamas, al-Quds (Jerusalem) Radio by Islamic Jihad, Al Shabab (Youth) Radio by Fateh, and Alwan (Colors) Radio by a security service member and run by a security officer of the same service.[63] At present, there are 20 Palestinian radio stations, 19 newspapers and 33 TV stations, according to the Palestinian Ministry of Information.[64]

The PNA engaged in a type of censorship that prevented independent radio stations from presenting views that disagreed with political positions taken by the government on Iraq.[65] Political censorship was also imposed on people who disagreed with the conduct of peace negotiations with Israel. The American and Israeli governments pressured Palestinian officials to curb anti-Israeli sentiments in the press. President Yasser Arafat did not hesitate to close stations that did not see eye to eye with his policies toward Israel and the United States or Iraq.[66] He has also allowed the imprisonment of journalists, including Daoud Kuttab for running, live, Legislative Council deliberations about corruption.[67]

Calls for controlling unregulated growth of independent stations came, in part, from the more established independent broadcasters. In two meetings in 2000 that the Ministry of Information arranged for the broadcasters to examine the draft of the new audiovisual law, broadcasters charged that poorly run stations gave broadcasting a bad name. Despite the meeting, nothing was done because of the 2000 Uprising.

There were advantages to the delay. Radio and TV companies were free to experiment and develop themselves according to private communication models. Furthermore, internal pressure by progressive Palestinians, coupled with international funding, encouraged the Palestinian government to make the audiovisual law now being finalized compliant with international norms for broadcasting through technical assistance and comment.[68] The pressure to reform the stations that were too poor to spend money on reporting led to the consolidation of several broadcast stations, strengthening the profession.

Ma'an Network established in 2002 has brought together nine independent TV stations and production studios located in the major cities of the West Bank and Gaza.[69] Ma'an News Agency, which began operating in December 2004 online, publishes up-to-the-minute news in Arabic, English, and Hebrew and supplies news and photos free of charge to local, regional, and international readers and media professionals. The agency is one of the main projects of the Ma'an Network, a nongovernmental organization that says it aims "to improve local Palestinian media production." On its Web site (www. maannews.net), it states its goals as being

> dedicated to promoting understanding of the Palestinian situation by strengthening cooperation between local and international media. The network shares a vision of fomenting democracy and freedom of thought and ideas in Palestine. It uses both technical and academic expertise in achieving these goals as it strives towards sustainable development and human rights for the Palestinian people.

The station may well be attempting to do all of that, but this language that it uses to describe its goals suggests foreign funding. The network receives financial support from the Netherlands and Denmark.[70] The funding allows the stations to function at a professional level, something small independent stations cannot afford.

PNN is similar to Ma'an and attempts to network local radio stations and turn the content into a kind of a wire service. The news PNN carries, however, has the mark of the organization that funds it, the Holy Land Trust, and pays special attention to nonviolence news. The PNN was established in 2002 when it appeared on the World Wide Web for the first time. In 2003, the Holy Land Trust took PNN under its wing, encouraging it to produce an English-language site and giving it a new design. Later, French and Hebrew pages were added to the site with both Spanish and German sites expected to be launched later. PNN simultaneously broadcasts four news bulletins over thirteen local Palestinian radio stations in the West Bank and Gaza via satellite and on PNN's Web site. PNN has also begun broadcasting its tickertape on eight local television channels in the West Bank and expects to increase the number of participant channels to twelve. It has begun sending SMS breaking news via mobile phones in Jordan and plans to extend this service to other Arab countries. The Network's TV production center was officially opened in early 2005.[71] PNN is also negotiating with the International Committee of Local Radio so that the network's news bulletins can be broadcast over several European radio stations."[72]

## THE STRUGGLE OVER PALESTINIAN
## BROADCASTING

A number of people and countries are attempting to influence Palestinian communication. A comparison between PNN and Fateh news headlines online reveals differences in emphasis between organizations that are funded by outside sources and those that are not. On August 25, 2006, for instance, Fateh highlighted the misdeeds of the occupation and resistance to it, while PNN ran more developmental items. Furthermore, the English version, which has a non-Arab editor, ran a headline that read, "Palestinians in Al Khader Village nonviolently resist the Israeli Wall, despite violent response," and placed it in a section called "Nonviolent Resistance." In Arabic, the same item ran under a section called "Culture," and it read, "With foreign participation: Mass March in Al Khader against the wall met by teargas." PNN included a feature about Palestinian children "functioning beyond stereotype" and putting on plays in their tour to France, instead of being depicted only as throwing stones. PNN also has an item on the Council of Tribes attempting to ban the firing of weapons in celebrations, and an account of a prisoners' strike. The only headline PNN published on Fateh deals with its distributing school bags. In contrast, Fateh's Center of Information and Communication's news on the same day has an item noting that "The most well-known leader of Fateh, Imad Maghniyyeh, leads the Islamic resistance in the South of Lebanon." Another Fateh headline provides statistics: "Since the Beginning of the *Intifada* and until June 2006, 4,464 martyrs fell and 47,440 were wounded and more than 9,800 are imprisoned."[73]

As Foucault has noted, power may be thought of in terms of strategy and tactics, and where there is power there is resistance.[74] One detects a bit of rebellion against external funding sources in the publication of items that do not fit into the let's-all-get-along category, such as this item in PNN, "The Popular Front for the Liberation of Palestine in Megiddo [prison] salutes its secretary general, the martyr, Abu Ali Mustafa [assassinated by Israel]."[75]

Israelis have not confined themselves to closing stations, but have destroyed them more than once. Israel attacked the transmission towers and other technical facilities used by the Voice of Palestine in Ramallah in October 2000. In November, Israeli helicopters bombed the offices of Palestine TV in Gaza.[76] Israel destroyed the Voice of Palestine radio station broadcasting headquarters in the West Bank city of Ramallah, then toppled a ninety-foot radio and television tower and destroyed the station's transmitter, which is also used by Palestine

TV. In an act of defiance, the Voice of Palestine went back on the air immediately, using one of the frequencies of an independent radio station in Ramallah. Israel has repeatedly accused Palestinian radio and television of inciting Palestinians to violence against Israel—a charge that Palestinians have rejected. In 2002, Israel reoccupied the city of Ramallah, took over seven stations, broadcast pornography out of them before destroying their equipment.[77] Most of the destroyed stations have since bought new equipment and resumed operation after an outpouring of support from various quarters.

## CONCLUSION

Rather than attempting to determine whether or not the press is "independent," I have distinguished the private news media's stance from the official positions of the Palestinian and Israeli governments, as well as their relative positions vis-à-vis international donors interested in Palestinian communication. All are competing to shape the Palestinian vision of the social world.

This chapter plotted the position of the Palestinian field of broadcasting and Internet development vis-à-vis the economic and political fields of the donor countries and agencies, the Palestinian expatriate community, as well as Palestinian academics. Even though donors have funded both official and independent media, the independent media have flourished most through experimentation. There is no doubt that the economic field has determined, through funding, the type of communication that is desirable. On the other hand, the nature of power and resistance suggest that even funded stations manage to slip in items of interest to them. As Benson tells us, professionals who share a field are constrained by the forces inscribed in it but are also able to act "in ways that are partially preconstrained, but with a margin of freedom." [78]

Palestinian independent radio and TV stations gave themselves a wide margin of freedom and managed to take advantage of the forums they had built. And because fields are arenas of struggle in which individuals and organizations compete to valorize those forms of capital that they possess,[79] Palestinian journalists have attempted to parley their symbolic capital and valorize it, even when they depend on international aid for survival. The result was the rise of vibrant radio and TV "from below" in a region where government broadcasting is the norm.

The Palestinian government has mostly kept out of the way of the development of independent media, in part because it wanted to reserve the most substantial portion of the broadcast spectrum in case

Israel bombed government TV. As a result, Palestinians have more independent radio and TV stations than any country in the Arab world. The involvement of Palestinian expatriates in the development of Internet policy under a weak regulatory body tilted Internet provision toward the capitalist model, but the involvement of educational institutions in Internet policy ensured that the weakest in society, the refugees, get a share of the Internet through programs designed to reach them. So the absence of the Palestinian state, itself under Israeli occupation, strengthened independent radio and TV that was established "from below" in response to the needs of the north and south of the country, areas not served well by the daily press.

There is no indication that the Palestinian government, even a Hamas one, is about to reverse the independent development of the media, even though Hamas's share of media real estate is small. Thus, in an interesting twist for the Arab world, the main danger to the media is not from the Palestinian government, but from lawless armed Palestinian groups from all political factions that threaten journalists who disagree with them.[80]

So, the absence of a strong state has helped the rise of broadcasting, but its inability to deal with lawlessness is not serving the media well. If Palestinians manage to reconcile their warring factions while keeping the Israeli war machine at bay, their broadcasting promises to be the most lively and diverse in the Middle East.

## NOTES

1. To audio of the song available online at: <http://www.underhouse.com/michael/song.wma>
2. "The Israeli Wages War against the Song 'Salute, Eagle of Lebanon . . . Salute, Hassan Nasrallah,'" *al-Quds al-Arabi* (London), August 17, 2006, available online at: <http://207.150.170.110/look/amin/press.htm>
3. Area A—full control of the PNA; Area B—Palestinian civil control, Israeli military control; Area C—full Israeli control. Until a final status accord was established, West Bank and Gaza would be divided into three zones: Area A—full control of the PNA; Area B—Palestinian civil control, Israeli military control; Area C—full Israeli control. *Israel-Palestine Liberation Organization Agreement: 1993. The Avalon Project at Yale Law School Text*, available online at <http://www.yale.edu/lawweb/avalon/mideast/isrplo.htm>
4. Rodney Benson, "Mapping field variation: Journalism in France and the United States," in R. Benson and E. Neveu (eds.), *Bourdieu and the Journalistic Field* (Cambridge: Polity Press, 2005), p. 30.

5. John Levi Martin, "What Is Field Theory?" *American Sociological Review*, vol. 109, no. 1 (July, 2003): 1–49.
6. Hallin, Daniel and Paolo Mancini, *Comparing Media Systems: Three Models of Media and Politics* (Cambridge: Cambridge University Press, 2004).
7. Benson and Neveu, *Bourdieu and the Journalistic Field*, 19; Benson, 204, 276.
8. R. Benson, "Mapping Field Variation: Journalism in France and the United States," in R. Benson and E. Neveu (eds.), *Bourdieu and the Journalistic Field* (Cambridge: Polity Press, 2005), p. 33.
9. R. Benson, "Mapping field variation: Journalism in France and the United States," in R. Benson and E. Neveu (eds.), *Bourdieu and the Journalistic Field* (Cambridge: Polity Press, 2005), p. 55.
10. Benson and Eric Neveu, *Bourdieu and the Journalistic Field*, 4
11. Timothy Lenoir, *Instituting Science: The Cultural Production of Scientific Disciplines* (Stanford, CA: Stanford University Press, 1997)
12. Benson and Neveu, *Bourdieu and the Journalistic Field*, 9.
13. Ibid., p. 18.
14. "Revolution until Victory," Antonym/Synonym: The Poster Art of the Palestinian Israeli Conflict, Liberation Graphics, 2003, available online at: <http://www.liberationgraphics.com/ppp/Revolution_until_victory.html>
15. A rotating exhibit of Palestine posters may be viewed at "Advancing Popular Democracy, Downwards and Outwards, via the Arts," available online at: <www.liberationgraphics.com>
16. Orayb Najjar, Palestine Press Service, in Derek Jones (ed.), *Censorship: A World Encyclopedia* (London: Fitzborn Dearborn Publishers, 2001), pp. 1801–1802.
17. Nigel Parry, "The Past and Future of Information Technology in Palestine: An introduction for the Palestinian NGO community," paper presented at the International NGO Meeting/European NGO Symposium on the Question of Palestine at the United Nations, August 25–28, 1997), available online at: <http://www.nigelparry.com/mideastinternet/unitednationspaper.html>
18. Phillip Ein-Dor, Seymour E. Goodman, and Peter Wolcott, "From *Via Maris* to Electronic Highway: The Internet in Canaan," *Communications of the ACM*, vol. 43, no. 7 (July 2000): 19–23, available online at: <http://mosaic.unomaha.edu/Canaan_2000.pdf#search=%22The%20growth%20of%20the%20Palestinian%20internet%22>
19. Iain Guest, "The Communications Revolution in the Palestinian Territories," available online at: <http://www.odihpn.org/report.asp?ID=2674>
20. Assad Barsoum, "Market Brief for West Bank and Gaza. United States of America Department of Commerce," available online at: <http://www.buyusa.gov/easternmed/ictmarketbriefs_nov04.html>

21. About PALTEL, available online at: <http://www.padico.com/paltel.htm>

22. "Letter of Support: A Copy of the Letter Written in Support of the Right to Education at Birzeit University," *The Guardian*, July 30, 2002, available online at: <http://education.guardian.co.uk/higher/worldwide/story/0,,765649,00.html>

23. Sam Bahour. "Telecommunications in Palestine: Self-Inflicted Paralysis." *Palestine Business Report*. June 21, 2005, available online at: <http://64.233.167.104/search?q=cache:rn3CcV_1KSMJ: www.epcc-jerusalem.org/report/pointofview.htm+Sam+Bahour+PALTEL+monopoly&hl=en&gl=us&ct=clnk&cd=1>

24. E-mail from Sam Bahour, August 31, 2006.

25. Sam Bahour. "De-development Israeli style," *Dissident Voice*. August 9, 2004, available online at: <www.dissidentvoice.org>

26. For a map of Israeli checkpoints at one point in time, see <http://www.poica.org/editor/case_studies/Checkpoints-north.jpg>

27. E-mail from Sam Bahour, August 31, 2006.

28. "Ritaj," The Great Portal Opens Access to Birzeit University, Birzeit University Web site, and October 15, 2002, available online at: <http://www.birzeit.edu/news/news-d?cnews_id=5231>

29. Introduction to Palestinian Art-(Online Course) access available only for BZU students via Ritaj, available online at: <http://virtualgallery.birzeit.edu/education_university_course>

30. Betsy Hiel, "Democracy's Challenges are Daunting, Played out Against the Backdrop of the Limping Peace Process," Reprinted from the *Toledo Blade* (Fall 1998), available online at: <http://www.journalismfellowships.org/stories/westbank/westbank_democracy.htm>

31. The Palestinian NGO Network (PNGO) Work Strategies, available online at: <http://www.pngo.net/pngo.htm>

32. Salim Tamari. Treacherous Memories: Electronic Return to Jaffa. Posted on November 2, 2000, available online at: <http://www.palestineremembered.com/Jaffa/Jaffa/Story152.html>

33. Palestine Maps, available online at: <http://www.palestineremembered.com/Maps/index.html>

34. Sabeel Ecumenical Liberation Theology Center, East Jerusalem, available online at: <http://www.sabeel.org/>

35. Reporters without Borders, "Al-Jazeera Website Reporter Freed for Lack of Evidence After Six Months," available online at: <http://www.rsf.org/article.php3?id_article=15804>

36. Internet World Stats, available online at: <http://www.internet-worldstats.com/middle.htm> (Accessed: August 22, 2006).

37. About Us. Ma'an News Agency, available online at: <http://www.maannews.net/en/index.php?opr=Content&Do=Aboutus>

38. Across Borders Portal, available online at: <http://www.acrossborders.ps/PORTAL/about.cfm>

39. Rodney Benson, "Mapping field variation: Journalism in France and the United States," in R. Benson and E. Neveu (eds.), *Bourdieu and the Journalistic Field* (Cambridge: Polity Press, 2005), p. 33.

40. Salim Tamari, "Tourists with Agendas," *Middle East Report*, vol. 25, no. 5 (September/October 1995), available online at: <http://www.hartford-hwp.com/archives/51/061.html>

41. Julie Salamon. "Israeli-Palestinian Battles Intrude on Sesame Street," *New York Times*, July 30, 2002, available online at: <http://www.toughpigs.com/extrasesamebattles.htm>

42. Daoud Kuttab, "Forced off the Air in Ramallah," *New York Times*, April 6, 2002. Section A, Page 15, Column 1,

43. BZU Outloud, available online at: <http://home.birzeit.edu/outloud/>

44. Ghada Karmi, with no Palestinian state in sight, aid becomes an adjunct to occupation. *The Guardian*. December 31, 2005. available online at: <http://www.guardian.co.uk/comment/story/0,3604, 1675672, 00.html>

45. Rima Merriman, "Rewriting H.R. 4681 so that it Actually Produces Peace" *The Electronic Intifada*, March 24, 2006, available online at: <http://electronicintifada.net/v2/article4587.shtml>

46. Osservatorio di Pavia Media Research. Media in Palestine December 2005, available online at: <http://www.osservatorio.it/interna.php?section=mediazoom&m=v&pos=0&idsection=000015>

47. "Palestine, Live, Unedited and Free, Index on Censorship," May 28, 1998. This talk, entitled *Challenges for Freedom of Expression in the Middle East*, was the keynote address at the IFEX Conference held at UNESCO, Paris and delivered on May 14, 1998.

48. Daoud Kuttab, "Palestine, Live, Unedited and Free," Index on Censorship May 28, 1998. This talk, titled *Challenges for Freedom of Expression in the Middle East*, was the keynote address at the IFEX Conference held at UNESCO, Paris and delivered on May 14, 1998.

49. Benaz Batrawi, "Echoes, Gender and Media Challenges in Palestine," in Naomi Sakr (ed.), *Women and Media in the Middle East: Power through Self-Expression* (London: I.B. Taurus, 2004), p. 113.

50. Francois Joutet, "Caught in the Net: The Internet in Palestine," *Connected: The whole universe in each of us*, August 1999, available online at: <http://www.connected.org/develop/palestine.html>

51. Ethan Zuckerman, AmmanNet, and the Future of Radio. The means of Expression-Media, Creativity and Experience, interview available online at: <http://www.worldchanging.com/archives/001693.html>
    Boing Boing: A Directory of Wonderful Things. January 3, 2005 Jordanian net-radio station gets state OK for FM broadcast

52. "Interview with Daoud Kuttab: Virtual Activism, Closing the Digital Divide," available online at: <http://www.virtualactivism.org/partnerfeatured/interviews/kuttab.htm>

53. Ibid.

54. Innovating Online Journalism in the Arab World. Submitted by mbridges Date Submitted: January 25, 2005, 3:11 pm, available online at: <http://cyber.law.harvard.edu/home/home?func=view Submission& sid=662&wid=10>

55. "2005 Middle East and North Africa Program Descriptions," The National Endowment for Democracy, available online at: <http://www.ned.org/grants/05programs/grants-mena05.html>

56. Seminar on the History of Broadcasting, Poetry House, Al-Bireh, May 14, 2000.

57. Jump TV, August 22, 2006, available online at: <http://www.jumptv.com/channels/palestine/overview.ch2?language=english>

58. Deutsche Welle. "Sesame Street Joins Middle East Peace Process." October 22, 2003, available online at: <http://www.dw-world.de/dw/article/0,,1006824,00.html>

59. According to a World Bank Report, in the year 2003, the number of obstacles of all kinds exceeded 700 resulting "in severe fragmentation of the West Bank." The World Bank Group: West Bank and Gaza Update, April 2006, p. 18.

60. Seminar on the History of Broadcasting, Poetry House, Al-Bireh, May 14, 2000.

61. IPI Public Statements: "New Law to Restrict Availability of Broadcasting Licenses," International Press Institute, September 30, 1996, available online at: <http://www.freemedia.at/cms/ipi/statements_detail.html?ctxid=CH0055&docid=CMS11472503116 75&year=1996>

62. Interviews with the head of each station: Tareq Jabbar, Qalquilia TV, June 8, 2000; Hamdi Farraj, Shepherd's TV of Bethlehem, June 12, 2000; Rimah Kilani, Gama TV of Nablus, June 8, 2000, Omar Nazzal, Wattan TV of Ramallah, May 30, 2000.

63. Palestine Free Voice, available online at: <http://palestine-freevoice.blogspot.com/2006/08/help-israel-will-in-2-hours-bomb-gaza.html> (Accessed: August 22, 2006).

64. Matthew Gutman, "Media in Middle of Palestinian Power Struggle," USA Today, July 6, 2006, available online at: <http://www.usatoday.com/printedition/news/2006007/a_hamaspress06.art.htm>

65. IPI. World Press Freedom Review 1998. PNA, available online at: <http://www.freemedia.at/cms/ipi/freedom_detail.html?country=/KW0001/KW0004/KW0101/&year=1998>

66. CPJ: Letter from Ann Cooper to President Arafat. Palestine: Open Season on Broadcast Media. June 2, 2000, available online at: <http://www.cpj.org/protests/00ltrs/Palestine02june00pl.html>

67. Kuttab has been awarded The Press Freedom Award by the Committee to Protect Journalists, Freedom to Write Award by PEN USA, Press Freedom Hero by the International Press Institute, Courage and Future of the Media by the Leipzig Media Institute, Germany. Daoud Kuttab Vita, available online at: <http://www. daoudkuttab.com/cv.html>

68. Toby Mendel and Ali Khashan. "The Legal Framework for Media in Palestine and Under International Law. Global Campaign for Free Expression." Article 19. May 2, 2006, available online at: <www.article19.org/pdfs/analysis/Palestine-media-framework.pdf>

69. The local TV partners are: Al-Amal TV—Hebron; Al-Salam TV—Tulkarem; Al-Nour TV—Jericho; Pase TV—Nablus; Al-Quds educational TV—Ramallah; Bethlehem TV—Bethlehem; Farah TV—Jenin; Nablus TV—Nablus; Qalqilia TV—Qalqilia.

70. Ma'an News Agency. About Us, available online at: <http://www.maannews.net/en/index.php?opr=Content&Do=Aboutus>

71. About US PNN, available online at: <http://www.holylandtrust.org/index.php?option=com_content&task=view&id=26&Itemid=1>

72. Palestine News Network, available online at: <http://english.pnn.ps/index.php?option=com_content&task=view&id=42&Itemid=33>

73. Voice of Palestine—Center for Information and Communication. August 25, 2006, available online at: <http://news.palvoice.com>

74. Michel Foucault, in James D. Faubion (ed.), *Power: Essential Works of Foucault 1954–1984*, vol. 3 (New York: The New Press, 2000), p. 346.

75. The Tribal Council in Jenin demands strict measure to prevent weapons being fired during weddings and celebrations, available online at: <http//Arabic.pnn.ps/index.php?option+com_content&task+view&id=1634&Itemid=40> (Accessed: August 25, 2006).

76. Israel: CPJ condemns destruction of Palestinian radio facility. December 13, 2001, available online at: <http://www.cpj.org/news/2001/Israel13dec01na.html>

77. "Number of hours Israeli soldiers in Ramallah broadcast pornography on seven Palestinian television stations in March: 48," "Events related to television: July 2002," *Harper's Magazine*, available online at: <http://www.harpers.org/Television.html>

    Palestine Emergency Committee. "Destruction of Palestinian Public Institutions"

    April 14, 2002 see the description of the destruction of six stations, available at MIFTAH, available online at: <http://www.ccmep.org/hotnews2/destructionofpalestinianpubli041402.html>

78. Rodney Benson, "Mapping field variation: Journalism in France and the United States," in R. Benson and E. Neveu (eds.), *Bourdieu and the Journalistic Field* (Cambridge: Polity Press, 2005), p. 30.

79. Benson and Eric Neveu, *Bourdieu and the Journalistic Field*, 4.

80. Kuttab, "Palestine, Live, Unedited and Free."

# CHAPTER 12

# New Media, New Audience, New Topics, and New Forms of Censorship in the Middle East

## Ahmed El Gody

### INTRODUCTION: INTERNET DIFFUSION IN THE MIDDLE EAST

The Arab world is generally known as laggard in adopting and utilizing new technologies, and the Internet was no exception. Tunisia was the first Arab country to link to the Internet in 1991 on an experimental level[1]; the first network connection was introduced in 1992 when Egypt established a 9.6k gateway through France. Then several Arab states started joining the new networked world; however, the pace of Internet diffusion in Arab states was slow for various reasons[2]. To many Arab States, such as Libya, the Internet is seen as the new arm of colonization; to others, such as Saudi Arabia, questions of morality and culture hindered adoption of Internet; and to still others, such as Syria and Sudan, fear of the Internet's liberalizing effects on their authoritative regimes slowed its adoption.[3]

Between 1992 and 2000, the Middle East—with the exception of Israel—was ranked among the lowest Internet penetrated regions in the world, with fewer than 2 million users and 0.1 percent penetration rate.[4] Analysts list four main reasons for this[5]:

1. *Poor telecommunications infrastructure*: Although some Arab telecommunication indicators can be compared with those of developed countries, the overall poor regional networking led to low usage and subsequently higher Internet infrastructural cost.

2. *Low economic development*: In most Middle Eastern states, Internet technologies develop faster than relatively poor Arab economies can handle. On the macro level, low income is another factor hindering the spread of the Internet in the Arab world. The cost of Internet access and the attendant charges are prohibitive factors for the development of Internet technologies.
3. *Low illiteracy*: The high illiteracy rate for this region ranges between 40 and 60 percent, making it among the least literate regions worldwide. Even with the introduction of Arabization of the Internet projects, the number of Arabic-based applets over the Internet is low (only 1 percent).
4. *Cultural factors*: Arab culture does not accept new technologies and does not allow their diffusion easily within a system motivated by religious ideals. Also, Arabs still fear innovations coming from the West, seeing them as aspects of neocolonialism.

Globalization forced Arab countries to recognize the power of Information and Communication Technologies (ICTs) as one of the most important factors in achieving sustainable development. Genuine efforts have been implemented by Arab governments during the last decade to utilize Internet technologies and promote their usage.[6] The Egyptian government, for example, initiated a personal computer for every student project that was followed by a free Internet initiative that increased Internet access 500 times in three years. The Moroccan government integrated Internet studies within its education system, and Lebanon and Jordan launched massive media campaigns to promote Internet usage[7].

Arab governments' initiatives paid off. The 2006 Internet World Statistics revealed that the number of Internet users in the Middle East increased significantly from around 1.8 million users in 2000 to over 33 million users by mid-2006 (see graph 12.1).

Although the Middle East is still lagging behind the more developed world in terms of the number of Internet users, as table 12.1 demonstrates, the Arab world possesses the highest Internet growth rate over the past six years with an average of over 600 percent exceeding European, North American, and Asian counties combined. Internet penetration increased from 0.1 percent at the turn of the century to 18.4 percent, exceeding Asian, Latin American, and African nations.

On the country level, as indicated in table 12.2, Iran has the largest Internet population in the Middle East with 7.5 million users, followed by Egypt and Morocco with 5.3 million and 3.5 million users respectively; on the other hand, between 2005 and 2006, the new

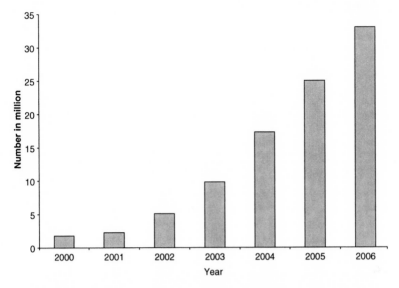

**Graph 12.1**   Internet Development in the Middle East (2000–2006)

*Source*: Internet World Statistics, ICT Challenges for the Arab World

**Table 12.1**   Regional Connectivity Figures (2006)

| Region | Number of Internet Users | Percentage of Internet Penetration | Percentage of Usage Worldwide | Percentage Growth Rate (2000–2006) |
|---|---|---|---|---|
| Asia | 380,408,000 | 10.4 | 36.5 | 232 |
| Europe | 294,100,000 | 36.4 | 28.2 | 179.8 |
| North America | 227,500,000 | 68.6 | 21.8 | 110 |
| Latin America | 79,965,000 | 14.7 | 7.8 | 350 |
| **Middle East** | **33,000,000** | **18.4** | **3.4** | **650** |
| Australia/Oceania | 18,000,000 | 52.6 | 1.7 | 134 |
| Africa | 12,200,000 | 1.3 | 1.4 | 300 |

*Source*: Internet World Statistics

Iraqi Internet network included 30,000 new Internet users, although most of them are expatriates. Yemen's 13,667 percent increase makes it among the leading global Internet new markets. Morocco and Saudi Arabia are considered among the fastest growing Internet markets in the region; whereas the Egyptian market maintained a 400 percent growth rate over the past four years. Sixteen Arab Internet markets have been increasing nine times more than the world average of 200 percent during the past six years.

**Table 12.2**  Internet Diffusion in the Arab World (2006)

| Country | Internet Users | Percentage of Internet Users to Population | Percentage in Comparison to the Arab World | Growth Rate during the Past Five Years |
|---|---|---|---|---|
| Algeria | 1,000,000 | 3 | 3.3 | 1,590 |
| Bahrain | 160,000 | 21.1 | 0.5 | 281 |
| Egypt | 5,300,000 | 7 | 17.7 | 1,100 |
| Iran | 7,500,000 | 11 | 25 | 2,900 |
| Iraq | 30,000 | 0.2 | 0.1 | 188 |
| Israel | 3,200,000 | 45 | 10.6 | 152 |
| Jordon | 600,000 | 11.5 | 2 | 372 |
| Kuwait | 650,000 | 22.8 | 2.2 | 300 |
| Lebanon | 600,000 | 13.3 | 2 | 100 |
| Libya | 300,000 | 4 | 1 | 1,950 |
| Morocco | 3,500,000 | 11.6 | 11.7 | 3,400 |
| Oman | 245,000 | 10.1 | 0.9 | 172 |
| Palestine (WB) | 160,000 | 4.9 | 0.6 | 360 |
| Qatar | 170,000 | 20.7 | 0.6 | 450 |
| Saudi Arabia | 2,600,000 | 11 | 9 | 1,170 |
| Sudan | 1,140,000 | 3.2 | 4 | 3,700 |
| Syria | 800,000 | 4.2 | 2.7 | 2,600 |
| Tunisia | 900,000 | 9 | 3 | 735 |
| UAE | 1,400,000 | 35 | 5 | 88.4 |
| **Yemen** | 230,000 | 1.1 | 0.8 | 13,667 |

*Source*: Internet World Statistics

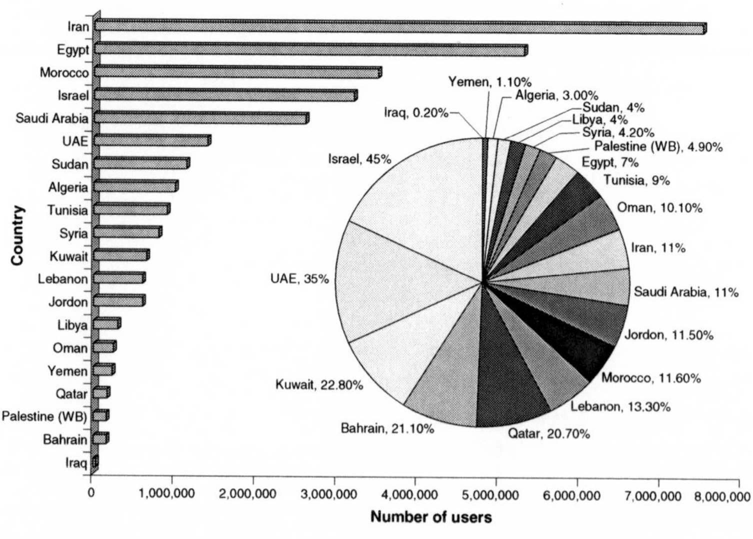

**Graph 12.2**  Internet Diffusion in the Arab World (2006)
*Source*: Internet World Statistics

The UAE posses the highest Internet penetration rate in the Arab world with 35 percent of the population. (In the region, Israel leads with 45 percent of the population connected.) Kuwait and Bahrain have a distant third and fourth penetration rate with 22.8 percent and 21.1 percent respectively.

As seen in graph 12.2, we cannot assume that Internet diffusion in the Arab world is homogeneous, as individual countries differ greatly in education standards, financial strength, and willingness to innovate. The level of political acceptance of the new medium also varies. As a result, some relatively wealthy countries with a large high-tech potential have only a few Internet ports, whereas the number of users is growing much faster in other, structurally weaker countries.[8]

## INTERNET: NEW MEDIA OFFERING A NEW AGENDA

Arab governments underestimated the power of new technologies and the Internet's effect on societies—it was always seen as a mere economic tool, never as a social empowerment force.[9] Even with the evolution of the Internet as a medium, Arab governments saw the technology as a new voice for their propaganda. Western studies saw the Internet as a medium of the young elites. Several were doubtful about the impact of the "open network" on Arab "closed regimes,"[10] some even saw the Internet as the Arab governments' new mechanism for repressing their citizens.[11]

Media ecology of the Arab world for the past 50 years has been shaped by authoritarian regimes. One can still use William Rugh's 1979 description of media in the Arab world as being authoritarian. By definition, an authoritarian media system is controlled by the government either by direct ownership or through strict laws and regulations that set the media agenda and directions of news.[12]

Authoritarian media follow government policies that prescribe the media role as serving as a propaganda tool to promote the government's political, cultural, and economic programs and to filter what the audience hears and sees. Arab citizens did not reach beyond the limits of a traditional system of relationships between the political class and the rest of the population—a system governed by principles of obedience and respect for the political establishment.[13]

Since the eighteenth century, Arab media have operated in an environment affected by frequent censorship. Direct censorship by the state and censorship by journalists themselves (self-censorship and censorship by editors and publishers) are commonplace in the Arab news media. Journalists are convinced that authorities use the new monitoring and surveillance technologies to record their actions and punish them if they cross government lines.

Hopes that the advent of new digital technologies of satellite broadcasting and the Internet would broaden Arab media horizons and ease government monopoly were broken by strict centralized political systems. Arguments for limiting freedom of expression in the region usually cluster around one reason: the preservation of the state unity and cultural hegemony.[14]

For Arab governments, it is apparent that controlling the means of communication is important for dominating mass public opinion to stabilize the political system. Arab media still favor protocol news that "registers state power, enforces nation political solidarity, and shows the unity of the society." In this media system, citizens are not encouraged to participate in the communication process.[15]

However the technology had an agenda of its own,[16] providing a great number of citizens in the Arab world a new public space for a "New transnational realm of civil society . . . an arena in which individuals participate in discussions about matters of common concern, in an atmosphere free of coercion or dependencies (inequalities) that would incline individuals toward acquiescence or silence."[17] The new communication revolution did lead to a more horizontal and less vertical communication model, enabling Arab societies to bypass Arab regimes and controlled traditional mass media. This allowed societies to create a new medium of their own.

The robust presence of the Internet in public consciousness raised an important question: What does the Arab see online that led to this new communication model? Few studies have focused on Arab citizens' attitude toward Internet usage.

Data provided in table 12.3 shows that general search engines and service Web sites Yahoo, MSN Arabia, and the Arabic version of Google are the top viewed Web sites in the Arab world, news and information Web sites, including MSN Arabia, Al Jazeera, and Al Ahram newspaper Web sites, are second in terms of categorization. A study conducted Stephen Quinn[18] on new media's role during the third Gulf War showed that many Arabs relied primarily on the Al Jazeera Web site to get news about the war. The survey showed that the number of searches for the name "Al Jazeera" was three times more than searches for the word "sex." This shows how Internet technologies became an alternative source of information. Religious Web sites come third, followed by blogging and file-sharing host Web sites. Women's issues and entertainment Web sites are the least accessed Web sites in the Middle East.

**Table 12.3** Top 15 Web Sites Viewed in the Middle East

| Site Name | Country | Description |
|---|---|---|
| Yahoo | USA | Search Engine |
| MSN Arabia | Egypt | Search Engine News and Information, Email |
| Google Saudi Arabia | Saudi Arabia | Search Engine |
| Maktoob | UAE | Email, News and Information |
| AmrKhalid | Egypt | Religious Teachings |
| MySpace | UAE | File Photo Sharing and Blogging |
| Yallakora | Egypt | Arab Soccer News |
| DVD4Arabs | UAE | Arab Movies File Sharing |
| Islam Online | UAE | Religious Teachings |
| Hi5 | USA | Chatting and File sharing |
| Al Jazeera | Qatar | News and Information |
| 6arab | Kuwait | Music Sharing and Downloads |
| Al Ahram | Egypt | News and Information |
| Hawaaworld | Saudi Arabia | Women Issues |
| Arb3 | Saudi Arabia | Married Women Issues |

*Source*: Arab Advisory Group, Alexa, Open Net Initiative Internet Filtering

Most Web sites come from the relatively heavy Internet users, UAE, Egypt, and Saudi Arabia, which constitute almost 33 percent of the total number of users in the Arab world and possess high Internet penetration.

The statistics findings are controversial because most studies profiling Arab Internet users had suggested that Arab societies would be swept by entertainment and chatting programs, and that news and information will be the least of Arab priorities.

Three main groups benefited most from the power of new technologies. First, political activist, especially Leftists, Islamists, civil society, and human rights groups that were historically deprived of their freedom of expression and coerced into silence for decades. Religious groups especially Shiites, Bahais, Christians, and Islamic radicals found in the Internet a venue where they could express their ideologies and concerns. Finally social groups that challenge Arab social norms and traditions find the Internet to be a medium where they can meet and create pressure groups to make their voices heard.[19]

## INTERNET: THE CREATION OF A NEW POLITICAL WILL

Media expert and former editor in chief Jihad El Khazen in his article "Censorship and State Control of the Press in the Arab World"[20]

explained how the Internet replaced traditional media. Statistics showed a general 30 percent decline in traditional media usage, as a result of increased reliance on the Internet. El Khazen believes that the migration to new technologies is a natural outcome given the political corrosion caused by Arab authoritarian regimes in a globalized era. The Internet introduced itself as a transnational weapon for political activists crossing boundaries and evading traditional censors.

Opposition parties and banned political groups and organizations such as the Jordanian Muslim Brotherhood groups, the Syrian Communist Party, Saudi Democratic Front Party who were Leftists, and human rights groups who were deprived of their freedom of expression to approach masses in their homeland found in the Internet a tool to engage users through newsgroups and chat rooms in hot discussions about political reform.

"Gaining access to the Internet was a great triumph to voice our opinion and gain political ground," said Mahdi Akef, a Muslim Brotherhood leader, in an interview with Al Masry Al Youm[21] in response to the movement's overwhelming success in winning over 25 percent of the 2005 Egyptian parliamentary elections. The Egyptian movement used Internet technologies creating Web sites for their candidates to show their program and interact with their local electorates as the Egyptian authorities, according to Akef, put pressure on traditional forms of campaigning.

Similarly Tunisian Islamists interact with their audience through publishing a monthly newsletter *Tunisia Insight* online.[22] The Web site states that they have launched an online newsletter due to the "lack of independent sources of information offering impartial news and analysis of the Tunisian situation on various levels: political, socioeconomic and human rights. This is due to the Tunisian government's absolute control of local media transforming it simply into a tool to enhance the government's image inside the country and abroad."[23] The Algerian Front Islamique du Salut (FIS) created numerous Web sites tackling sociopolitical issues to capture the attention of Algerians in their campaign to build a new image of Islamists in Algeria, an image that would replace the one of a group that terrorized citizens for almost 20 years.[24]

Other opposition groups from Saudi Arabia, Egypt, Lebanon, and Libya are using Internet technologies to send emails through specialized mailing lists expressing their opposition to government practices; through emails and Web sites they created intimacy with their publics and gained their support. This same pattern has been repeated, albeit with some differences, in other Arab states such as Syria, Morocco, Sudan, and Bahrain.[25]

## Arab Blog: A Redefinition of Journalism

Dan Gillmor, in his book *We the Media*, wrote that it was the Salam Pax blog chronicling life in Baghdad during the third Gulf War that made blogging a global phenomenon. Blogs have revolutionized the way writers can communicate with their audiences while gaining their readers' feedback instantly through the use of interactive comments.[26]

In Iran, 7.5 million Internet users and 7 million bloggers discuss all forms of political ideologies through very networked and organized webrings. From President Ahmadinejad, who created a blog about his policies and vision of a new Persia, to the simple individuals who want to express themselves building virtual home for themselves where they are in control and could nurture an intimate community of the likeminded, it is becoming customary to have the blog

The Egyptian political blogrings—including the Kefaya (Enough!) movement, Shayfenkom (we are watching you), Manalla, Baheya—are considered the best example of how Internet political activities can be taken from the virtual to the real world. During the 2005 presidential elections, the webring opposed a fifth term for President Mubarak or the succession of his son Gamal, seeking genuine democratic reforms in Egypt, organized tens of thousands of citizen protests on several occasions using the Internet for their cause. During the parliamentary elections that followed the presidential elections, both Kefaya and Shayfenkom established monitoring committees over the elections, becoming the main reference against fraud cases committed during the elections and gaining international recognition for their blogging.

Indeed the Arab version of blogging *al-mudawwenoon* became a powerful tool of democratization that has enthused millions of ordinary people. Passive consumers of information have become energetic participants or potential editors in a new kind of journalism, at a time when the mainstream media is under pressure. Bloggers became a form of independent news agencies, giving the grassroots up-to-the-minute news and other information. That is why many bloggers from Algeria, Tunisia, Egypt, Jordan, Syria, and Iran have been hounded or thrown into prison by authoritarian regimes.

## Internet: A Religion Empowerment Tool

Media analysts noticed that between 35 and 65 percent of the total number of Arabic Web sites are either describing Islam or preaching for Islam. This estimate measures the exceedingly large number of

Web pages with Islamic content that multiplied especially after 9/11 in response to the growing hate campaign against Islam. Some of these Web sites such as Islam.net became internationally acknowledged in cultural dialogues. In 2005, Alexa Web site announced that Islamic preacher Amer Khalid's Web site amrkhaled.net scored second as the most individual personal Web site (first being Oprah Winfrey's site).[27]

It is noticeable, however, that a growing number of Web sites are calling for adoption of the extremist interpretation of religion. There is also the rise of cyber-terrorism sites and blogs promoting xenophobia and hate speech. An Iraqi suicide bomber stated that he learned how to make explosives from the very Web site he adopted his ideologies from!

For religious minorities, Internet technology grew to be a tool used by Shiite Muslims to unite their voice and appear as a powerful movement across the Arab world from Iran, Iraq, and Bahrain in the East to Syria, Palestine, and Egypt in the Middle to Morocco on the western coast. For Egyptian Copts, several Web sites were launched to express Christian problems. The same can be applied to the Bahais who use Internet technology as a double-edged tool to create awareness about their beliefs as well as to seek international recognition.

## INTERNET: A CALL FOR SOCIAL CHANGE

The Internet has changed the way Arabs live by giving them unfettered access to an unprecedented amount of information around the globe. As Arabs start joining the hybrid world, many started to address the social rigidness in the region, making their voice heard. By the time their tone of voice changed, becoming more active, they had enlarged their social networks and gained more confidence in their ability to change some of the pragmatic Arab traditions. They created a parallel community of activists that was strengthened by the participation of individuals who normally would not be involved in activism but who now are speaking out and expressing themselves on the Internet.

Kuwaiti women used Internet technologies effectively creating a "virtual activity" in their successful quest for gaining political representation in the Kuwaiti parliament for the first time in their history. Moroccan women, on the other hand, used Internet technologies to create a network lobby to improve women's health care and raise the level of women education.

Homosexuals may be the only social group in the Arab world that was completely unable to declare publicly its existence until the appearance of the Internet. Through Internet technologies gay and lesbian societies in Egypt, Lebanon, and even Saudi Arabia, known as an extreme conservative society, established several Web pages to announce themselves as a social group, expressing themselves publicly. Ironically, the more the Arab governments crack down on their Web sites and arrest them for "social misconduct," the more the number of such Web sites increase.

## New Media: New Forms of Censorship

The rise of Internet has definitely shaken the Arab world. As Internet-based democratization steadily develops, Arab authoritarian regimes are trying to tighten their grip on it. The situation has worsened during the past three years and today more than 25 cyber-dissidents are in prison and censorship is increasingly effective.

**Table 12.4**   Censorship Cases in the Middle East (2000–2006)

| Country | 2000 | 2001 | 2002 | 2003 | 2004 | 2005 | 2006 | Total (2000–2006) |
|---|---|---|---|---|---|---|---|---|
| Algeria | 1 | 1 | 3 | 4 | 5 | 4 | 3 | 21 |
| Bahrain | 0 | 1 | 2 | 2 | 3 | 3 | 4 | 15 |
| Egypt | 1 | 2 | 3 | 5 | 6 | 8 | 5 | 32 |
| Iran | 2 | 4 | 5 | 7 | 7 | 8 | 6 | 39 |
| Iraq | 1 | 2 | 2 | 1 | 0 | 0 | 1 | 7 |
| Israel | 0 | 1 | 1 | 2 | 1 | 2 | 2 | 9 |
| Jordon | 1 | 2 | 3 | 4 | 3 | 4 | 4 | 20 |
| Kuwait | 0 | 1 | 1 | 2 | 2 | 3 | 2 | 11 |
| Lebanon | 1 | 1 | 0 | 1 | 2 | 2 | 5 | 12 |
| Libya | 0 | 0 | 1 | 2 | 2 | 3 | 2 | 10 |
| Morocco | 1 | 1 | 1 | 2 | 2 | 2 | 4 | 13 |
| Oman | 0 | 1 | 1 | 1 | 1 | 2 | 2 | 8 |
| Palestine (WB) | 1 | 1 | 1 | 3 | 2 | 2 | 2 | 13 |
| Qatar | 0 | 1 | 1 | 2 | 1 | 2 | 2 | 9 |
| Saudi Arabia | 0 | 1 | 3 | 2 | 4 | 3 | 3 | 16 |
| Sudan | 0 | 0 | 1 | 1 | 1 | 3 | 2 | 8 |
| Syria | 0 | 2 | 3 | 5 | 8 | 4 | 5 | 27 |
| Tunisia | 1 | 2 | 4 | 6 | 7 | 8 | 8 | 36 |
| UAE | 0 | 1 | 1 | 1 | 3 | 3 | 3 | 12 |
| Yemen | 0 | 0 | 0 | 0 | 1 | 1 | 3 | 5 |
| Total | 12 | 25 | 37 | 56 | 64 | 66 | 68 | 265 |

*Source*: IFEX, RSF, Silenced Report, Internet Under Surveillance, Freedom House

In six years (see graph 12.3), 265 cases of censorship and/or offenses against Internet users were reported, as shown in table 12.4. Of these, 60 percent were reported during the past three years, which matches the increase not only in the number of Internet users, but also in technology usage as a reform tool. We can also deduce that the third Gulf war considered a turning point, as a number of cases show clearly that the number of offences increased by almost 20 percent

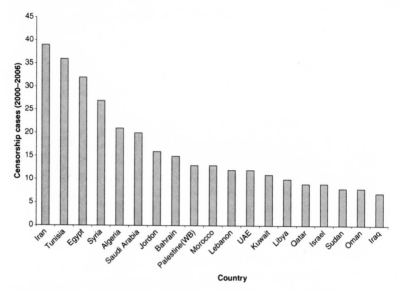

**Graph 12.3**   Censorship Cases in the Middle East (2000–2006)
*Source:* IFEX, RSF, Silenced eport, Freedom House

The Internet clearly is alarming Arab systems. Each Internet user is a potential regime opponent. That is why Arab governments have ended "romancing the net" and are trying to find solutions to control it. Although Internet technologies cannot be controlled easily, Arab governments are applying different measures to censor the medium. These measures put seven Arab countries on the list of the top 15 enemies of Internet freedom.[28]

### (1) Applying Laws and Licenses

Nine Arab countries established Internet laws and regulations to govern citizens' Internet usage. Tunisia has developed the region's most detailed Internet-specific laws. Tunisia also explicitly extends to the Internet existing press laws limiting free expression, something that few other countries in the region have done. However, the existing press laws of several countries, in their delineation of offenses, define "publishing" or "disseminating" information in so broad a fashion that no new laws are needed to bring Internet speech under their purview. Although the Tunisian government stated that the new law is to regulate the usage of the Internet and to assure "fair usage," the Tunisians—under these laws—established Internet police to keep an eye on Internet users, especially in Internet cyber cafes frequented by dissidents.[29] Between 2005 and 2006, twelve Tunisian Internet activists were serving prison sentences due to "disturbing social welfare."[30]

In Syria, the government established a licensing body under security police where any citizen who needs to buy a PC, fax, modem, or register as an Internet user must obtain a government clearance. Citizens need to sign a contract with the Syrian Internet Society before carrying any Internet activity (see table 12.5).[31]

### (2) Content Filtering

This is another major scheme used by Arab states to regulate Internet access. Saudi Arabia, Yemen, and the United Arab Emirates publicly announce they are filtering the Internet under the claim of legal right by imposing router IP blocking and DNS redirection, which are devices that are interposed between the end-user and the Internet in order to filter and block specified content.

**Table 12.5** Arab Countries being Part of the International Covenant on Civil and Political Rights (ICCPR)[32]

| Country | Adopted |
| --- | --- |
| Algeria | √ |
| Bahrain | X |
| Egypt | √ |
| Iran | √ |
| Iraq | √ |
| Israel | √ |
| Jordon | √ |
| Kuwait | √ |
| Lebanon | √ |
| Libya | √ |
| Morocco | √ |
| Oman | X |
| Palestine (WB) | X |
| Qatar | X |
| Saudi Arabia | X |
| Sudan | X |
| Syria | √ |
| Tunisia | √ |
| UAE | X |
| Yemen | √ |

*Source*: Open Net Initiative[33]

The Saudi government, for example, established the King Abdul Aziz City for Science and Technology (KACST) to act not only as the governing and regulatory body for the Internet but also as the sole provider of Internet content. A KACST team monitors and filters incoming material and then redistributes it to local Internet Service Providers (ISPs).[34] Currently the Saudi censored material list includes more than 900,000 sites varying from pornographic and gambling sites to political opposition, human rights, and freedom activist sites.

The Egyptian government imposes no restriction on material downloaded from the Internet through satellite communication. However, uploading and publishing material is a different story. The Egyptian government established a fiber optic network for uploading content over the Internet, so it could be monitored easily by officials. The United Arab Emirates, Bahrain, Iran, Yemen, and Tunisia also block Web sites, using a variety of technical means available to filter and block content. For example, they use proxy servers (programmed to send messages such as "host not found" or "connection timeout") to deny users access to sites marked inappropriate by governments (see graph 12.4).[35]

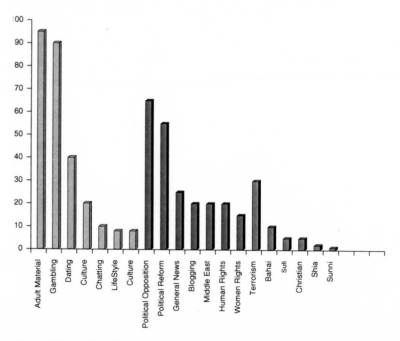

**Graph 12.4** The Most Censored Google Search Topics in the Middle East

### (3) Tapping and Surveillance

According to Human Rights Watch, Arab governments have also pursued old-fashioned forms of surveillance of online expression. Bahraini authorities detained webmaster of www.bahrainonline.com for transmitting information opposing the king of Bahrain, the detention was made through traditional methods of the secret police, including the interrogation of third parties and the use of informants.[36]

On several occasions, the Palestinian National Authority complained that the Israeli government had surveillance programs linked to the government network system, and accused the Israeli government of installing Internet bugs to gather information about the Palestinian government.[37]

Tunisia and Syria routinely tap the phones of dissidents and activists, and Internet users, especially those in cyber cafes who search for information that the government considers "inappropriate." In recent years, many Arab governments are increasingly using computer hackers who create viruses and other software to sabotage or at least block access to "undesirable" publications and to download information, activities, and user logs.

### (4) Pricing and Taxation Policies

In many countries such as Bahrain, Jordan, Saudi Arabia, and Lebanon pricing is a means to control Internet access. Imposing high prices on Internet services is a means to prevent the middle class from using the Internet (see table 12.6).[38] Taxation on telecommunications policies, as in Morocco, renders Internet access expensive and thus beyond the means of many—whether or not this is the objective of these policies.[39]

### (5) Infrastructure

For many Arab countries, hindering the upgrading of Internet telecommunication network projects is a means to prevent Internet access. In Palestinian territories, Israeli troops hit telecommunication network to stop Palestinian online opposition.[40] Saudi Arabia, one of the wealthiest countries in the Arab world, does not encourage the Internet network upgrade so as to minimize Internet usage.[41]

### (6) Telecommunication Manipulation

In most Arab states telecommunication is a government monopoly. Even with privatization that marked the globalization process, Arab

**Table 12.6**   Internet Pricing in the Arab World

| Country | 20 hours Charge ($) |
| --- | --- |
| Algeria | 18 |
| Bahrain | 40 |
| Egypt | 2.5 |
| Iran | 6.5 |
| Iraq | 23 |
| Israel | 18 |
| Jordon | 28 |
| Kuwait | 19 |
| Lebanon | 27 |
| Libya | 20 |
| Morocco | 22 |
| Oman | 26 |
| Palestine (WB) | 20 |
| Qatar | 22 |
| Saudi Arabia | 35 |
| Sudan | 18 |
| Syria | 15 |
| Tunisia | 9 |
| UAE | 13 |
| Yemen | 18 |

*Source:* ICT Challenges for the Arab World

governments have sought to limit the number of ISPs in order to keep them monitored and loyal. In many cases, government telecommunication companies serve as the sole ISPs, as in Yemen, Sudan, and Algeria. In Saudi Arabia, ISP licenses are given to members of the royal family or the royal family's business associates to keep the Internet under control.

Etisalat, the ISP of the UAE government, has longed tapped Web sites dedicated for Bahai faith so that the government can easily detain their participants.[42] The Syrian government ISP has a record of every online activity including creation of and access to emails and Web sites and accordingly can easily restrict email access or shut down Web site constructions.[43]

### (7) Hardware Manipulation

Public access to the Internet can be altogether denied by manipulating the hardware market, as seen in Arab states such as Libya and Syria where even obtaining a computer-modem needs government approval. Through this measure, governments restrict Internet access to limited few, who in most cases are government officials. Syria, for example, has placed strict restrictions on the possession of facsimile machines, and PC owners must register with a military authority.

### (8) Software Manipulation

Software control is yet another method used by governments to strengthen Internet censorship. Special software are developed on the basis of so-called children's protection software, such as Netnanny or Cyberpatrol, and are used to censor banned material. Such programs are usually sold by online services such as CompuServe in order to allow the home user to childproof their PCs, however, most of them are either imposed in cyber cafes and ISPs or offered as free downloads on the ISPs' Web sites.[44] The Bahraini government in its steps to censor the Internet, in order to protect Islamic values and morals from indecent material, came up with a pragmatic solution, by offering links to free software programs designed to protect surfers.

### (9) Self-Censorship

In addition to technical and legal means, all governments create an atmosphere of fear to intimidate Internet users so that they would practice what is known as social responsibility censorship. Arab states use their media control to propagate special programs to monitor and punish those who cross the Internet line. In Jordan, for example, threats and intimidation techniques are used to prevent inappropriate discussions in chat rooms. Fears of government surveillance or reprisals fostered chat room self-censorship.[45] After implementing this law to intimidate Internet users, the Jordanian government captured at least two persons who were reportedly summoned for questioning by the police because of articles or comments they had posted on electronic bulletin boards or in chat rooms—forums whose contents can be read by everyone, including the police.

## CONCLUSION: NEW MEDIA AND NEW FORMS OF CENSORSHIP IN THE MIDDLE EAST

The speed with which Middle Eastern governments censor the Internet, as shown in graph 12.5, testifies the citizens' appetite for alternative means of getting and transmitting information. In countries where the media is rigidly controlled, the Internet opened a window for a new agenda that has room for greater freedom of expression. The

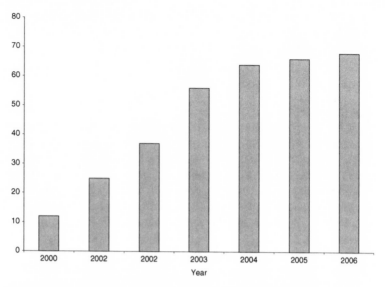

**Graph 12.5**   Number of Internet Offences in the Middle East

*Sources:* Internet under Surveillance, Silenced Report, False Freedom

2005 Human Rights Watch report on Internet censorship in the Middle East states that the penetration of Internet in Arab societies is unpredictable in both magnitude and possible effect. "Anyone with access to a computer, Internet connection, and 'blogging' tools can publish to a potential audience of millions, free of charge, within minutes."[46]

Tim Berners-Lee predicts that the Internet will be more of a social creation than a technical one has come true[47]. The Internet is a tool used by societies across boundaries to help individuals and grassroots organizations develop their existing world. Internet technology has not only introduced itself to the Middle Eastern world as an "alternative medium" but is also the Arab society's hope for a growing freedom of expression and the creation of a democratic region.

The Internet provided opportunities for Arab citizens to participate in forums to discuss and debate issues that concern them. The new communication revolution did lead to more horizontal and less vertical communication. The power of the Internet has allowed Arab society to more fully participate in the decision-making process not only in the virtual world but also in the real world, locally, regionally, and internationally. Through the Internet, Arab societies are able to plant the seeds of democracy and freedom and nourish its growth.

**Table 12.7** Forms of Internet Censorship in the Middle East

| Country/Censorship | Laws/Regulations | Content Filtering | Tapping and Surveillance | Pricing | Infrastructure Control | Telecom Control | H/W Control | S/W Control | Self-Censorship |
|---|---|---|---|---|---|---|---|---|---|
| Algeria | ✓ | ✓ | ✓ | | ✓ | ✓ | | | ✓ |
| Bahrain | ✓ | ✓ | ✓ | ✓ | ✓ | ✓ | | | ✓ |
| Egypt | ✓ | ✓ | ✓ | | ✓ | ✓ | | | ✓ |
| Iran | ✓ | ✓ | ✓ | ✓ | ✓ | ✓ | | ✓ | ✓ |
| Iraq | | ✓ | | ✓ | ✓ | | | ✓ | |
| Israel | ✓ | ✓ | | ✓ | ✓ | ✓ | | | |
| Jordon | | ✓ | ✓ | ✓ | ✓ | | | | |
| Kuwait | | ✓ | ✓ | ✓ | | | | | ✓ |
| Lebanon | | ✓ | | ✓ | ✓ | | ✓ | ✓ | ✓ |
| Libya | ✓ | ✓ | | ✓ ✓ | | | | | |
| Morocco | | ✓ | | | | ✓ | | | ✓ |
| Oman | | ✓ | | | ✓ | ✓ | | | |
| Palestine (WB) | | ✓ | ✓ | | ✓ ✓ | ✓ | | | |
| Qatar | | ✓ | ✓ | | | ✓ | ✓ | ✓ | ✓ |
| Saudi Arabia | | ✓ | | | | ✓ | | | ✓ |
| Sudan | | ✓ | | | | ✓ | ✓ | | ✓ |
| Syria | ✓ | ✓ | ✓ ✓ | | | ✓ | | ✓ ✓ | ✓ |
| Tunisia | ✓ | ✓ | ✓ | | | ✓ | | | ✓ |
| UAE | ✓ | ✓ | | | | ✓ | | | ✓ |
| Yemen | | ✓ | ✓ | | | ✓ | | | ✓ |

It is no wonder that many authoritarian Arab regimes/governments fearing Internet technology's power to change the status quo have imposed policies (see table 12.7) ranging from regulation and state monopolization of infrastructure to hacking and cracking Web sites in an attempt to prevent citizens from gaining access to Internet information.

The tussle between Arab governments and citizens on the issue of democracy continues, however, this time citizens know that by the effective usage of the Internet they will force their governments to take action to promote civil democratic society.

## NOTES

1. Deborah Wheeler, "Empowering publics: Information Technology and democratization in the Arab World—Lessons from Internet cafés and beyond" *Oxford Internet Institute*, vol. 11, no. 1 (July 2006): 2–3.

2. Ahmed El Gody, in Roland Stanbridge (ed.), *African Media and ICT4D: A Baseline Study on the State of Media Reporting on ICT and Information Society Issues in Africa* (London: Economic Commission for Africa, 2003), pp. 27–47.

3. Ahmed El Gody, "New Media, New Politics, and New forms of Censorship," paper presented to the 25th Conference and General Assembly of the International Association for Media and Communication Research (Cairo: AUCPRESS, 2006).

4. Ibid.

5. Hussein Amin, *Civic Discourse and Digital Age Communications in the Middle East* (Greenwood: Ablex, 2000), p. 14.

6. S. Dutta, "ICT Challenges for the Arab World," development gateway [Cited August, 2006], available online at: <http:// topics. developmentgateway.org/knowledge/rc/filedownload.do~itemId= 290684>

7. D. Hassan, "ICT Capacity Building," Eforesee [Cited August, 2006], available online at: <http://www.eforesee.info/conferences andevents/malta2003/presentations/diab.ppt>

8. Karen D. Loch "Diffusing the Internet in the Arab World: The Role of Social Norms and Technological Culturation," *IEEE Transactions on Engineering Management*, vol. 50, no. 1 (February 2003): 45–63

9. Helmi Noman, "Internet in the Arab World: A Catalyst for Power Shift," Harvard University [Cited July 2006], available online at: <http://cyber.law.harvardedu/home/home?wid=10&func= viewSubmission&sid=981>

10. Shanti Kalathil and Taylor C. Boas. *Open Networks, Closed Regimes: The Impact of Internet on Authoritarian Rule* (Washington, DC: Carnegie Endowment for International Peace, 2003), pp. 22–41.

11. Gamal Eid, "The Internet in the Arab World: A New Space of Repression?" Arab Network for Human Rights Information. [Cited April 2006], available online at: <http://www.hrinfo.net/en/reports/net2004/all.shtml>

12. William Rugh, *The Arab Press* (New York: Syracuse University Press, 1987), p. 11.

13. William Rugh, *Arab Mass Media: Newspapers, Radio, and Television in Arab Politics* (Westport, CT: Praeger, 2004), pp. 8–10.

14. Ibid., p. 12.

15. Jon Alterman, 2005. "IT Comes of Age in the Middle East," The Voice of Foreign Service [Cited July, 2006], available online at: <http://www.afsa.org/fsj/dec05/alterman.pdf#search=%22Alterman%20Jon%20New%20Media%20Arab%20World%22>

16. Andrew Feenberg, *Transforming Technology: A Critical Theory Revisited* (New York: Oxford University Press, 2002), p. 23.

17. Ibid.

18. Stephen Quinn. "A Broadcaster Creating Ripples in a Stagnant Pool," in Ralph D. Berenger (ed.), *Global Media Go to War: Role of News and Entertainment Media During the 2003 Iraq War* (Spokane, WA: Marquette Books, 2004), pp. 57–73

19. Eid, "The Internet in the Arab World."

20. Jihad El Khazen, "Censorship and State Control of the Press in the Arab World," Project Muse [Cited July, 2006], available online at: <http://muse.jhu.edu/journals/harvard_international_journal_of_press_politics/v004/4.3khazen.html> (Accessed: August 24, 2006).

21. Magdy El Galad, "The Unorthodox Methods of Campaign proven Success for the Banned Group," *AlMasry AlYoum* Saturday, December 17, 2005, Sec.1.

22. Tunisia insight [Cited August, 2006], available online at: <http://www.iol.ie/~afifi/ BICNews/Mag/mag6.htm>

23. Ibid.

24. Islamic front for salvation [Cited August 2006], available online at: <http://www.fisweb.org>

25. Eid, "The Internet in the Arab World."

26. Dan Gillmor, *We the Media: Grassroots Journalism by the People for the People* (Cambridge: O'Reilly, 2004), p. 44.

27. Alexa [Cited August 2006], available online at: <http://www.Alexa.com>

28. Freedom House [Cited August 2006], available online at: <http://www.freedomhouse.org>

29. Simon Davies, "Silenced: Censorship and Control of the Internet." Privacy International [Cited August 2006], available online at: <http://www.privacyinternational.org/article.shtml?cmd[347]=x-347-83814>

30. Julien Pain, "2004 Internet Under Surveillance," *Reporters without Borders* [Cited August 2006], available online at: <http://www.rsf.org/rubrique.php3?id_rubrique=433>

31. El Gody, "New Media, New Politics."

32. One of the most widely subscribed human rights treaties, the International Covenant on Civil and Political Rights (ICCPR), reiterates these protections. Article 19 of the ICCPR provides that everyone's right to freedom of expression "shall include the freedom to seek, receive and impart information and ideas of all kinds, regardless of frontiers, either orally, in writing or in print, in the form of art, or through any other media of his choice."

33. Open Net Initiative. "Internet Filtering in the United Arab Emirates in 2004–2005," Open Network Initiative [Cited July 2006], available online at: <http:// www.opennetinitiative.net/studies/uae/ONI_UAE_Country_Study.pdf>

34. Human Rights Watch. "False Freedom: Online Censorship in the Middle East and North Africa," Human Rights Watch [Cited May 2006], available online at: <http://www.hrw.org/doc/?t=mideast> (Accessed: August 28, 2006).

35. Ibid.

36. Pain, "Internet Under Surveillance."

37. Space and Tech. "Israel Launches Surveillance Satellite," Space and Tech [Cited July 2006], available online at: <http://www.space-andtech.com/ digest/flash2002/flash2002-048.shtml>

38. S. Dutta, "ICT Challenges for the Arab World."

39. Pain, "Internet Under Surveillance."

40. Ibid.

41. Alterman, "IT Comes of Age."

42. Human Rights Watch, "False Freedom."

43. Ibid.

44. Davies, "Silenced."

45. Pain, "Internet Under Surveillance."

46. Human Rights Watch, "False Freedom."

47. Tim Berners-Lee, *Weaving the Web: The Original Design and Ultimate Destiny of the World Wide Web by its Innovators* (San Francisco: Harber, 1999), p. 123.

# CHAPTER 13

# Terrorism and the Making of the "New Middle East": New Media Strategies of Hezbollah and al Qaeda

*Maura Conway*

## INTRODUCTION

When U.S. defense secretary Donald Rumsfeld was asked about soft power in 2003, he replied, "I don't know what it means."[1] In February 2006, in a speech at the Council on Foreign Relations in New York, however, Rumsfeld was forced to concede:

> Our enemies have skillfully adapted to fighting wars in today's media age, but for the most part we, our country, our government, has not adapted. Consider that the violent extremists have established media relations committees—these are terrorists and they have media relations committees that meet and talk about strategy, not with bullets but with words. They've proven to be highly successful at manipulating the opinion elites of the world. They plan and design their headline-grabbing attacks using every means of communication to intimidate and break the collective will of free people . . . They know that communications transcend borders and that a single news story handled skillfully can be as damaging to our cause and helpful to theirs as any other method of military attack. And they're doing it. They're able to act quickly. They have relatively few people. They have modest resources compared to the vast and expensive bureaucracies of Western governments. Our federal government is really only beginning to adapt our operations to the 21st century. For the most

part, the U.S. government still functions as a five and dime store in an eBay world.²

This chapter explores the use of new media technologies: satellite television and the Internet by Hezbollah³ and al Qaeda (and affiliated groups and individuals) respectively. The argument put forward here is twofold: firstly, while both groups are savvy users of new media technologies, which they employ in conjunction with their hard power resources to amplify their soft power, the style and substance of their new media strategies, and hence their larger goals, differ quite dramatically; second, however, is the assertion that, despite these differences, both of these groups are potentially substantial contributors to the making of a "new" Middle East, albeit one very different from that envisaged by the U.S. administration when they employ this terminology.

## Old Media, New Media:
## The Evolution of the
## Terrorism-Media Relationship

Nobel's invention of dynamite in 1867 was the technological breakthrough that ushered in the era of modern terrorism. The economy of means afforded by the use of dynamite ensured that terrorist bombings proliferated. High levels of illiteracy in nineteenth century Europe imposed serious limitations on conventional text-based propaganda. Conversely, "propaganda by deed" could show, as the French anarchist Paul Brousse explained lucidly at the time, "the weary and inert masses . . . that which they were unable to read, teach them socialism in practice, make it visible, tangible, concrete."⁴ When the anarchist Albert Parsons was arraigned for his alleged involvement in the Haymarket bombing in Chicago in 1886, he insisted in court that dynamite "made all men equal and therefore free."⁵ However, while modern terrorists may still seek to convey a message through their violent performance, they must also employ written and spoken language in an effort to legitimize, rationalize, and, ultimately, advertise their actions. With the advent of new media technologies, however, they are no longer reliant on intermediaries to interpret their deeds; instead they may employ the former as soft power tools in order to amplify their hard power resources, thus adopting, in Nye's terms, a "smart" approach to conflict.⁶

Since the advent of the printing press using industrial age technologies in the nineteenth century, terrorists and extremist movements have employed every available mass communications technology. This is evidenced in everything from Carlos Marighela's advice to his comrades to the use of photocopying machines to produce large numbers of pamphlets and manifestos on Hezbollah's establishment of its al Manar television station in the early 1990s. The year that witnessed the birth of modern international terrorism, 1968, was the same year in which the United States launched the first television satellite, heralding the second great revolution in mass communications that directly impacted terrorism.[7]

Much of the explanation of the power of terrorism is said to hinge on how the news media operate: "Journalists are attracted to drama and few political spectacles offer greater dramatic appeal than violence."[8] Terrorists are cognizant of this and use it to their advantage. In his seminal 1975 paper, Brian Michael Jenkins argued that "terrorist attacks are often carefully choreographed to attract the attention of the electronic media and the international press."[9] The news media have proved unable to ignore events "fashioned specifically for their needs."[10]

Terrorist "spectaculars" can hijack media attention: witness the attack on the Israeli athletes at the Munich Olympics, the hijacking of TWA flight 847, the events of 9/11 and their aftermath. This is not to suggest, however, that the terrorists themselves actually control the news agenda or that they can determine the ways in which their behavior is framed. In their repackaging of events, even where terrorists gain "disruptive access" to the media, the media still largely rely on official sources and dominant understandings of where legitimacy lies.[11] In the British case, for example, the tabloid press often exceeded the language of the state in stigmatizing the IRA as "scum," "cowardly murderers," and "bastards."[12] In the past, those characterized as "terrorists" were rarely accepted by the mass media as legitimate or authoritative sources of news in their own right. Neither were they accepted as reliable commentators on the political situation that had given rise to the violence: "Certainly, on the few occasions when the BBC or ITV interviewed Republican paramilitaries in the 1970s and 1980s, they were emphatically not, as a matter of policy, treated as individuals whose opinions could be accorded the same respect and due consideration as others."[13] By concentrating almost exclusively on the violent dimension of terrorism, making no attempt to contextualize its causes, media reports often leave readers, viewers, or listeners mystified as to the motivation of violent acts.[14] The upshot of this is that many in the media audience take these acts to be simply the senseless, inexplicable behavior of psychotic fundamentalists or extremist lunatics.[15]

For this reason, terrorists generally accompany their violent acts with a flurry of threats, communiqués, and manifestos, leading one commentator to assert that "the violence of terrorism is positively verbose."[16] Previous to the widespread use of the Internet and other new media technologies, the mainstream media were held by many to be complicit in the attainment of the terrorists' objectives. This was because media attention to terrorist violence was held to be considerably more significant than the terrorists' own propaganda: "[the terrorists'] own self-generated posters, manifestos, leaflets, and broadcasts are unlikely, after all, to reach a wide audience and even less likely to convince any other than the already converted."[17] This may have been true when cultures and politics could be contained within national borders. Historically, leaders and elites were generally the only ones who knew the world first hand. Thus they were relied upon to interpret the motives and behaviors of other leaders and elites, and to formulate responses. Today, that reliance has all but vanished. The Internet and satellite television present those with access and the requisite interest with the opportunity to know and interpret the world for themselves and, therefore, decreases the historical control by the media and political elites over individual worldviews.[18]

"In the modern era, the truism that 'information is power' is very clearly understood by the media and governments; it is also understood by terrorists, their audiences, and their adversaries."[19] If victory, in the information age, is ultimately about "whose story wins,"[20] the crucial questions become what messages are sent and received by whom under which circumstances, and how that affects the ability of actors to obtain the outcomes they want.[21] Terrorists now have the ability to tell their own stories via their Web sites and television stations. The level of editorial control afforded to terrorists by their access to new media technologies has added a significant new tool to terrorists' soft power arsenal. This chapter is composed of two case studies: the first of these details Hezbollah's use of its satellite television station, al Manar, in their information warfare strategy, while the second case describes and analyses the adoption of a heavily Net-centric posture by al Qaeda and affiliated groups and individuals. Considering that both of these groups are heavy users of new media and that the tech-savvy among them have already made an impact in the Middle East, they are both potentially significant contributors to the future remaking of the region in terms of their politically violent initiatives and the undoubtedly central role new media technologies will play in the groups' amplification of the latter. Relevant also is the way in which efforts by Western governments to muzzle these groups has rebounded on the former and led to widespread derision in the Middle East region (and, indeed, father afield).

## New Media Strategy 1: Hezbollah's Al Manar TV[22]

The major focus of this section is the way in which Hezbollah has wielded its television station, al Manar—the "Beacon" or "Lighthouse," in Arabic—as a weapon in their information war. The argument put forward here is that Hezbollah has met with high levels of success in this regard—to the extent that they may recently be seen to have become the victims of their own success, with the institution of multiple bans on transmission of al Manar globally and the repeated targeting of the station by Israeli forces during the summer 2006 crisis. On the other hand, these difficulties may also be viewed by the organization as blessings in disguise, as they have forced the station to streamline its processes that may, in the long term, not only ensure its continued existence, but even allow it to access a larger audience.

Although Hezbollah's political goals are narrower than al Qaeda's, "[s]ymbolism and the projection of messages to internal and external audiences have occupied a central place for Hezbollah throughout its evolution."[23] Donald Rumsfeld would clearly be surprised to learn that during the crisis precipitated by the hijacking of TWA flight 847 in 1985, Hezbollah deftly manipulated the U.S. television networks: "There were graduates in media studies from American colleges at meetings at Nabih Berri's house in West Beirut while ['spin doctoring'] tactics were being worked out."[24] Later, during the 1990s, Hezbollah utilized its media apparatus to wage successful campaigns against both the Israeli Defense Forces (IDF) and South Lebanese Army (SLA) when they adopted a two-pronged military strategy, combining guerrilla and psychological warfare. According to Schliefer, "Hezbollah's unique contribution to PSYOP lay in the way it combined conventional and psychological warfare, creating a whole new PSYOP idiom."[25] Al Manar was at the center of this campaign from its inception.

Al Manar has, since its foundation, been a television station devoted to the goals of Hezbollah, and although these have been subject to change over time, the overarching theme of resistance has persisted. From its establishment in 1991 to the Israeli withdrawal from the south in 2000, the bulk of the station's programming was aimed at sustaining and, if possible, strengthening the Lebanese public's support for Hezbollah's campaign of resistance again the IDF in south Lebanon, while at the same time pressuring Israeli viewers to push their government for a unilateral withdrawal.

The eventual withdrawal was celebrated live on air for days, but this "triumph" came tinged with distress: what was to be the station's purpose without the "hook" the resistance provided? The answer presented itself in the form of the outbreak of the so-called *al-Aqsa Intifada*. Al Manar became "the secret weapon of the Palestinian *Intifada* against Israeli occupation, the loyal supporter of armed resistance, devoting at least half its 24-hour-a-day satellite broadcasting to the battle between Palestinians and Israelis in the West Bank and Gaza."[26] The nature of some of this programming eventually resulted in the widespread banning of the station, however.

### Banning Al Manar's Satellite Transmissions

The campaign to have al Manar banned from transmitting via satellite began with an opinion piece that appeared in the *Los Angeles Times* in October 2002. The article, penned by Avi Jorisch,[27] accused American companies that advertised on the station of promoting terrorism. PepsiCo, Proctor and Gamble, Western Union, and a number of other major U.S. and European companies were named as advertisers on al Manar's local broadcasts (the satellite broadcast was, at that time, commercial-free).[28] Jorisch followed up with a letter to the U.S. Congress, asking its members to put pressure on these companies. The majority of U.S. advertisers duly pulled out, and pressure to ban the transmission of the station itself increased. The Coalition Against Terrorist Media (CATM), an offshoot of the U.S.-based neoconservative organization Foundation for Defence of Democracy (FDD), was also founded at this time in order to generate further momentum for the ban. Representatives of FDD and CATM—including Jorisch, who came on board as the latter's executive director—have issued numerous statements claiming "al Manar runs graphic videos encouraging viewers, even children, to become suicide bombers and calls for acts of terrorism against civilians . . . Al Manar is an operational weapon in the hands of one of the world's most dangerous terrorist organizations."[29]

Al Manar was, at the same time, coming under pressure in Europe. While claims about incitement to suicide bombing are contested, this is not to deny that some measure of al Manar's programming is objectionable by Western standards. The French move against al Manar began after the station caused an uproar in October 2002 by broadcasting a Syrian-produced drama series entitled *al Shattat* (The Diaspora), which is based on the controversial text known as the

*Protocols of the Elders of Zion*, a nineteenth-century publication that depicts a Zionist conspiracy to take over the world.[30] Scenes from the multipart miniseries include a dramatization of a rabbi slaying a young boy in order to use his blood to make Passover *matzoh*.[31] Another episode includes a scene depicting a secret Jewish government allegedly plotting to drop an atomic bomb on Hiroshima, Japan.

The transmission of this series caused an uproar in France, where incitement to racial hatred and anti-Semitism are criminal offences, and led France's higher audiovisual authority to instruct al Manar to change the tone of its programming or face a ban. However, when in December 2004 a guest on a live show said that Zionists were deliberately trying to spread diseases, including AIDS, to Arabs, the authority decided to take the station to court. On January 6, 2005, France's highest administrative court, the *Conseil d'État* (Council of State)—which had jurisdiction over the channel because it broadcast via a satellite based in France—decided that the programs al Manar broadcast "were in a militant context, with anti-Semitic connotations" and banned transmission of the station, warning the satellite provider Eutelsat that if it failed to stop broadcasting al Manar on its satellite within 48 hours of the decision, it would be subject to a large fine.[32] For its part, the station said it was unfair to ban a channel on the basis of one live caller, and it denies it is anti-Semitic.[33] Al Manar voluntarily stopped broadcasting several days before the ban was to take effect, a move that prevented other stations on the same satellite network from being removed from the airwaves as well.[34] As regards the U.S. ban, it followed shortly thereafter. In December 2004, al Manar was placed on an "exclusion list" by the U.S. State Department. This was followed up in March 2006 with al Manar's designation as a terrorist organization by the U.S. Department of the Treasury.[35] As a result, no one associated with the broadcaster is allowed entry to the United States and any U.S. company found to be doing business with al Manar will be subject to sanctions and possible prosecution. The result is al Manar is effectively prohibited from transmitting in the United States. Although they result in the same outcomes, it is worth noting that the French and U.S. bans rest on different legal foundations, with the French ban focusing on constitutional issues of expression, and the U.S. ban based on laws prohibiting the material support of terrorist organizations, which, according to Yadav, means that "At least in theory, then, the U.S. is suggesting that their own struggle against al Manar is not based on the substance of what it says, but rather on what it does."[36] Being unavailable in North America, and with only restricted access in Europe, al Manar is also no longer available for satellite viewing in South America, nor in Australia or much of Africa; however, it is still broadcast throughout the Middle East, parts of Europe, and North Africa by Nilesat, whose major shareholder is the government of Egypt, and by Arabsat, which is owned in part by the government of Saudi Arabia. In any event, the station has all but entirely circumvented the satellite bans by providing free continuous live streaming online.

The above notwithstanding, al Manar officials were some of the most vociferous critics of the bans imposed on the broadcast of their satellite signals. The station responded in a statement that the U.S. action amounted to "intellectual terrorism" and an attack on press freedom.[37] The Lebanese minister of information declared the ban proof of censorship of any opposition to Israel, and students demonstrated in support of al Manar. In response to the French ban, the Lebanese foreign minister Mahmud Hammud commented "we consider this to be against the freedom of expression that the entire world, including the EU demands. We believe this attitude is not in harmony with the call for freedom of expression these countries advocate, and we believe there is a contradiction."[38] The banning was also criticized by organizations ranging from Hamas[39] and Palestinian Islamic Jihad[40] to Reporters without Borders, with the latter warning against confusing anti-Israeli positions with anti-Semitism.[41]

### Al Manar's Role in the Summer 2006 Crisis

In the summer of 2006, events in Lebanon put Hezbollah and al Manar back in the spotlight. During the crisis precipitated by a cross-border raid made by Hezbollah, al Manar reverted to its original role as mouthpiece of the Lebanese "resistance." Although this time around the Israelis, cognizant of the role played by al Manar in the previous conflict between the two sides, quickly sought to neutralize the station, they had little success.

Following Israel's withdrawal from Lebanon in 2000, and believing itself relatively safe from the threat of Israeli aerial bombardment, al Manar invested in high-specification antennas, which allowed it to extend its broadcasts farther into Israel. As a result, residents of Haifa, Israel's third largest city—which is located some 30 miles from the Lebanese border—are now within al Manar's transmissions range. Al Manar's headquarters in Haret Hreik and the above-mentioned antennas—one of which was located near Baalbek, northeast of Beirut, and another in Maroun al-Ras in southern Lebanon[42]—were some of the first targets of IDF air attacks when hostilities erupted between Israel and Hezbollah in early July 2006. Al Manar's Beirut headquarters was first struck by the Israeli Air Force on Thursday, July 13, the second day of the crisis. The complex was bombed again on July 16, resulting in a fire in the station and surrounding buildings. Although the station's broadcasts continued uninterrupted during the first attack—which severely damaged the upper stories of the building—the second attack caused the station's signal to be briefly unavailable on several occasions before returning to full strength.[43] Also, on the second day of the crisis, the first-ever Hezbollah rocket attacks on Haifa commenced.

Indeed the IDF—in addition to conventional attacks on media targets in Lebanon—is also said to have broadened its PSYOP activities over the course of the crisis. The first reports of intercepts of al Manar's satellite transmissions were carried by Egypt's Middle East News Agency, which said that, on Sunday, July 23, Israel managed "to intercept the satellite transmissions of Hezbollah's al Manar TV channel for the third successive day, replacing them with Israeli transmissions that reportedly showed Hezbollah command sites and rocket launching pads which Israel claimed it has raided."[44] A little over a week later, Al Jazeera reported that a series of still photos with captions appeared on the screens of al Manar viewers for several minutes during the evening news. Al Jazeera attributed the interruption to "Israeli-backed hackers." One of the images showed the corpse of a khaki-clad man lying face-down with accompanying Arabic text reading: "This is the photograph of a body of a member of Hezbollah's special forces. Nasrallah lies: it is not we who are hiding our losses." The Al Jazeera report is also accompanied by what appears to be a screen shot that shows a photograph of Nasrallah accompanied by the text "member of Hezbollah: watch out," which, Al Jazeera said, also appeared on TV screens.[45]

The Israeli bombing of Hezbollah's media outlets received harsh criticism from journalistic and human rights organizations. The Committee to Protect Journalists, the International Federation of Journalists (IFJ), Human Rights Watch, and others agreed that the attacks were a violation of international law, as the station's broadcasts were not serving any direct military function (e.g., sending military communiqués).[46] Aidan White, the IFJ's general secretary, said, "The bombing of al Manar is a clear demonstration that Israel has a policy of using violence to silence media it does not agree with. This action means media can become routine targets in every conflict. It is a strategy that spells catastrophe for press freedom and should never be endorsed by a government that calls itself democratic."[47] Human

Rights Watch agreed, insisting that "Lebanese civilian opinion might influence how the Lebanese government responds to Hezbollah is not a sufficiently direct contribution to military action to render the media used to influence that opinion a legitimate military target. Rather, broadcasts should be met with competing broadcasts, propaganda with propaganda."[48]

## New Media Strategy 2: Islamists and the Internet

Islamic texts and discussion venues have been accessible online for about twenty-five years. Anderson discerns three phases in the growth of an Islamic presence on the Internet characterized by the predominance of three different groups:

1. *Technological adepts:* People who uploaded scanned texts and added a generally laic discourse
2. *Activists and official voices:* Individuals at two ends of the ideological spectrum, competing for adherents
3. *Spokespersons and audiences:* People representing the "online advent of moderate Islam."[49]

The assertion here is that, after September 11, a fourth phase was developed and spearheaded by radical Islamic fundamentalists, particularly those supportive of Osama bin Laden and al Qaeda. Throughout the maturation process identified by Anderson, the principal actors in each phase employed—in many cases, even furthered the development of—the best publicly available technology.[50] The representatives of phase four were no different.

In his discussion of Islam and the Internet, Anderson champions the role of the Net in the emergence of an "activist but distinctly moderate Islam, for which the Internet seems peculiarly congenial."[51] This is in keeping with much of the early work on the positive effects of new Information and Communications Technology (ICT) for global civil— read "positive"—society actors. The spread of information does not necessarily encourage increased civility or, indeed, stability, however. On the contrary, "Johannes Guttenberg's invention of movable type in the mid-fifteenth century led not only to the Reformation but to the wars of religion that followed it, as the sudden proliferation of texts spurred doctrinal controversies and awakened long dormant grievances."[52] Such impacts are not restricted to Christianity; historically, the salience of technology in precipitating change within Islam has been vast.

According to Mandaville, it was the experience of European colonialism and the concomitant perceived decline in Islamic civilization that paved the way for the embrace of print technology within the Muslim world in the nineteenth century. "The book, pamphlet, and newsletter were taken up with urgency in order to counter the threat which Europe was posing to the Muslim *ummah*."[53] In theory at least, this resulted in Islam's sacred texts being made available for the first time to anyone who could read them, to "be consulted by any Ahmad, Mahmud, or Muhammad, who could make what he [would] of them."[54] In a similar fashion, just as "the move to print technology meant not only a new method for transmitting texts, but also a new idiom of selecting, writing and presenting works to cater for a new kind of reader,"[55] the advent of the Internet has resulted in not only a new method for transmitting text, audio, and video, but also a new idiom of selecting, producing, and arranging data to cater to a new kind of audience.

In a videotaped statement that was released in December 2001, in which he comments upon the 9/11 attackers, Osama bin Laden stated,

> [T]hose youths who conducted the operations did not accept any *fiqh* in the popular terms, but they accepted the *fiqh*[56] that the Prophet Muhammad brought. Those young men . . . said in deeds, in New York and Washington, speeches that overshadowed all other speeches made everywhere in the world. The speeches are understood by both Arabs and non-Arabs—even by the Chinese.[57]

Bin Laden thus describes the events of 9/11 not as primarily hostile or vengeful actions, which they undoubtedly were, but underlines instead their essentially communicative aspect(s).[58] The centrality of communication(s) and communication technologies, especially the Internet, to al Qaeda and its affiliates was not immediately clear to researchers, analysts, or policymakers, however. Michael Scheuer admits in the introduction to *Imperial Hubris* (2004) that a major problem with his previous book, *Through Our Enemies Eyes* (2003), was that in it he seriously underestimated the role of the Internet in al Qaeda's activities.[59] Of course, one reason for this may be the rapidly evolving nature of al Qaeda's Internet use and thus its impact.

Clearly interesting things can happen when a "complex world discourse" such as Islam comes into contact with a force that can claim an equally wide geographic spread: the socially and politically transformative effects of the Internet. Islam—political Islam in particular—has exhibited a wide range of responses to this relatively new information and communication technology with certain features being eagerly appropriated and others vociferously rejected.[60] Bin Laden himself has observed that "In the past there was imperfection, but it was partial. Today, however, the imperfection touches the entire public because of the communications revolution and because the media enter every home."[61] However, citing the Western media's "vicious campaign" against Islam, bin Laden, in a 2002 Internet posting, called on Muslim publishers and broadcasters to take "[their] rightful position and play [their] required role in confronting . . . [the West's] visual, audio, and written organs."[62]

### Al Qaeda's Internet Use

Al Qaeda's Internet presence increased after January 2002 when the group began to employ two sites, in particular, to spread their message. Al Qaeda never claimed ownership of the sites *Al-Neda* and *Al-Ansar*, but senior al Qaeda commander Abu-al-Layth al-Libi provided the following recommendation as regards the *Al-Neda* site—also known as the Center for Islamic Studies and Research—to visitors to *Islamic Jihad Online*:

> It is a website run by reliable brothers . . . and financed by brothers that you know. It is a good website and we hope that God will accept its actions . . . [W]e will not spare any effort or withhold anything we can offer to this website.[63]

*Al-Neda* and *Al-Ansar* published, amongst other things,

- Audio and video clips of Osama bin Laden, al Qaeda spokesman Sualaiman Abu Ghaith, and others.
- Biweekly electronic journals containing analyses of the conflicts in Iraq and Afghanistan.
- Islamic scholars' and clerics' evaluations and explanations of al Qaeda's past attacks, future plans, and admonishments to others to act. These included a series of articles claiming that suicide bombings aimed at Americans are justifiable under Islamic law
- Essays describing al Qaeda's war aims and assessments of how achieving these goals would benefit the Muslim *ummah*.[64]

There was also media speculation that the *Al-Neda* site was being used to direct al Qaeda operational cells. According to one report the site has carried low-level operational information: for example, in February 2002, it was said to have published the names and home phone numbers of al Qaeda fighters captured by Pakistan following their escape from fighting in Afghanistan with the aim that sympathizers would contact their families and let them know they were alive.[65] Click on alneda.com today and the following appears: "Hacked, Tracked, and NOW Owned by the USA. The site is described as 'a mostly unmoderated discussion board relating to current world affairs surrounding Islamic Jihad [*sic*] and the U.S.-led war on terrorism (plus other conflicts around the globe).'"

Michael Scheuer has argued that since 9/11, bin Laden has maintained a deliberately low profile for two reasons: firstly, to prevent the United States and its allies from locating him and, secondly, because he knows his continued silence induces fear amongst Western publics. The latter notwithstanding, however, Internet sites maintained by al Qaeda and its supporters provide not just bin Laden's followers, but also those he is seeking to incite to holy war, with a regular, easily accessible flow of information and comment carrying al Qaeda's imprimatur.[66] Discussing the impact of these Web sites, Paul Eedle goes further asserting, "As a result of the al Qaeda viewpoint, it now takes great courage to speak out against the jihadi view. . . . [and] public debate in the Muslim world is now very radical."[67]

### *Abu Musab al-Zarqawi and al Qaeda in Iraq's Cyber Strategy*

Every participant in the al Qaeda movement has used the Internet since 9/11 to pursue its goal of destroying American power in the world, but Abu Musab al-Zarqawi was perhaps the most melodramatic and successful player of them all. The world first heard of Zarqawi on February 5, 2003, the day that the then U.S. secretary of state Colin Powell appeared at the United Nations, making the case for the invasion of Iraq. In his statement Powell told the Security Council that "Iraq today harbours a deadly terrorist network, headed by Abu Musab al-Zarqawi, an associate and collaborator of Osama bin Laden and his al Qaeda lieutenants."[68] Throughout the remainder of 2003, Zarqawi's name arose again only as a result of leaks from American and Jordanian intelligence to media outlets. However, in a little over four weeks in April and May 2004, "he rocketed to worldwide fame, or infamy, by a deliberate combination of extreme violence and Internet publicity."[69]

In early April 2004, Zarqawi posted online a thirty-minute audio recording that explained who he was, why he was fighting, and details of the attacks for which he and his group were responsible. Paul Eedle has described the latter as "a comprehensive branding statement":

> The Internet gave Zarqawi the means to build a brand very quickly. Suddenly the mystery man had a voice, if not a face, and a clear ideology which explained his violence . . . But what is the point of an insurgent group building a brand, establishing a public profile in this way? The answer is to magnify the impact of its violence.[70]

Another of the functions of this original audio statement was to alert audiences that Zarqawi viewed the world rather differently than Osama bin Laden. Within the context of the Iraq conflict, Zarqawi was anxious to stress that the enemy included not just the American troops, but also the Kurds and the Shi'ite Muslims. According to Zarqawi, the former are in league with the Israelis and the latter are not true Muslims.[71]

Amongst the claims of responsibility were the attacks on the UN's Baghdad headquarters, the shrine in Najaf, the Red Cross headquarters, and an assortment of attacks on Iraqi police stations (carried out in 2003). It was difficult to conclusively link these and other attacks prior to Zarqawi's admission of responsibility, nor was it entirely clear what precise message should be taken from the attacks, which were open to differing interpretations. It is also worth noting that prior to the initiation of his Internet-based PR campaign, each of Zarqawi's attacks had to kill large numbers of people in order to get noticed in the chaos and mounting daily death toll in Iraq. By going online, however, Zarqawi was able to both control the interpretation of his violent message and achieve greater impact with smaller operations. By the end of April 2004, his group was issuing communiqués via the *Al-Ansar* Web site. The first claimed responsibility for a suicide speedboat attack on Iraq's offshore oil export terminal in the Gulf; although the operation failed, it shook oil markets because of Zarqawi's efforts at publicizing the attack through the Internet.

In May 2004, Zarqawi took things a step farther when he used the Internet's force-multiplying effect to the maximum effect for the first time when

> he personally cut off the head of an American hostage live on video, and had the footage posted on the Internet . . . . The entire purpose of the beheading was to video it, to create images that would grip the imaginations of friends and enemies alike. It worked. Zarqawi risked almost nothing in this operation; but he started a withdrawal of foreign contractors which has paralysed reconstruction in Iraq and done as much if not more to undermine US plans as a bomb that killed

100 people in Najaf. And he made himself a hero to jihadis across the world.[72]

No other figure has yet emerged from within the ranks of al Qaeda–affiliated groups to fill the cyber-gap left by Zarqawi's death in June 2006. But the emergence of such a figure is not crucial to the continued buoyancy of al Qaeda's online presence.

## Other Voices

Official and semiofficial Web sites are not the only important jihadi cyber spaces. An increasing number of Islamist groups and individuals (re-)post articles and analyses, exchange information, voice opinions, and debate ideas on Web sites and forums that they themselves have established. Writing in *The National Interest*, David Martin Jones observed that "the *ummah* is no longer a geographical concept; the 'virtual' world of the potential cybercaliphate knows no conventional boundaries."[73] Today's Internet "allows militant Muslims from every country to meet, talk, and get to know each other electronically, a familiarization and bonding process that in the 1980s and early 1990s required a trip to Sudan, Yemen, Afghanistan, or Pakistan."[74] A majority of the postings to these Web sites are explicitly pro–bin Laden, praising him as a hero and applauding al Qaeda's attacks. The proliferation of these sites acts as free publicity for al Qaeda's cause, but the more important impact of this development may be the increase in the number of Muslim groups and individuals who become aware of jihad-related activities and the religious justifications for them. For example, mainstream Muslim religious leaders such as Sheikh Yusuf Qaradawi, whose Web site is one of the top three visited Arabic-language Web sites in the world, support attacks even on some Western civilians in Iraq on the grounds that they are all part of an illegal occupation of an Islamic-majority country.[75]

New Web sites appear—and also disappear—frequently, and popular chat rooms are said to have lists of applicants awaiting admission. Most producers of these sites are technically savvy, and almost all the sites include audio, video, and the like. Together these contributions add up to a tremendous input into what bin Laden has repeatedly said is his and al Qaeda's top priority: the instigation to violent jihad of as many Muslims in as many locales worldwide as possible. Al Qaeda does not provide financing, have any management role, or provide dedicated content for most of these sites; nonetheless, they act as an invaluable force-multiplier for its cyber-based incitement strategy.

Recognizing this benefit, al Qaeda has assured its "Internet brothers" that "the media war with the oppressive crusader enemy takes a common effort and can use a lot of ideas. We are prepared to help out with these ideas."[76] Interestingly also while most Islamic extremist sites are in Arabic, Urdu, and Indonesian languages, there are an increasing number available in English, French, German, and Dutch. This signifies both the rise of Islamism in the West and the growing efforts by extremist Islamic voices to reach Western Muslim populations online.[77]

As regards U.S. government attacks on al Qaeda Web sites: these may make security sense but will also serve to validate bin Laden's and al-Zawahiri's claims of American hypocrisy by showing that freedom of speech is extended only to America's friends and allies. For example, a statement appearing on the *Al-Neda* site in 2002 read:

> Every time you [the United States] close a site, you only further expose yourself to the world and the truth about the democracy you brag about. It is a democracy that is tailored to your measurements only. And when people oppose you, your democracy turns into the ugliest forms of domination, tyranny, and despotism on earth.[78]

In addition, Scheuer suggests that the United States and its allies have increased the appeal and presumed importance of the al Qaeda sites by subjecting them to repeated cyber attacks, which have taken them offline and forced their owners to hunt for new host servers. The U.K.-based Arabic daily *Al-Hayat* reported that *Al-Neda* was the target of some twenty U.S. attacks. While such targeting undoubtedly made the sites more difficult for interested readers to locate, they are doubtless interpreted by Islamists on the other hand as evidence of American fear of al Qaeda's "voice" and as validation of bin Laden's claim that freedom of speech is not extended to Muslims, while also potentially resulting in a readership boost.[79]

## CONCLUSION

Almost from the outset, bin Laden and his associates "thought big" by integrating local causes and conflicts into a global campaign shaped "to resonate with Muslims of all stripes and cultures." Bin Laden has made globalization work for him; he has a capacity for what business executives term "strategic control," that is tailoring himself, his "workforce," and his "product(s)" to the changing "marketplace," while at the same time making the most of the best available technologies.[80] The seriousness of the implications of such a strategy was remarked upon by a number of analysts, prior to being commented upon by Rumsfeld. In an article that appeared in *Foreign Policy* in 2004, Jason Burke offered the following admonition:

> Bin Laden is a propagandist, directing his efforts at attracting those Muslims who have hitherto shunned his extremist message. He knows that only through mass participation in his project will he have any chance of success. His worldview is receiving immeasurably more support around the globe than it was two years ago, let alone 15 years ago when he began serious campaigning. The objective of Western countries is to eliminate the threat of terror, or at least to manage it in a way that does not seriously impinge on the daily lives of its citizens. Bin Laden's aim is to radicalize and mobilize. He is closer to achieving his goals than the West is to deterring him.[81]

One of the most significant aspects of al Qaeda's post-9/11 reshaping has been the significant increase in its reliance on the Internet as a soft power tool.[82] Bin Laden's cadres had employed the Internet for communication and propaganda purposes prior to the U.S. attacks,[83] but their use of the Internet increased exponentially thereafter. Michael Scheuer has put this down to the loss of al Qaeda's Afghan base and the consequent dispersal of fighters, along with rapid development of the medium itself and the proliferation of Internet cafes globally, which has made Internet access easier.[84] Indeed al Qaeda's increased virtuality after 9/11 inspired one analyst to coin the descriptor "al Qaeda 2.0"[85] and another to liken al Qaeda's deployment of cyber-based tools to their own "stealth 'revolution in military affairs.'"[86]

On the other hand, although Hezbollah was an early adopter of Internet technology,[87] up until quite recently this was secondary in terms of the group's new media strategy in its satellite television-based information campaign, with some estimates putting al Manar's local and satellite audience in 2003–2004 at a combined 10 million viewers worldwide.[88] All this changed with the widespread banning of the station's satellite transmissions in 2006. On a practical level, if the goal of the French, U.S., and other bans on al Manar's satellite transmission was to make the station unavailable to large numbers of people worldwide, it translated into an own-goal when, almost immediately on the announcement of these, the station commenced live online streaming. Eventually, this may mean that the station will draw more viewers via its freely available Internet service than via more costly satellite connections. The U.S. ban was likely doubly ill-advised because by blocking al Manar's transmission, Washington not only increased the station's notoriety and thus popularity but also ignored political logic that upholds interests. Commenting on how counterproductive this was for the United States and its attempts to reach out to the "Arab street," the chairman of Hezbollah's executive committee Hashim Safiy-al-Din summed up the feelings of presumably a great many people in the Middle East when he spoke about the ban:

> [T]his impudent attack against our rights, with all their media, political, cultural and economic dimensions, is not a sign of strength but a sign of the U.S. weakness and powerlessness. By doing this it has proved its tyranny and oppression, which we have been talking about . . . [T]he U.S.A. is talking about democracy and freedom of speech, but at the same time it cannot tolerate a sound or an image despite all the media it has available throughout the world.[89]

If, as Burke suggests, bin Laden is closer to achieving his goals than the West is to deterring him, the same is almost certainly true for Hezbollah. Recent events, much of them played out live on al Manar, have ensured that Hezbollah and its leader Nasrollah have gained considerably in stature right across the Middle East. It is no surprise then, in the context of the Lebanese crisis, when George Bush and Condoleezza Rice called for the birth of a "new Middle East," that many in the Arab world felt that just such a birthing was already in the offing but, as one opinion writer put it, "it will not be exactly the baby [the United States] has longed for. For one thing, it will be neither secular nor friendly to the United States. For another, it is going to be a rough birth."[90] There are myriad complex reasons for this, but at least one relates to the increased availability of new media technologies and their powerful effects, and to the first-hand knowledge available to at least two powerful actors in the Middle East drama that in the information age "the ability to take command and control of the global info-sphere is every bit as important as any other weapon on the military, intelligence, financial or any other fronts."[91]

## NOTES

1. As quoted in Joseph Nye, "Think Again: Soft Power," *Foreign Policy*, vol. 26 (February 2006).
2. From a transcript of remarks made by Rumsfeld at the Council on Foreign Relations, New York, February 17, 2006, available online at: <http://www.cfr.org/publication/9900/>
3. It is worth pointing out that Hezbollah are a legitimate political party with a wide base of support in Lebanon; however, they are

considered a terrorist organization by a large number of governments including the United States and the member states of the European Union.

4. Charles Townshend, *Terrorism: A Very Short Introduction* (Oxford: Oxford University Press, 2002), p. 55.
5. Ibid., p. 25.
6. Nye, "Think Again."
7. Bruce Hoffman, *Inside Terrorism* (London: Indigo, 1998), pp. 136–137; see also Susan L. Carruthers, *The Media at War* (Hampshire, U.K.: Palgrave Macmillan, 2000), p. 168; Gerard Chaliand, *Terrorism: From Popular Struggle to Media Spectacle* (New Jersey: Saqi Books, 1985), p. 13–14; Alex P. Schmid and Janny De Graaf, *Violence as Communication: Insurgent Terrorism and the Western News Media* (London: Sage, 1982), p. 16.
8. Steven Livingston, *The Terrorism Spectacle* (Boulder, CO: Westview Press, 1994), p. 2.
9. Brian M. Jenkins, "International Terrorism: A New Mode of Conflict," in David Carlton and Carlo Schaerf (eds.), *International Terrorism and World Security* (London: Croom Helm, 1975), p. 16.
10. J. Bowyer Bell, "Terrorist Scripts and Live-Action Spectaculars," *Columbia Journalism Review*, vol. 17, no. 1 (1978): 50.
11. Bethami A. Dobkin, *Tales of Terror: Television News and The Construction of the Terrorist Threat* (Westport, CT: Praeger, 1992); David L. Paletz & Alex P. Schmid, *Terrorism and The Media: How Researchers, Terrorists, Governments, Press, Public, Victims View and Use the Media* (Newbury Park, CA: Sage, 1992), p. 19.
12. Carruthers, p. 191.
13. Ibid.
14. Gus Martin, *Understanding Terrorism: Challenges, Perspectives, and Issues* (Thousand Oaks, CA: Sage, 2003), p. 280.
15. George Gerbner, "Violence and Terrorism in and By the Media," in Mark Raboy and Bernard Dagenais (eds.), *Media, Crisis and Democracy: Mass Communication and the Disruption of Social Order* (London: Sage, 1992), p. 96.
16. Stephen Segaller, *Invisible Armies: Terrorism Into the 1990s* (Orlando, FL: Harcourt Brace Jovanovich, 1987), p. 62.
17. Carruthers, p. 170.
18. Arjun Appadurai, *Modernity At Large: Cultural Dimensions in Globalization* (Minneapolis & London: University of Minnesota Press, 1996).
19. Martin, p. 279.
20. John Arquilla and David Ronfeldt, *The Emergence of Noopolitik: Toward an American Information Strategy* (California: Rand, 1999), p. 53, available online at: <http://www.rand.org/publications/MR/MR1033/>. See also David Bollier, *The Rise of Netpolitik: How the Internet Is Changing International Politics and Diplomacy*

(Washington, DC: The Aspen Institute, 2003), pp. 32–36, available online at: <http://www.aspeninstitute.org/AspenInstitute/files/CCLIBRARYFILES/FILENAME/0000000077/netpolitik.pdf>

21. Joseph Nye, *Soft Power: The Means to Success in World Politics* (New York: Public Affairs, 2004), p. 44.

22. For a detailed analysis of al-Manar's establishment and evolution, see Maura Conway, "Terror TV? Hezbollah's Al Manar Television," in James Forest (ed.), *Countering Terrorism in the 21st Century* (3 vols.) (Connecticut: Praeger Security International, 2007).

23. Magnus Ranstorp, "The Strategy and Tactics of Hizballah's Current 'Lebanonization Process,'" *Mediterranean Politics*, vol. 3 (1998): 109.

24. Bruce Hoffman, *Inside Terrorism* (London: Indigo, 1998), p. 134.

25. Ron Schliefer, "Psychological Operations: A New Variation on an Age Old Art: Hezbollah Versus Israel," *Studies in Conflict & Terrorism*, vol. 29, no. 1 (January–February 2006): 5.

26. Robert Fisk, "Television News Is Secret Weapon of the Intifada," *The Independent* (London), December 2, 2000, available online at: <http://www.findarticles.com/p/articles/mi_qn4158/is_20001202/ai_n14356264.>

27. Jorisch is the author of *Beacon of Hatred: Inside Hizballah's Al-Manar Television* (Washington, DC: Washington Institute for Near East Policy, 2004).

28. Available online at: <http://www.washingtoninstitute.org/pdf.php?template=C06&CID=453>

29. Press releases available online at: <http://www.stopterroristmedia.org/News/DocumentQuery.aspx?DocumentTypeID=357>

30. In 2002, the U.S. State Department objected, but it failed to prevent the broadcast by Egyptian television of the Ramadan miniseries *Horseman without a Horse*, which was also based upon *The Protocols of the Elders of Zion*. The *Protocols*—which the U.S. State Department calls "racist" and "untrue" and which claims to describe a Jewish plot for world domination and was used in Nazi Germany as a pretext to persecute Jews—is a work of fiction masquerading as fact.

31. "Matzoh" is Yiddish for a brittle, flat piece of unleavened bread.

32. BBC Monitoring, "IFJ Criticizes French Ban on Al-Manar TV," *International Federation of Journalists*, December 16, 2004.

33. Kim Ghattas, "Al-Manar Network Feels World's Heat," *The Boston Globe* December 21, 2004, A24.

34. Anna Marie Baylouny, "Al-Manar and Alhurra: Competing Satellite Stations and Ideologies," *CSRC Discussion Paper* 05/49 (2005): 12, available online at: <http://www.da.mod.uk/CSRC/documents/Special/csrc_mpf.2005–10–17.5799702381/05(49).pdf>

35. This was carried out pursuant to Executive Order 13224, which was signed into law by U.S. president George W. Bush on September 23, 2001 as a response to the 9/11 attacks. It describes

powers designed to disrupt the financial activities of named terrorist organizations.

36. Stacey Philbrick Yadav, "Of Bans, Boycotts, and Sacrificial Lambs: Al-Manar in the Crossfire," *Transnational Broadcasting Studies (TBS) Journal*, no. 14 (2005), available online at: <http://www.tbsjournal.com/Archives/Spring05/yadav.html>

37. Ghattas, A24.

38. BBC Monitoring, "Lebanese Syrian Ministers Criticise European Ban on Al-Manar TV," *Lebanese National News Agency* [translated from Arabic], March 21, 2005.

39. BBC Monitoring, "Hamas Expresses Solidarity with Al-Manar TV After French, US 'Harassment,'" *Palestinian Information Centre* (online), December 19, 2004.

40. BBC Monitoring, "Islamic Jihad Condemns US Campaign Against Lebanese Al-Manar TV," *Information Bureau of the Islamic Jihad Movement* (online) [translated from Arabic], December 20, 2004.

41. Federal News Service, "Interview with Robert Menard, Secretary-General of the French Group *Reporters Sans Frontieres*, Discussing the French Ban on Lebanese Al-Manar TV Broadcasts in France," *Monday Morning Magazine* (Beirut), January 18, 2005.

42. These transmission stations were also used by Future TV and the Lebanese Broadcasting Corporation (LBC). According to the BBC, attacks on these transmitters on July 22 resulted in the death of an LBC technician. See Peter Feuilherade, "Israel Steps Up 'Psy-Ops' in Lebanon," *BBC Monitoring*, July 26, 2006, available online at: <http://news.bbc.co.uk/1/hi/world/middle_east/5217484.stm>

43. Committee to Protect Journalists, "Lebanon: Israeli Forces Strike Al-Manar TV Facilities," July 13, 2006, available online at: <http://www.cpj.org/news/2006/mideast/lebanon13july06na.html> The Beirut HQ of Hezbollah's al-Nour radio was also attacked on July 16.

44. Feuilherade, "Israel Steps Up 'Psy-Ops' in Lebanon." Feuilherade's article also details the hacking, presumably also by the Israelis, of local FM radio stations and Lebanese mobile phones.

45. Agence France Press, "Israeli 'Hackers' Target Hezbollah TV," *Aljazeera.net*, August 2, 2006, available online at: <http://english.aljazeera.net/NR/exeres/1DCBA43C-C892–4F02–8964–83BDA9081FC8.htm>

46. See Human Rights Watch, "Can Israel Attack Hezbollah Radio and Television Stations?" July 31, 2006, available online at: <http://hrw.org/english/docs/2006/07/17/lebano13748.htm#1>

47. International Federation of Journalists, "IFJ Accuses Israel Over Pattern of Targeting After Strike on Beirut Broadcaster," July 14, 2006, available online at: <http://www.ifj.org/default.asp?Index=4064&Language=EN>. The Israeli Association of Journalists

withdrew from the IFJ due to this criticism, claiming that al-Manar employees "are not journalists, they are terrorists." See Gil Hoffman, "Israeli Journalists Pull Out of IFJ," *Jerusalem Post*, July 20, 2006, available online at: <http://www.jpost.com/servlet/Satellite? pagename=JPost/JPArticle/ShowFull&cid=1153291961355>

48. Human Rights Watch, "Can Israel Attack Hezbollah Radio and Television Stations?" For an alternative perspective, see CATM's press release entitled "Hezbollah's Al-Manar Television Station Legitimate Target of Israeli Response," available online at: <http://www. stopterroristmedia.org/News/DocumentSingle.aspx?DocumentID= 16668>

49. Jon Anderson, "Muslim Networks, Muslim Selves in Cyberspace: Islam in the Post-Modern Public Square," paper presented at the Japan Islamic Area Studies Project conference on *The Dynamism of Muslim Societies*, Tokyo, October 5–8, 2001, available online at: <http://nmit.georgetown.edu/papers/jwanderson2.htm>

50. Ibid.

51. Ibid.

52. Robert Kaplan as quoted in Michael Scheuer, *Imperial Hubris: Why the West Is Losing the War on Terror* (Washington, DC: Brasseys, 2004), xx.

53. Peter Mandaville, *Transnational Muslim Politics: Reimagining the Umma* (London: Routledge, 2001), p. 155.

54. Francis Robinson as quoted in Mandaville, p. 155.

55. Mandaville, p. 156.

56. *Fiqh* is a generic term used to describe a School of Islamic law.

57. As quoted in Faisal Devji, *Landscapes of the Jihad: Militancy, Morality, Modernity* (New Delhi: Foundation Books, 2005), p. 13.

58. Devji, p. 14.

59. Scheuer, p. xx.

60. Mandaville, p. 153.

61. As quoted in Scheuer, p. 152.

62. Ibid., p. 132.

63. Ibid., p. 79.

64. Anwar Iqbal, "Site Claims bin Laden's Message," *United Press International*, February 20, 2002, available online at: http:// www.upi.com/view.cfm?StoryID=20022002–075528–9498r; Jack Kelley, "Agents Pursue Terrorists Online," *USA Today*, June 20, 2002, available online at: <http://www.usatoday.com/life/cyber/ tech/2002/06/21/terrorweb.htm; Scheuer, p. 79>

65. Paul Eedle, "Terrorism.com: Al Qaeda on the Net," *The Guardian* (U.K.) July 17, 2002.

66. Scheuer, p. 79.

67. As quoted in Scheuer, p. 79.

68. Loretta Napoleoni, "Profile of a Killer," *Foreign Policy* (November/ December 2005): 37.

69. Paul Eedle, "Al Qaeda's Super-Weapon: The Internet," paper presented at conference entitled *Al-Qaeda 2.0*, New America Foundation, Washington, DC, December 1–2, 2004, available online at: <http://www.outtherenews.com/modules. php?op=modload& name=News&file=article&sid=89&topic=7>

70. Ibid.

71. Ibid.

72. Ibid.

73. David Martin Jones, "Out of Bali: Cybercaliphate Rising," *The National Interest*, no. 83 (Spring 2003): 83.

74. Scheuer, p. 81.

75. Eedle, "Al Qaeda's Super-Weapon."

76. As quoted in Scheuer, p. 81.

77. Madeline Gruen, "Terrorism Indoctrination and Radicalization on the Internet," in Russell D. Howard and Reid L. Sawyer (eds.), *Terrorism & Counterterrorism: Understanding the New Security Environment*, 2nd edition (Iowa: McGraw Hill, 2006), pp. 363–364.

78. As quoted in Scheuer, pp. 79–80.

79. Scheuer, p. 79.

80. Larry Seaquist as quoted in Scheuer 2004, p. 117.

81. Jason Burke, "Think Again: Al Qaeda," *Foreign Policy* (May/June 2004): 26.

82. Eedle, "Al Qaeda's Super-Weapon."

83. See Maura Conway, "Reality Bytes: Cyberterrorism and Terrorist "Use" of the Internet," *First Monday*, vol. 7, no. 11 (November 2002), available online at: <http://www.firstmonday.org/issues/issue7_11/conway/index.html>

84. Scheuer, p. 78.

85. Peter Bergen, "Al Qaeda's New Tactics," *New York Times*, November 15, 2002.

86. Magnus Ranstorp, "Al-Qaida in Cyberspace: Future Challenges of Terrorism in an Information Age," in Lars Nicander and Magnus Ranstorp (eds.), *Terrorism in the Information Age: New Frontiers?* (Stockholm: National Defence College, 2004), p. 61.

87. See Maura Conway, "Cybercortical Warfare: Hizbollah's Internet Strategy," in Sarah Oates, Diana Owen, and Rachel Gibson (eds.), *The Internet and Politics: Citizens, Voters and Activists* (London: Routledge, 2005).

88. Office of the Coordinator for Counterterrorism, *Country Reports on Terrorism 2004* (Washington, DC: United States Department of State, 2005), p. 100, available online at: <http://www.state.gov/documents/organization/45313.pdf>

89. BBC Monitoring, "Hezbollah Official Criticizes Decisions against Al-Manar TV," *Al-Manar* (Beirut) [translated from Arabic], December 20, 2004.

90. Saad Eddin Ibrahim, "The 'New Middle East' Bush Is Resisting," *Washington Post*, August 23, 2006, A15, available online at: <http:// www.washingtonpost.com/wp-dyn/content/article/2006/08/22/AR2006082200978.html>

91. Philip Taylor, "Desert Storm Blowback: Psychological Operations in Operation Iraqi Freedom, 2003," in Lars Nicander and Magnus Ranstorp (eds.), *Terrorism in the Information Age: New Frontiers?* (Stockholm: National Defence College, 2004), p. 108.

# INDEX

Printed in the United States
202683BV00002B/1-105/P